Shechem

SHECHEM

The Biography of a Biblical City

G. Ernest Wright

McGRAW-HILL BOOK COMPANY
New York   Toronto

To Bernhard W. Anderson,
Lawrence E. Toombs,
Edward F. Campbell, Jr.,
and the members of the staffs of
the Drew-McCormick Expedition,
without whom this book could **not**
have been written.

The Norton Lectures
of the
Southern Baptist
Theological Seminary

First Published in 1965

Library of Congress
Catalog Card Number: 64-24611

First Edition

72063

Contents

v

Table of Archaeological Periods

		Leading Events
Neolithic	*ca.* 7000–4000 B.C.	
Chalcolithic Age	*ca.* 4000–33d cent. B.C.	
Early Bronze Age	*ca.* 33d–24th cents. B.C.	
Dark Age	*ca.* 24th–21st cents. B.C.	Invasions
Middle Bronze I	*ca.* 20th–19th cents. B.C.	"Amorite" invasions
II A	*ca.* 1850–1750 B.C.	Egyptian magical texts
II B	*ca.* 1750–1650 B.C.	Age of Mari and Hammurabi
II C	*ca.* 1650–1550 B.C.	Height of Hyksos Period
Dark Age	*ca.* 1550–1500 B.C.	Egyptian conquest, followed by slow recovery

Late Bronze I	*ca.* 15th cent. B.C.	Thutmose III's Conquest of Megiddo, 1468 B.C.
II A	*ca.* 14th cent. B.C.	Amarna Letters, *ca.* 1376–1350 B.C. Conquest of Seti I, *ca.* 1300 B.C.
II B	*ca.* 13th cent. B.C.	Egyptian-Hittite Peace Mernepthah Stele, 1220 B.C.
Dark Age	*ca.* 1230–1150 B.C.	Israelite Conquest *ca.* 1230–1200 B.C. "Philistine" Conquest, *ca.* 1175–1150 B.C.
Iron Age I A	*ca.* 12th cent. B.C.	Destruction of Shechem and Megiddo, *ca.* 1130–1100 B.C.
I B	*ca.* 11th cent. B.C.	Destruction of Shiloh, 1050 B.C. Height of Philistine Power
I C	*ca.* 10th cent. B.C.	Israel's United Monarchy Division of Kingdom, *ca.* 922 B.C.
II A	*ca.* 9th cent. B.C.	Ben-hadad's Conquest of Israel, *ca.* 860–855 B.C. Battle of Qarqar against Assyria. 853 B.C. Hazael's Conquest of Israel, *ca.* 810 B.C.

II B   *ca.* 8th cent. B.C.

Tiglath-pileser III's Conquest of Israel, 733/732 B.C.
Shalmanezer V's and Sargon II's destruction of Israel and Samaria, 724–721 B.C.

II C   *ca.* 7th–early 6th cents. B.C.

Unification of Israel and reform by Josiah, *ca.* 628–620 B.C.
Conquests of Judah by Nebuchadnezzar, 597 and 587 B.C.

Abbreviations

Illustrations

xii Shechem

Foreword

This book tells the story of a city, one which played an especially interesting and important role in the life of ancient Palestine. Its name was Shechem, pronounced by the author *shĕk'-um*, though *shee'-kum* is also proper in English; a purist would insist, however, on the Hebrew pronunciation, *shĕ-kém*. As is the case with most cities of old, the literary references to this one are too few in number to present a full picture of its life and time. As a result, it has been necessary to excavate, and the story herein told concerns itself primarily with the manner in which two expeditions have gone about their work in ferreting history out of the dust, stones and layers of debris which remain in modern Tell Balâṭah, a mound of ruins forty-one miles north of Jerusalem in the Hashemite Kingdom of Jordan.

Here once stood the predecessor of modern Nablus, today the third largest city of Jordan. How can one be sure of that?

The first chapter will begin with this question, which will be continued in the second with a brief description of why the site was important and what traditions were associated with it. Then will follow chapters on the excavators and their work, with special reference to the Drew-McCormick Expedition, whose digging since 1956 has made this book possible. In the unraveling of the mound's story there will be much talk about walls, floors, layers and the like, but primary attention will be focused upon the magnificent fortifications and how they have been dated, upon the history of the sacred area and upon the attempt to understand the biblical traditions afresh in the light of the archaeological history. In this area we can seldom work with certainties. Instead, it is necessary to construct hypotheses which always possess greater or lesser degrees of probability. The truth in them rests upon their ability to interpret and hold together a variety of disparate data, but new information at any moment may make it necessary to change a given hypothesis, or cause a scholar to express it somewhat differently. It is to be hoped that the fresh hypotheses set forth herein will be found by readers to have been put together with care, or, if at any point found weak or unacceptable, will stimulate further consideration of the problems and perhaps fresh answers.

The work at Shechem has been conducted by those who for the most part are ordained clergymen and specialists in biblical studies, and who teach in theological seminaries for the training of clergy or in departments of religion in colleges or universities. On the one hand, it is not infrequent that our motives and our methods are suspect, especially by historians and archaeologists in other fields, for many of whom the terms "Bible" and "Palestine" smack of "religion" and everything that is unscientific. It is often felt that biblical scholars at work in Palestine can only have an interest that is mainly apologetic, not historical. One can only hope that what is here written may suggest that this stereotyped view is untrue to the actual situation, and that Palestinian and biblical archaeologists are no less rigorous in their use of archaeological and historical method than are their colleagues in other fields.

On the other hand, within theological circles generally we

are suspect because it is felt that archaeology does little of importance for the ongoing life of church and synagogue, or for
the discipline of thought about biblical faith in modern dress.
It has been my own experience during almost a quarter of a
century of teaching in theological schools that the more interest
a student or colleague has in theology or philosophy, the less interest he will generally have in archaeology. This is a rather peculiar situation. In no small part the reason for it lies in the fact
that theologians generally have rarely been interested in history,
and there are varieties of biblical theology which have so sev-
ered their relation to history that existentialism must now be
used as the ladder by which feet can again reach solid ground.
I suggest that this is peculiar because one would suppose that
the religious perspectives which the Bible presents would require
that those of us who take it seriously be deeply concerned with
history for religious reasons. In any event, the recovery of the
biblical world and the vast scholarly attempt to place the Bible
in its proper context in ancient history have revolutionized the
understanding and teaching of it until we can say that it is almost a "new" book.

The substance of the text which follows was first presented
as the Norton Lectures at the dedication of the Nicol Museum
of Biblical Archaeology in Southern Baptist Theological Seminary, Louisville, Kentucky, on March 5–8, 1963. I should like to
express my gratitude to President Duke McCall and the members of his faculty for their hospitality, and for the opportunity
it afforded in drawing scattered material into one unified presentation. I am especially indebted also to the various members
of the Drew-McCormick Expedition's staff, whose individual work
and scholarship has made this book possible. I cannot overstress
the teamwork nature of our operation; it is completely impossible and entirely inappropriate for any one of us involved to
take all the credit for the work of the expedition. In this case I
am serving as a spokesman for a group, though this does not
mean that the entire staff is agreed on all that is here written.
For this and for many inadequacies I alone must bear the responsibility. I am under especial obligation to Lawrence E.
Toombs, Associate Director, who went over the manuscript and

offered many suggestions for its improvement. S. Dean McBride of Harvard University's Department of Near Eastern Languages and Literature has done a great deal of work as a draftsman for a large number of the illustrations in the text, including the preparation of the map of the Shechem area in Fig. 2. In order to visualize more adequately what the text is attempting to describe, it seemed advisable to attempt certain visual-aid reconstructions. These are of fortification walls and gates in Figs. 21 and 31, of the original fortress temple, Fig. 47, of one of the courtyard temples, Fig. 58, and of the eighth-century House 1727, Fig. 79. These were done by my son, Daniel S. Wright.

G. E. W.

March 28, 1964
Lexington, Massachusetts

The map in Fig. 1 is adapted from Plate 1, *The Westminster Historical Atlas to the Bible*, rev. ed., George Ernest Wright and Floyd Vivian Filson, eds. Copyright 1956, W. L. Jenkins. The Westminster Press. By permission.

The quotation in Chapter 2 from Edward F. Campbell, Jr., "The Amarna Letters and the Amarna Period," *The Biblical Archaeologist*, Vol. XXIII, 1960, pp. 19–20, is used by permission of the journal's publisher, The American Schools of Oriental Research.

1

Locating an Ancient City

In 1903 a party of German scholars was making a tour of Palestine, investigating the country's geography and looking for places
where ancient cities had once existed. At that time such trips
had to be made on horseback, and one slept in the open air or
accepted such lodging as the villages could provide. Travel,
therefore, was much slower than it is today, though for historical
investigation a leisurely pace had its advantages. Yet it demanded
a rugged constitution, one that was able to endure, not simply
the outdoor life, but the almost inevitable maladies which still
afflict the Westerner when he consumes native Arab food and
drinks from a village spring.

One of the travelers, Prof. Hermann Thiersch, wrote the
following entry in his diary for June 26:[1]

> The horses are still too tired from yesterday to go any
> farther. Therefore, a day of rest. The question of old She-
> chem discussed. On the small hill of ruins which the Eng-
> lish map shows directly north of Balata near Kubr Yusuf
> [the traditional Mohammedan location of the tomb of
> Joseph], we discovered to our great joy and surprise a
> piece of "cyclopean" wall, lying exposed for a distance of

1

some 8 m(eters) and to be traced further a distance of
30 m. This is on the west side of the flat hill. The surviving
piece still reaches as high as 3 m. above the present soil,
but surely goes on down. The blocks are completely unhewn, in part attaining 2 m. in length, though they are
laid in fairly regular courses. . . . The further course of this
obviously very old wall can be followed only on the north
side, where in fact it follows an irregular curve and then
with a sharp corner turns inside. . . . Among the multitude
of sherds [pottery fragments] we found none which we
with certainty could designate as very old. Though the hill
at first seems unimportant and not very striking, yet its
extent is considerable and its situation remarkable. It controls the plain of Askar and at the same time blocks the
pass. These two together are not true of modern Nablus.
From this the situation of old Shechem is fixed with certainty and the earlier supposition (Nablus) is refuted. All
historical conditions are satisfied completely in this regard.
Here in any case the investigation must begin. The place
is somewhat under cultivation with vegetables and seed-
crops.

Professor Thiersch writes as one who has made an important
discovery. By archaeological observation he believes he has discovered where the ancient city of Shechem once existed, thus
correcting a previously held opinion.

The place where this discovery was made lies today in the
territory of the Hashemite Kingdom of Jordan, forty-one miles
directly north of Jerusalem (Fig. 1). To reach it we follow the
central ridge of western Palestine through the hills and valleys
of a territory which in ancient times was known as "Ephraim."
About five miles before we reach the site the road suddenly dips
down over the hills into a long, narrow plain running directly
north to northeast. At the left the hills gradually gather together
into a large massif known in biblical times as Mt. Gerizim. At
the northeastern foot of this mountain a critical parting of the
ways occurs. Turning a sharp left one can enter a deep and narrow pass, bounded on the north by another massif, known as
Mt. Ebal (Fig. 3). This is the main road west and north. The
pass is filled today by the third-largest city of Jordan, the city
of Nablus. At the foot of Gerizim, one can also go directly
northeast on the road to the Jordan valley, to Transjordan and
to Syria. Or one could turn directly east along the old border

between the tribal areas of Ephraim and Manasseh and descend rapidly into the Jordan valley (*see* maps, Figs. 1 and 2).

It is at this road junction that Jesus met the Samaritan woman at the traditional Well of Jacob (John 4). In that story we are told how Jesus, wearied with his journey, sat down beside the well and asked for a drink from a woman drawing water. In the ensuing conversation he is reported as uttering the familiar words: "The time is coming when neither on this mountain nor in Jerusalem will you worship the Father . . . true worshipers will worship the Father in spirit and truth . . . God is spirit, and those who worship him must worship in spirit and truth" (John 4:19–24). The woman was a Samaritan, a member of a dissident Jewish sect who believed that Mt. Gerizim was the proper place for the worship of God. Jesus, along with most Jews, was heir of an old tradition which since the time of King David had associated proper worship with the hill in Jerusalem where the central sanctuary and temple of the Israelite people was still standing. In other words, the area to which we have come has had a long history with religious associations rivaling those of Jerusalem. The story of how this came about is part of the story which our excavations have unearthed.

One clue to the situation is the traditional association of the Hebrew Patriarchs, Jacob and his son Joseph, with places still held in reverence today. "Jacob's Well" still exists—a deep, hand-dug, stone-lined well, enclosed by the walls of an unfinished Greek Orthodox church (Figs. 4 and 5). It was certainly old in Jesus' time, but whether it is actually as old as the time of Jacob we have no way of proving. The sacred enclosure around the well is at the southeastern edge of the Arab village, Balâṭah, the people of which own and care for a Moslem shrine, just north of the well, which is supposed to house the Tomb of Joseph (Fig. 3). Here today women with their children will come once or twice a week, sometimes from considerable distances, for an all-day picnic and song festival whenever there is something to celebrate. Here, too, individual women not infrequently come to pray when facing trouble of one kind or another. One important factor in the religious history of the area, then, is its long association with Patriarchal figures, specifically with the traditions of the family of Jacob.

Today the most spectacular sight in the area is the vast refugee camp (Fig. 5) filling one whole sector of the plain south of Jacob's Well—a major extension of the small village of Balâṭah, whose copious spring supplied most of the water for the people, before Nablus water was piped into the village during 1961–1962. In the village itself are some three hundred people, separated into the families which own the cultivated land round about. Rising beneath the northern side of the village and continuing directly behind it is a low mound, some ten to twelve acres in extent, used by the villagers for fruit and vegetables until modern excavations made that impossible in certain areas.

Around the western and eastern edges of this mound are some of the largest extant fortifications from ancient Palestine. It was a portion of these which Professor Thiersch first discovered in 1903. An important ancient city was once located here, one that was created as a great fort for control of the main roads in north central Palestine. It was made strong enough to guard the pass behind it and the great plain which supplied its food directly east and south of it. Nothing comparable to this site in size and strength existed during the second millennium B.C. between Jerusalem and ancient Gezer to the south, Megiddo and Taanach in the great Esdraelon plain to the north and Bethshan at the opening of that pass into the Jordan valley to the northeast.

Judging from the strength of the fortifications, therefore, and from a survey of the major tells in the region, there can be no doubt that the ancient city which once stood here controlled a city-state that bordered on those of Jerusalem and Gezer to the south and of Megiddo to the north. And the date of the archaeological remains shows Shechem to have been in existence through most of the second millennium B.C. While the size of this city-state is difficult to compute because of so many unknown factors, it is probable that during the period of its greatest power Shechem controlled an area of the hill country at least 1,000 square miles in extent.[2] Ancient Tirzah, modern Tell el-Fârʻah, some five miles to the northeast, and Tappuah, modern Tell Sheikh Abū Zarad, some five miles to the south, are the largest tells besides Shechem in the area. During Balâṭah's heyday, however, they were surely dependencies, well fortified indeed, but subservient to and allied with the Balâṭah site.

Modern Nablus bears a name that derives from "Neapolis" ("New City" in Greek). This was a Roman city established in A.D. 72 during the reign of Emperor Vespasian; and indeed Roman-Byzantine ruins can still be seen in Nablus. Its predecessor was Shechem. A city with that name seems to be mentioned in Egyptian sources as early as the nineteenth century B.C.[3] In one of them an official of Pharaoh Sesostris III (1878–1843 B.C.) says that during a campaign in Asia "his majesty reached a foreign country of which the name was *skmm*. Then *skmm* fell, together with the wretched Retenu." We also note that Shechem is the first Palestinian city mentioned in the Bible, for it is there that tradition credited Abram with receiving the news of the divine promise of the land of Canaan—Palestine, Lebanon and southern Syria—to his descendants (Gen. 12:6–7). It is Jacob and his family, however, who are most closely connected with the city (cf. Gen. 33:18–20; 34), while Joseph is said to have been buried there in the plot of ground which his father had purchased (Josh. 24:32).

We shall have occasion to refer later to the significance of these and other biblical traditions, in the light of the excavations.

Biblical passages indicate that ancient Shechem was near the border of the tribal areas Ephraim and Manasseh (Josh. 17:7), and in the vicinity of Mt. Gerizim (Judg. 9:7). The Jewish historian Josephus about A.D. 90 says that the city was located between Mts. Ebal and Gerizim.[4] The early Church historian Eusebius (d. ca. A.D. 340), a contemporary of the first Christian emperor, Constantine, prepared the first dictionary of biblical sites and their locations as far as he could determine them. His book, the *Onomasticon*, was a badly needed guide to pilgrims whose numbers swelled into a flood when Christianity became the official religion of the Roman Empire. Eusebius places Shechem in the suburbs of Neapolis by Jacob's Well. A pilgrim from Bordeaux in the same period (A.D. 333) wrote an account of his travels in the Holy Land, and he gives Shechem the same location.

From the country's period of Christian control comes the earliest-known map of Palestine, a mosaic map which was once the floor of a Byzantine church of the mid-sixth century in the Transjordanian town of Madeba. This map places "Sychem" or "Sikima" by the traditional Tomb of Joseph between the

Well of Jacob and Sychar in a direction that can be only east or southeast of Neapolis.[5] This means that pilgrims between the fourth and sixth centuries were directed precisely to the place where today the village of Balâtah stands, with the traditional Tomb of Joseph and the Well of Jacob on its northeastern and southeastern outskirts, respectively. Sychar, identified with a village where the modern Arab 'Askar with its spring now is, was still farther to the northeast on the slope of Mt. Ebal (see Fig. 2).[6]

Less than a century after the appearance of Eusebius' *Onomasticon*, a great biblical scholar, Jerome (d. A.D. 420), translated it into Latin, revising it as he did so. While he allows the location of Shechem to stay where Eusebius had placed it, elsewhere in his writings he appears to have decided that the tradition was false. Instead, the ancient city name is simply the predecessor of Neapolis, and "Sychar" is a mistake for "Sychem."[7]

Jerome's views were followed by most modern scholars before about 1910. Thus Edward Robinson, America's first great biblical topographer, wrote after his Palestinian trip in 1838 that Jerome was undoubtedly correct, and that the views of Eusebius and the Bordeaux pilgrim are to be charged to the uncritical speculations at the beginning of the era of Christian pilgrimages to the holy places. Robinson says that earlier travelers, namely Maundrell in 1697 and Schubert in 1837, had claimed that they had seen thick walls still visible near Jacob's Well, but that he and his companion, Eli Smith, "were not able to make out anything of this sort; and saw only the ruins of the church [at Jacob's Well] and the hamlet Belât."[8] The great British *Survey of Western Palestine*, which produced the first modern detailed map of the country, followed Jerome and Robinson because the old mound at Balâtah was not recognized as a tell.[9] Indeed, in the word of a German scholar whose dissertation was the first scholarly monograph to be written about the historical importance of our city, "Whether this new city [Neapolis] was built on the site of ancient Shechem or in its vicinity, Shechem since Vespasian's time has completely disappeared from sight."[10]

It is clear, then, that Thiersch had indeed made an important discovery—and this because his party was on horseback and the horses needed a day of rest! It should be noted, however, that he refrained from giving publicity to his conclusion because he did not want a nation other than his own to act upon it.[11] Then in 1908 a Balâṭah family, building a new house on the slope of the old mound, came upon a hoard of bronze swords, daggers, spear points and the like. These objects attracted wide attention. Prof. F. W. Freiherr von Bissing, who purchased them, subsequently gave them to the Museum Lunsingh Scheurleer in The Hague, Netherlands. That Museum has long since been closed and its collections distributed elsewhere. Thus far our staff has been unable to find anyone who knows what happened to the hoard.[12]

In any event, a group of scholars in Germany before World War I knew the secret of old Shechem's location. The belief now needed archaeological testing. This came in two small reports of the first excavations published in March and July of 1914 by the German biblical scholar, Prof. Ernst Sellin.[13] After completing his successful work at Jericho (1907–1909) with the aid of the classical architect, Carl Watzinger, he had made an exploratory trip to Shechem in 1911. Between September 4 and 20, 1913, the first digging was conducted with a work force ranging from 50 to 100 men. This was followed by a second campaign lasting from March 26 to May 7, 1914, during which time an average of 150 workmen were employed.

Work began on the western side of the mound where the old wall which Thiersch had found protruded. This wall was traced toward the northeast for some 60 m. (nearly 200 ft.), where a city gate was encountered, jutting out from the wall 4.40 m. (14½ ft.), and possessing three entryways, one behind the other, which once were heavily fortified. Huge blocks of stone were used in both wall and gateway, the largest of which were up to 2.20 m. (nearly 7¼ ft.) long. The wall turned slightly as it went north; its face had a slight slope—i.e., a "batter"—and its foundation was on packed clay, which smoothed the surface of the bedrock. A number of trenches were dug to test the inner parts of the mound, and four strata were discerned. The topmost was called Greek because of imported wares, and dated between the fourth and second centuries B.C. Next was the "Jewish" or "Samaritan" level, dated between the eighth and fifth centuries. Then followed the "Israelite" level, and finally the "Canaanite."[14]

Among the objects found were: a large jar containing about

850 bronze arrowheads and 7 of iron from the "Greek" or Hellenistic period, a small jar containing some 200 pieces of silver and 10 small silver rings from the same era, and from other periods bronze fibulae (safety pins), alabaster jars, painted ceramics, jar handles impressed with scarabs, etc.[15]

Sellin, then, was quite justified in writing: "The results of the work carried out so far leave no doubt that the hill of Balata represents the site of the Canaanite-Israelite Shechem, and that continued excavations there promise rich rewards in every respect."[16] The problem of the location of a great city was solved. Eusebius was right after all, and Jerome was wrong.

2

Shechem, "The Uncrowned Queen of Palestine"

Though we are accustomed to focus on Jerusalem as the center of Palestine, the German scholar Albrecht Alt has emphasized that this is not due to Jerusalem's location or geography. The advantage of Jerusalem, Alt said, was accorded it by history, not by nature: King David chose it as his capital because it happened to be a non-Israelite city which he could capture and make his own, and because it was located precisely on the border between northern and southern tribal groups which he had to bind together. From David's time Jerusalem's historical and religious associations were such as to maintain it as the country's central city.

Yet if one were to search for a *natural* capital in the hills of the country, Alt correctly says that the one place which meets all requirements can be only ancient Shechem. He names this site "the uncrowned queen of Palestine." Shechem is almost in the exact center of western Palestine. It is surrounded and protected by mountains, located in the most important mountain pass in the country, from which in antiquity highways radiated in every direction.[1] Along the eastern base of the old tell runs

9

the 500-m. contour: at the traditional Tomb of Joseph the land
lies 500 m. above the level of the Mediterranean. Scarcely a
quarter mile farther west within the pass is the watershed contour, separating the waters that flow to the Jordan from those
that run to the Mediterranean. Shechem's historical and religious
associations were far older than those of Jerusalem; as we shall
see, they ran deep within the life of early Israel, especially in
pre-Davidic times. It is believed to have been a center where
legal and liturgical forms were used which survived in the collected writings of Israel and formed the basis of at least one
sweeping reform in later Jerusalem—that of King Josiah in
622 B.C. Stephen, the first Christian martyr, in his final words to
his persecutors cites a tradition that the Patriarch Jacob and
members of his family who died in Egypt "were carried back to
Shechem and laid in the tomb that Abraham had bought for a
sum of silver from the sons of Hamor in Shechem" (Acts 7:16).[2]
This tradition is surely one preserved by a Jewish sect, because
orthodox tradition recalls the parcel of ground at Shechem as
having been purchased, not by Abraham but by Jacob himself
(Gen. 33:18–20), and further records that Jacob was buried in
the Cave of Machpelah in Hebron which Abraham had bought
from Hittites (Gen. 23; 50:13).

Nature worked hard and at length in the creation of Shechem's area as the country's natural capital. The coastlands of
Syria, Lebanon and western Palestine were for one long geological age—the Cretaceous, or period of great limestone and chalk
deposits some 150 million years ago—a shelf under a greatly
expanded version of the Mediterranean, one often called the
Sea of Tethys. During this time up to 600 ft. of limestone were
formed by the deposits of the water, so that the hills, valleys and
water supply of the country are first of all a history of this limestone. Yet the stone is by no means all of one kind, because the
happenings within the Cretaceous Age, and subsequently, were
most complex.

The oldest large deposit is Cenomanian in the middle of
the Cretaceous Age. This was then raised, faulted and worn until
a great basin of Cenomanian limestone was formed. The ridges
of the basin lie to the east and south near at hand, but are farther
away to the north in the Gilboa and Carmel ranges. Then came

a lowering of the land and another great deposit of limestone in the Eocene period, some fifty million years ago, which in its turn was pushed up, faulted and eroded. Thus the Ebal and Gerizim mountains are Eocene limestone massives which protrude in the older Cenomanian basin. The cracking or faulting of the Eocene deposits occurred both in an east-west and northeast-southwest direction. The east-west fault produced the deep Shechem Pass as well as the surrounding plains. These were then filled with a comparatively soft chalk or marl which the Arabs call ḥuwwar. The erosion of the chalk formed the present topography, including the shape of the pass through which one must go if he wishes a direct road to the Mediterranean, uninterrupted by modern political boundaries. Through it and around the Ebal range runs the road to the Esdraelon plain and Galilee.

The chalk erosion also formed the great plain which was the primary food-basket of the ancient city. This plain stretches east of Shechem for over five miles before the ridges and valleys start tumbling rapidly and steeply to the Jordan valley. The plain extends approximately the same distance to the south-southwest before the hills of Ephraim cut it off. Going northeast, the plain quickly ends and one enters a narrow defile between Mt. Ebal and the older Cenomanian Jebel el-Kebîr. By this route one can proceed northeast to the Jordan and thence to Syria, or he can round the corner of Jebel el-Kebîr, turn southeastward in the Wâdī Fâr'ah, and proceed to the Jordan valley, and thence to Transjordan or to Jericho.

Geological history thus created the natural setting for a great city to be established. The major tells of Palestine where the cities once existed all have sizable plains around them; otherwise the food supply would limit the concentration of economic and political power in a given spot. For a city there must also be an adequate supply of water and a good soil. The latter is very rich in the Shechem area, filled with an iron oxide that gives it a deep red color. The water table in the Shechem Pass, however, is far below the surface. Jacob's Well was dug 151 ft. deep, and a new well drilled a short distance west of the tell in 1957 had to go down to 34½ m. (113 ft.) (*see* Appendix 4). Mt. Ebal has comparatively little vegetation and no water issuing along its southern side because the slope of the tilted rock is north-

ward.[3] The slopes of Mt. Gerizim, on the other hand, are covered with trees to the very top of the ridge, and the slope of the
rock causes the main springs to issue on this side of the valley.
While the trees represent replanting since 1920, the contrast in
the amount of water on the two sides of the valley is very marked.

One of the finest springs in the region is that of the modern
village of Balâṭah. Villagers had told us that it flowed through
a long man-built aqueduct, and following the direction they
pointed out to us, we concluded that the aqueduct must lead
under the old tell to a source which once may have supplied
the city within its fortification walls. During the summer campaign of 1962, however, Prof. Robert J. Bull of our Drew-McCormick Expedition staff obtained the villagers' permission to
investigate the aqueduct on the Expedition's behalf. Together
with three companions, and armed with pressure lantern, flash-
lights, surveyor's tape measure, compass, camera and flashbulbs,
he succeeded in measuring and planning the tunnel. Much to
his and our surprise he found himself led by a circuitous route,
not under the tell but instead under the modern Jerusalem-
Nablus road into a cave at the base of Mt. Gerizim. Another,
though much shorter, tunnel leads water from a Gerizim spring
into the police post and prison a short distance farther within the
pass (see Appendix 4 and Fig. 108). Where ancient Shechem
got its water in time of siege, therefore, is still unknown. The
secret is probably hidden deep within the southern part of the
tell over which the modern village now stands. It must have been
either a well or a tunnel from Gerizim; Professor Bull argues
persuasively in Appendix 4 for the latter.[4] The main part of the
Balâṭah aqueduct probably goes back at least as early as the
time of the Roman-Byzantine village of Sychem, which Eusebius
and the makers of the Madeba map placed between the Tomb
of Joseph and Jacob's Well. It is improbable that Jacob's Well
was used by the whole village, because it was by then a place
of pilgrimage, a holy place with a church over it, even as is the
case today.

A rather dramatic discovery of a modern use of an ancient
water facility was made during the summer of 1957. An army
camp had been placed many years ago in the Shechem plain about
two miles south of Balâṭah village on a low ridge. The com-

mander of the Arab army unit quartered there had ordered the leveling of a playing field, and the bulldozer in doing so had struck ancient ruins. I was invited to bring some of our staff for tea one afternoon and to inspect the discovery. Upon examination of the potsherds among the ruins I concluded that they were late Roman and Byzantine in date. Furthermore, the name of the site, "Ruin of Maḥneh,"[5] reminds one strongly of an ancient word for "army camp." Consequently, I speculated that the British eye for a good spot to install a district military post matched that of the Romans some sixteen hundred years ago. The post commander told us that some time previously they had repaired the water conduit which brought water from the mountain, under the Jerusalem-Nablus road and across the plain to the camp. He said that an ancient pottery pipe from the spring was in such good condition that it was still used. However, it could not be followed near the highway and modern piping had been installed from that point to the camp. When the bulldozer had been making the playing field, it had inadvertently struck the camp's water pipe, only to discover the ancient Roman pipe following precisely the same course only a few inches below it!

The chalk or marl deposits still to be found along the lower slopes of the mountains were certainly an important factor in the life of ancient Shechem, as they are today to the inhabitants of Balâtah. Whenever an ancient Shechemite wished to make a street in the town or a watertight dirt floor in his home, he would simply dig beneath the red soil. The marl can easily be dug with hoe, mattock or pick. And the soils which the archaeologist digs in the Shechem mound seem mostly to be alternating layers of red and white (that is, field soil and marl), or a mixture of the two!

Most of the mound exists on the lower slope of Mt. Ebal as it descends into the alluvium of the valley. How much of a natural hill may have originally been there is unknown. We do know, however, that the city in its strongest period (± 1800 B.C.–1100 B.C.) was a human creation carved into the Ebal slope. The fortifications had to be huge in order to overcome the lack of the natural defense of scarped hillsides. We do know that the interior of the city within the fortifications sloped very rapidly to the south and southeast, that the inhabitants constructed a series of terraces to give stability to house foundations, and that a small valley of some sort crossed the site under the East Gate, where it was filled up. Hence the first impression the archaeologist obtains from the Shechem mound concerns the vast amount of filling, hauling and shifting of earth that the ancient inhabitants undertook in their effort at strong building and self-defense.

The original topography of the Shechem area was radically altered during the city's history, especially in the Middle Bronze Age during the eighteenth and seventeenth centuries. In 1956 and 1957, however, I was much puzzled by the huge amounts of marl and earth which towered over the western and northwestern defenses (Fig. 6). What is its meaning? It could not all be dump from the Sellin excavation of the western part of the mound. Indeed, if one looked closely, he could see the dark layer in the material which marked the surface before excavation began. This was still well above the level of the surviving ruins of the Northwest Gate and associated structures. A glance at the contour map of the site before excavation (Fig. 7) shows that the highest point on the mound before the post-World War I excavations was just east of the Northwest Gate (G–4 on the plans in Figs. 13 and 20). Since the material removed from the top of this whole sector was the same chalk-filled earth as that which once was piled against and over the western and northwestern defenses, we are led to the conclusion that this was the filling, and deep covering-over, of the whole western side of the mound. It was a purposive act, done at one time by man and not by erosion. (Indeed, it has been borne in upon us time and again how resistant to erosion a tamped marl fill can be.) This was a huge operation which piled dirt and chalk dug from the Ebal slopes over the western fortifications. On the outside it reaches depths of over forty feet. A large number of people put in a prodigious amount of labor here. And the purpose could only have been to cover over the western and northern fortifications so that they never again would be used.

When did this happen? Since the fill had to be dug through and removed to find the surviving constructions, we must conclude that the covering of the fortifications was the last thing that occurred when the city ceased to be a city. The approximate time when that happened became clear in our first excavations in 1956. It was during the latter part of the second century B.C. In possession of that date, one could then turn to ancient sources, particularly to the works of the Jewish historian Josephus. As the archaeological details of the city's final era have been gradually clarified and sharpened, the outlines of Shechem's final period of glory can be reconstructed (see Chapter 10). At the end of the second century B.C. the Jewish Hasmonean ruler in Jerusalem, John Hyrcanus (134–104 B.C.), decided to put an end to Samaritan independence and sectarian religion. We can only infer that he destroyed Shechem, which then was the Samaritan capital city, as he had earlier destroyed the Samaritan temple on Mt. Gerizim. After he had done so, he evidently used his army, and probably conscripted labor, to cover the city's fortifications where their foundations could not be entirely destroyed.

Excavations in areas F–H 3–5 (Figs. 13 and 20) in 1934 by Dr. Hans Steckeweh removed the surface soil between trenches of earlier excavations down into the levels of the first surviving houses. Next to the city fortifications in the northern part of this sector were badly burned houses from the end of the Middle Bronze Age. Farther south, again directly under the surface soil and approximately at the same level, were the remains of Iron Age houses, and south of these were Hellenistic remains. In other words, the building levels in the city sloped sharply southward from the Bronze Age walls, but for some unknown reason during the third, or perhaps early second century B.C., Samaritans had chosen to level off this sector, slicing off the earlier strata as they emerged in the slope in order to create a level area. It is possible that we found some of the fill from this leveling slice under a third-century house excavated in 1957 (Field II, F–7 in Figs. 13 and 20). If this is not true, then it is possible that the operation dates from the first half of the second century (our Stratum II; *see below*). Why it was done, we do not know, beyond the fact that the Samaritans went to great lengths to enlarge level areas for their houses and to eliminate some of the terraces.

These historical illustrations from the end of the city's life suggest the manner in which throughout its existence people were continually altering the site's topography—and this without the assistance of bulldozers!

The problem of the historian is to use every source of knowledge he can find to reconstruct what once happened. Hence, the more the archaeologist knows about all phases of a city's life, literary as well as non-literary, the better able he will be to make historical sense out of what he unearths. In prehistoric periods one must do the best he can with non-literary evidence. In the historical periods, however, all pertinent literature, as well as the stones and rubble, must be studied in detail, so that the two classes of evidence may be used together, the one supplementing and giving body to the other.

The most important literary source to give meaning to what is dug from Shechem's ruins is, of course, the Bible. There the references to Shechem are sufficiently frequent in varying literary forms as to make historical hypotheses about the city both possible and significant, though not all of them can be placed on the same level of probability.[6] Fortunately also a few scattered references to the city in non-biblical ancient literature prove exceedingly helpful. What, for example, can we infer from the first Egyptian references to the city in the Brussels magical texts and the Khu-sebek inscription mentioned in the first chapter? The second suggests that by *ca.* 1850 B.C. the Shechem city-state was of sufficient importance as to merit the imperialistic attention of the great Pharaoh of the Twelfth Egyptian Dynasty, Sesostris III (1878–1843 B.C.). Its mention among the chief Asiatic enemies of Egypt in the Brussels texts suggests the same thing, though unfortunately these texts cannot be dated precisely.[7]

During the Early Bronze Age of the third millennium B.C., Syria and Palestine took on the basic political system which remained in force for centuries. This was the city-state system, each small state controlled by a heavily fortified capital city. Competing claims of the rival city-state kings kept life anything but serene; political and military maneuvering was constant, as Edward F. Campbell, Jr. makes clear in Appendix 2.

The end of the third and the beginning of the second millennium were marked by political instability throughout the

Near East. Decline of power in the centers of political control made it possible for Semitic ("Amorite") groups living as semi-nomads around the inner fringes of the Fertile Crescent to move into the areas of the sown lands. In Palestine the movement began as early as the twenty-fifth century and probably continued for some time, until by about 2300 B.C. a dark age had descended upon the country following the destruction of every major city-state center, as far as these have been investigated. Shechem, judging from the archaeological evidence, shared in these events only in a minor way. The first important period in the city's life began during the nineteenth century.

The Egyptian references to Shechem come from the period of recovery from this dark age, when the re-urbanization and the re-establishment of the city-state system was rapidly under way. Archaeologically, this recovery must be connected with the MB II A period which is characterized by precisely these phenomena. And the only way we have to date the beginning of this period is an inference from the Egyptian references and from the number of Egyptian objects discovered in Syria and Palestine, particularly those representing high Egyptian officials: that is, when Syria and Palestine are deemed important enough for major Egyptian figures to leave statues or other mementos of themselves in important cities. This did not occur in the first part of the Twelfth Egyptian Dynasty during the twentieth century B.C., but by the time of Sesostris III we must assume that the new age had begun.[8] Thus the beginning of Shechem's great age is to be dated in the nineteenth century B.C.

The next group of documents in which Shechem plays an important role is the Amarna Tablets, dating from the third quarter of the fourteenth century B.C.[9] These are letters from Canaanite kings in lower Syria and Palestine to the Pharaoh in Egypt which were found in the archives of the government of the heretic king, Amenophis IV (Akhenaten), at his capital, Tell el-Amarna (Akhetaten) in Egypt. (An additional one was subsequently found in Palestine.) In the Amarna Letters the situation in Palestine is chaotic, each king picturing himself as a model of righteousness while he does his best to incriminate his enemies. The letters relating to Shechem are freshly translated and discussed by Professor Campbell in Appendix 2. Shechem was ruled by a man named Lab'ayu whose city-state appears to touch on those of Jerusalem and Gezer in the south and Megiddo on the northwest. There is frequent mention of a people called " 'Apiru" (a term related to "Hebrew"—'ibrî), who are the source of much trouble. In the past the texts have been interpreted as witness to a nomadic invasion, perhaps including groups which became a part of later Israel. This interpretation has been disproved, for the 'Apiru are local foreign groups of various kinds within the country—e.g., mercenaries who fail to receive their pay—who cause trouble and become a symbol of disloyalty to Pharaoh. Hence when one king calls another an 'Apiru, he is trying his best to put the blame for all trouble and rebellion on his enemy, but in such case the term of incrimination suggests nothing concerning the enemy's point of origin!

Be that as it may, there is no question but that the sense of safety which the hills of Shechem and the city's fortifications provided gave a certain independence to Lab'ayu. He is roundly accused before Pharaoh as a great troublemaker, presumably because he sought diligently to enlarge his territory at the expense of his neighbors. Edward F. Campbell, Jr., has recently described his role in the Amarna Letters, as follows:[10]

> It is Shuwardata [king of Hebron?] and Abdu-Kheba [king of Jerusalem] who introduce us to Lab'ayu. Neither has any use for him. Shuwardata writes after Lab'ayu's death that the threat of Lab'ayu is mitigated, but that Abdu-Kheba has become another Lab'ayu (280:30–35). This must have been a stinging condemnation! Abdu-Kheba, on the other hand, asks rhetorically whether the king would have his vassal do as Lab'ayu has done, "who gave Shechem to the 'Apiru." Once again, the view which sees the 'Apiru as an attacking force has been inclined to treat this quite literally and see Shechem as one of Lab'-ayu's cities which he gave to the 'Apiru as their camp. But it is at least as possible that the reading be understood "to make Shechem into 'Apiru territory" (the term here has a determinative sign used with names of countries), that is, to make it rebellious to the king. In that case, Shechem was Lab'ayu's headquarters, and the evidence for heavy Canaanite occupation there, which current excavation will hopefully clarify, is explained.
>
> Lab'ayu himself wrote three letters to the court, each rather cheeky by our standards. . . . Lab'ayu's truculence

is almost refreshing in the face of the rampant hypocrisy of his contemporaries. Nevertheless, he was a real scoundrel, and his contemporaries are universal in their opposition. Almost certainly Lab'ayu controlled all of the central hill country from not far north of Jerusalem to well north of Shechem. He is found raiding in Shuwardata's territory (see above) and he causes trouble to the west in Megiddo, as is learned from Biridiya, Megiddo's prince. Long threatened by Lab'ayu, Biridiya finally collected a posse and captured him so that he might be sent to Egypt for punishment. Lab'ayu was placed in the custody of Zurata of Accho, who promptly let him get away by payment of the ransom price. Incidentally, the theme of ransom is familiar in the Amarna Letters and seems to have been accepted practice. Ba'lu-shipti, writer of Letter 292, complains that Peya, an Egyptian official, has been charging too much ransom—100 shekels per man instead of the 30 shekels normal when one ransoms a man "from the mountains" (i.e., the hill country, probably, and perhaps from Lab'ayu, therefore).

Lab'ayu's escape was temporary, for another posse caught him again, and before Biridiya could intercede, they put Lab'ayu to death. It was not long, however, before his sons were following in their father's footsteps, Mut-Ba'lu of Pella being one of them.

We may safely infer from the size and strength of the Shechem city-state in the Amarna period that it was equally large and strong during the eighteenth and seventeenth centuries, when its great fortifications were originally erected.

The first important fact to be noted in the biblical traditions about Shechem is the close association of the Patriarchs, particularly the family of Jacob, with the city. Put another way, later Israel remembered Shechem and the relation of her ancestors to the place, with the result that the city and its district were deemed of such special importance that regular religious services of a special type were held there. The following may be noted especially:

(1) Both Abraham and Jacob erected altars and worshiped "the God of the Fathers" there, thus inaugurating a religious tradition continued in later times (Gen. 12:6–7; 33:18–20).[11]

(2) The Dinah story in Genesis 34 certainly preserves a bit of ancient tribal lore dealing with the relations of Jacob's family with the city, which is there personified after the Patriarchal

manner. "Shechem, son of Hamor," desired marriage with a daughter of Jacob. This suggests a treaty or covenant which would permit intermarriage between the two groups, the first such recorded, for otherwise the tradition recalls the sharp separation of the Patriarchs from the local inhabitants (cf. Gen. 24:2–4). On the other hand, the barbarous acts of two of Jacob's sons, Simeon and Levi, in violating the covenant and killing the men of the city (Gen. 34:25–30),[12] can be understood as meaning that the city was actually captured. A peculiar verse in Gen. 48:22 records Jacob as saying on his deathbed to his son Joseph, "I have given to you rather than to your brothers one Shechem which I took from the hand of the Amorites with my sword and with my bow." While later interpretative activity has made the meaning of the verse uncertain, the simplest interpretation is that Shechem was actually conquered—the sole tradition preserved about a conquest before the time of Moses.

In the narratives of Joshua, particularly those deriving from northern sources, Shechem also has a special position, unlike that of any other city. Most significant is the fact that there is no record of its conquest by Joshua.[13] Instead, the view of the Deuteronomic historian is that as soon as Joshua obtained a foothold in the hills north of Jerusalem, the Israelites immediately went north to Shechem where a covenant ceremony was held, one that officially brought the tribal league into being within the Promised Land (Josh. 8:30–35; 24; cf. Deut. 11:26–29; 27). Here, then, an enclave and great city entered the Israelite nation by covenant, accepted the Sinai traditions as normative, even though its inhabitants had probably not participated in the Sinai or the Exodus events.[14]

We shall return to Shechem's sacred traditions in a subsequent chapter. Here we need only point out that recent research has understood the Shechem tradition to suggest the special nature of an annual ceremony of worship at Shechem in early times, one in which covenant renewal was the central theme. The Book of Deuteronomy is composed of liturgical materials deriving ultimately from this ceremony, even though the present form of the tradition and the written text come from a later time, perhaps even after the ceremony had ceased to be observed. In any event, the old book found in the temple in the time of King Josiah has, since the days of the earliest Christian scholarship of the fourth and fifth centuries A.D., been assumed to be the Book of Deuteronomy or some part of it. It led to reform and religious revival because of its authentic and strong representation of the Mosaic covenant theology (in 622 B.C.; 2 Kings 22–23).[15]

As a special enclave, a city-state entering the Israelite tribal league by covenant, Shechem not surprisingly provides the clearest expression of the theology of the tribal league in pre-monarchical Israel. The first attempt to institute a monarchy within the league also happened there. After Gideon's great victory over the camel-riding Midianite invaders, the Shechemites asked him to be their king. He refused with the words: "I will not rule over you, nor shall a son of mine rule over you. Yahweh rules over you" (Judg. 8:23). That is, God's government is direct and immediate, the antithesis of human monarchy. Nevertheless a certain Abimelech, a son of Gideon who was a Shechemite on his mother's side, accepted the position after his father's death. Considering Shechem's history, we can reasonably infer that what was proposed here was the return of Shechem to the city-state pattern of government with a local king who still would remain within the Israelite confederation. For reasons which are not entirely clear other than Abimelech's lack of wisdom, the experiment ended disastrously. The city rebelled against him, and he in turn destroyed it and "sowed it with salt" (Judg. 9:45). The sowing with salt was evidently a symbolic act, "sowing" infertility on a city that had violated its solemn covenant with him.[16]

The story of this unsavory episode in Judges 9, however, provides us with considerable information about Shechem. For example, there is within it the Temple of El-berith (meaning, "God of Covenant," or "The Covenant God," or "God of the Covenant"). This building was the last stronghold of the city, and the sector in which it was located was the citadel, which obviously was in a special area, separated from the rest of the metropolis. With the destruction of the temple and citadel we may infer that the great Bronze Age strength of this pivotal spot was no more. We shall return to this point again as we attempt to interpret the archaeological discoveries.

When the city was rebuilt we do not know, though further discussion of the question is given in Chapter 9. After Solomon's death, his son, Rehoboam, did not automatically become king over the whole country upon his gaining control of the reins of government in Jerusalem. Instead, he had to journey to Shechem where "all Israel had come to make him king" (1 Kings 12:1). That is, Shechem as the old religious center of the north was the place for solemn meeting and covenant with the new monarch. When he refused to agree to certain of the northerners' demands, choosing to follow the counsel of his young companions rather than that of the wise old elders who had served his father, the people promptly rejected him and chose as king Jeroboam, one of their own leaders who had been a political exile in Egypt. And they further put themselves on record as ready to fight for their independence of action: "To your tents, O Israel! Look now to your own house, David" (1 Kings 12:16).

It is not surprising, therefore, that Jeroboam made Shechem his first capital and refortified it (1 Kings 12:25). Why he moved first to Penuel across the Jordan and then to Tirzah, five miles northeast of Shechem, we are not informed. The Omri Dynasty (*ca.* 876–842 B.C.) built a new capital at Samaria, five miles northwest of Shechem, on the other side of the Ebal range, a city owned by the monarch and independent of all old associations. From that time on we hear little about Shechem. People were still living there in the early sixth century, however, because representatives from the town, together with men from Shiloh and Samaria, went in mourning on a pilgrimage to Jerusalem to present offerings and incense at the site of the temple which the Babylonians had recently destroyed (Jer. 41:4).

The last sources of literary information for Shechem's history are non-biblical materials dealing with the period between the Old and New Testaments. During part of this time the Samaritans, who gained their name from the city of Samaria, are also called "Shechemites."[17] Yet the evidence for what actually went on is so confused and confusing that scholars have proposed a variety of theories without being able to reach a consensus. New evidence was needed. This archaeology has provided eloquently, until it can be said that a fresh view of the literature, and a new chapter added to ancient history, are now possible. This subject will be reserved, however, for Chapter 10.

3

The First Excavations of Shechem

After the preliminary work done in two brief campaigns in 1913–1914, Dr. Sellin returned to Shechem as soon as he could after World War I. Germany in defeat and inflation in the 1920s made the continued excavation of the ancient mound seem an irrelevant luxury. But Sellin was determined. His resources were small, but with financial aid secured in the Netherlands from Prof. F. M. Th. Böhl, from Methodist Bishop H. M. DuBose of North Carolina (Fig. 8), and from the government and Evangelical Church in Germany, he was able to carry out his third campaign between March 24 and May 3, 1926.

Long negotiations with the villagers who owned the tell were needed. Sharp bargainers, they held out for exceedingly high rental prices for their land. Normally, an excavator rents only the land he wishes to use in a given season—a few *dunams* at most—and he will renew the rental on that parcel only if he desires to leave it open and unfilled so that additional work in it can be conducted in another season. Dr. Sellin was finally forced into an arrangement whereby he had to pay rental each year on the whole northern sector of the mound, 54½ *dunams* (*ca.* 13½ acres). We of the American expedition have had to continue this arrangement.[1] While expensive, it has had this advantage: the digging areas can be left open, so that filling in after each campaign is unnecessary. Had Sellin's major discoveries been covered over after he finished, a good part of what appears in this book could not have been written!

Sellin's staff in the spring of 1926 included his companion in 1913–1914, Professor Dr. Praschniker of the German University in Prague, an architect named Heinz Johannes from Berlin and for three weeks a classical archaeologist, Dr. Gabriel Welter, who was delegated by the *Notgemeinschaft der Deutschen Wissenschaft*.

Sellin summarizes his spring work in 1926 as follows:

(1) An 80-m.-long trench, 5 m. wide, was dug from the House of Salim (also called in subsequent reports "the House of the Blind Man") in a northwesterly direction (K–M 7–11 in Fig. 13). It was during the erection of this house in 1908 that the bronze weapons are said to have been found (*see* Chapter 1). The stratigraphy was the same as that encountered before the War. Sellin reports that there were: "Greek," "Israelite" ("Early Iron") and "Canaanite" ("Middle and Late Bronze Age"). Of particular interest was the discovery of a Canaanite street, with a sewer 1 m. deep running beneath it to which drains from various houses connected.

(2) A second trench, 50 m. long and 5 m. wide, was dug from east to west (K–N 5–6, Fig. 13). Here in addition to an "Israelite house altar" (i.e., a small stone altar of incense with "horns" on the top four edges, an object called *ḥammān* in Hebrew),[2] there were found potsherds with "Aramaic letters" incised on them. Most important, however, was the discovery of a city wall, 3.20 m. (just over 11 ft.) wide which could be followed both north and south. It differed from the western wall in that it "jumped back and forth every fifteen meters" (*see below*, Chapter 5). Following it south, it was found attached to a tower of another city gate, the East Gate, the entrance and inner court of which are larger than those in the Northwest Gate.

(3) In 1913–1914 a north-south trench had been started in which a portion of a large Canaanite building and a square tower had been encountered (H–I 3–6, Fig. 13). Here a 20 by 20 m. square was marked out for stratigraphical excavation. A large

complex of the "Greek" era was encountered which had a side wall 30 m. long. Below it was an "Israelite" house with another incense altar, 90 cm. high, within it (but *see* note 2).

(4) The Northwest Gate had been in an excellent state of preservation when first excavated in 1913–1914. After the War, however, before antiquity laws could be instituted and enforced by the British mandate authorities, the villagers had used it as a stone quarry for the building of their own houses. Hence the imposing ruin was now in a state of complete disarray. Sellin salvaged what he could, and re-excavated the gate, this time from the new debris of stone chips. Proceeding south from the gate, excavation began in rooms built against the top of the great western wall which Sellin believed to be the "palace" of the city, one which was believed to possess at least two courts and a long-columned hall.[3]

The fourth campaign of the German expedition took place between June 17 and September 13, 1926. Dr. Praschniker was unable to be present and his place was taken by Dr. Welter. For the last month of the campaign the staff was augmented by Dr. Kurt Galling, at that time a *Privatdozent* in Berlin. As during the latter part of the spring campaign, an average of 200 workers were employed in the following areas:

(1) Work was continued on the "palace." A ramp led out of the gate tower to the south into a rectangular room (10 by 6 m.). In its center lay a large angular stone which must have carried a column to support a roofing beam. From this a door led into a small room (6 by 3 m.) and thence into "a large hall" which was originally supported by ten columns. There were also remnants of a stairway which led up upon the city wall. Two long parallel walls, attached to the inner tower, had been built over the outer edge of the rooms, and were, therefore, built in a later period. To the right or northeastern side of the gate there was another series of rooms built against city wall and gate-tower, but of a different type of masonry from that of the south-western side. Smaller stones had been used, and these had been covered by a white plaster. Indications were that this, too, was a later building, not contemporary with the palace (*see* Fig. 9 for plan). None of these structures, however, contained much in the way of objects. They had been cleared before destruction.

Sellin now was able to theorize that there were two main

periods of building activity in the Northwest Gateway area, and also two periods in the building of the fortifications: (a) the western wall and Northwest Gate which use such huge stone blocks; and (b) the eastern wall and East Gate which generally use much smaller stones.

(2) The most significant discovery of the campaign was a tremendous block of masonry, near the palace area. It proved to be the stone foundation of a rectangular building, 21 m. wide by 26 m. long (that is, ca. 69 by 86 ft.), with side walls 5.30 m. thick (over 17 ft.). With an atmosphere of suppressed excitement Sellin was thus able to announce the discovery of "the house of the Covenant-God" (El-berith) which Abimelech had destroyed, according to the story in Judges 9. We shall return to this building in Chapter 6 to look at it more closely (Figs. 39–41, 47).

(3) Directly in front or east of the temple, Sellin began excavation in a large area which had been the temple's courtyard. Here he found a long, well-preserved wall which ran in front of the temple and turned a right angle to ascend the hill toward the Northwest Gate. This was named the "*Temenos* Wall" because it enclosed the sacred court or temple precincts (*temenos*). A 41-m. length of it was uncovered in front (southeast) of the temple, and an 18-m. length to the northeast. Fig. 10 shows Dr. Welter's plan of the discoveries published in 1932, while Figs. 58, 59 and 63 show the long walls more clearly. The main architectural elements found were now for the first time given dates: (a) Erection of the great western wall, Northwest Gate and palace (southwest of the Gate)—*ca.* 1700 B.C.; (b) building of the eastern wall and the northeast wing of the palace—*ca.* 1500 B.C.; (c) building of the temple and its court—*ca.* 1300 B.C.; (d) renovation of the temple—*ca.* 1150 B.C. These dates have now to be revised, as we shall see.

(4) During the summer of 1926 the East Gate was completely excavated.

(5) Finally, the trench in the southeast by the House of Salim was widened at its southern end and excavations were undertaken in the courtyard of the house itself. Here two cuneiform tablets were discovered. One of them, a list of witnesses to a judicial proceeding or contract, was only half preserved, the other half having broken off in antiquity. It was found in

disturbed soil only 50 cm. below the surface. The second is a letter of which at first not enough could be made out to afford coherent sense. Later W. F. Albright published an article on it, explaining that it was written by a teacher to a father in Shechem, asking payment for his services! Albright dated it about 1400 B.C. Sellin found it in a Canaanite house which he believed to have belonged to a rich merchant. He dated it to the period *ca.* fourteenth to twelfth centuries.[4] The tablets are translated and discussed below by Edward F. Campbell, Jr., in Appendix 3.

The fifth campaign was a brief one, extending from March 10 to April 15, 1927, carried out by Drs. Sellin and Praschniker and Architect Johannes, and devoted to a continuation of projects under way in 1926. The *temenos* area and temple were given further clearance, as was also the northeast palace wing adjoining the Northwest Gate. "Trench K" is now the name given the southeast trench by the House of Salim, where additional work brought to light more remains of Canaanite houses. One of them, dating from the end of the Middle Bronze Age, is said to have been exceptionally fine, and to have been destroyed by fire. In the street next to the house were two skeletons, thought to be victims of the catastrophe which destroyed the house. In the court of the House of Salim another fine Bronze Age building was recovered in which were many objects. Of particular interest and importance is a clay mold in which bronze tools and weapons were cast. It is 37 cm. long and 11.5 cm. in height and breadth, and is today on exhibit in the Palestine Archaeological Museum in Jerusalem, Jordan.

For the summer campaign the German society for scientific research, the *Notgemeinschaft der Deutschen Wissenschaft*, purchased 300 m. of track for a small, hand-operated quarry railroad together with eight dump cars. With the very substantial aid of this machinery the foreman of the expedition spent July in removing part of a huge dump created southwest of the temple during the excavations. Earlier an earthquake had destroyed large sections of Nablus, but it had done no damage on the tell. Precise dates for the campaign are not given, but it appears to have lasted from early August into early September, the staff being Drs. Sellin, Welter, Böhl, and a new architect, named Heck. Because the railroad eliminated the need of a large number of basket-carriers, the working force was cut to 100 men.

The main effort was the continued excavation of the various walls and rooms of the *temenos* area southeast and south of the temple's entrance. Sellin writes: "Everywhere we found houses of the Hellenistic, Middle and Early Iron Ages, as well as of Late and Middle Bronze Ages, one lying on top of the other. They showed a rich content, especially in the Late Bronze Age level."[5] This is an extremely important observation, and it can now be interpreted, as a result of the Drew-McCormick Expedition's work. No detailed plans, however, showing the phases of walls, one above the other, were published, nor were the objects carefully preserved or published in groups by stratum. As a result, the history of the building arrangements in this critically significant area will never be known, except in the earliest periods where the remains were unexcavated or left in place after excavation. (We shall return to the history of this sacred area in Chapter 6.) Other areas of investigation included especially further tracing of city fortifications on the north and southwest, to be treated in the next chapter. A revision of dating was undertaken, including especially the dating of the great cyclopean western wall, Northwest Gate and palace to the first part of the Late Bronze Age (sixteenth–fifteenth centuries) rather than to the Middle Bronze Age. That is, Sellin now regarded them as a creation of the age of Laba'yu.[6] We need not go into detail about these views, however, because they have had to be revised.

At this point in the progress of the work, matters were interrupted. The German Archaeological Institute, a society supported by the government for the guidance and assistance of scientific investigations, intervened, removed Dr. Sellin from the direction of the excavations and elevated Dr. Welter to his place. Sellin returned for one month between March 10 and April 12, 1928. During this period his main object was the removal of a huge dump in the area of F–H 3–5 so that an area of 2,400 sq. m. would be free of debris and ready for excavations. While doing so he traced the cyclopean (western) wall and the eastern wall farther along the north and northeast, and found that they ran parallel to one another, some 10 to 13 m. apart. It is unfortunate that he had no architect with him; what was discovered was never put on the plans. At the same time he was able to make a special study of some peculiar stones found in the courtyard of the temple. In an article giving details about them, he maintained correctly that they were sacred stones with their sockets, objects which in Hebrew are called by the term, *maṣṣēbāh,* meaning "a sacred pillar."[7]

Dr. Welter resumed the work during the summer of 1928. What staff, if any, assisted him, as well as the precise chronology of his work between 1928 and 1932, is impossible to determine. He published very little, and his reports to the Department of Antiquities of the British mandate in Palestine are not sufficiently detailed to make clear what he did.[8] As far as we can determine, his main work consisted in the making of detailed plans and sections during 1928. These are very important because they are the best surviving plans available. In trenches on the west side which he dug in order to make a section through the debris (see Fig. 22), he found evidence of two stages of fortification earlier than the great cyclopean wall on the west. During August, 1928, he excavated an octagonal Byzantine church on top of Mt. Gerizim. At a subsequent time, in one source said to have been 1931, he excavated a fine Middle Bronze Age villa on the slope of Mt. Gerizim above the village, 18 by 18 m. square. He believed it to be a sanctuary,[9] the temple of Judges 9, but our present knowledge of temple plans does not permit this interpretation. The building was a fine private home erected in a choice location, precisely after the manner of well-to-do Nablus residents today. Dr. Welter did not believe that Sellin's temple was anything more than a fortress, though he conceded that in its final period it might have been used as a temple. He derogated Sellin's theory of sacred standing stones in front of the building. Indeed, he doubted that Tell Balâṭah was ancient Shechem at all. It was probably only the "Tower of Shechem" (Judg. 9:46–47), he believed, whereas the ancient city itself was probably beneath modern Nablus!

During 1933 Welter was removed as director, and Sellin was reinstalled on condition that the excavation be directed by a professional archaeologist. The services of Dr. Hans Steckeweh, an architect who had worked in Egypt, were obtained. The latter spent a month during the summer of 1934 at Bethel under the tutelage of W. F. Albright, where James B. Pritchard, John Bright and this writer, among others, were receiving their archaeological baptism. Then in September he spent a month removing the surface covering, revealing the first building walls in areas F–H 3–5, with results which were referred to in Chapter 2. While this work was intended to be preliminary to much more, it actually was the end of the German expedition's excavations. The direct financial support of the German Archaeological Institute was now evidently not available, and insufficient funds were at hand for 1935. Then the difficulty of changing German marks into Palestinian currency at the time, coupled with the Arab-Jewish uprisings, one center of which was at Nablus, prevented renewed work until the summer of 1939. Tickets had been purchased for the trip when the beginning of World War II brought the whole project to a halt.[10]

Sellin died on New Year's Eve, 1945/1946. A letter, written by request to a staff member of our expedition on November 22, 1960, by Erika Schneller-Sellin, a daughter, informed us that in her parents' home her father had the files, the cuneiform tablets, numerous small objects on loan from the Department of Antiquities and a completed manuscript on his excavations at Shechem. All were destroyed in the American fire-bombing of Berlin during the fall of 1943.

In an article published in 1932 Dr. Thiersch in an appended footnote wrote the following:

> After having had the good fortune of making an important discovery, it is bitter to observe that it does not receive the treatment which it deserved. This is my personal reaction to the excavation of Shechem. The excellent archaeological expert assigned to the excavation remains almost completely silent. The reports published by the theological director of the excavation are not only poor, as far as excavation techniques go, but also in the archaeological evaluation of the objects. It is for this reason that I now almost wish I had never made my discovery when I recognized on June 26, 1903, for the first time the girtle wall of Shechem, as it protruded from the soil of the fields.[11]

When this statement was published, Dr. Sellin finally broke silence with a frank but nevertheless dignified article about the situation. He did not wish myths to be formed about the alleged "personal quarrels between myself, 'the theological director,' and Dr. Welter, 'the excellent archaeological expert,'" with the resultant implication "that I am really the one that has to be blamed for these conditions." He offered little personal defense, nor did he desire to enter into personalities. He simply wished to suggest the little that had happened since Dr. Welter had taken over the direction of the work, to point to the important discovery of earlier defense walls on the west side and to correct certain of Welter's errors.

Welter had published his view that the temple was not a temple but a fortress which had been erected on a "pyramid." Four years later, Sellin continued, long after learning that his views regarding the supposed pyramid were unjustified, he nevertheless had not rectified his initial statements. The same is true about his supposed location of Shechem under modern Nablus.

As for the "sanctuary" on the slope of Mt. Gerizim, excavated in 1931, Sellin accepted the view that it was a sacred structure and gave certain details about the discovery. Yet he said that in a visit to the site he found that the pottery and small objects from the building had not been studied but simply thrown into boxes, without order or recording. If the building were the temple of Judges 9, then it should contain pottery of Abimelech's era. As a matter of fact, however, the pottery is all from the Middle Bronze Age with nothing later. Sellin wrote: "It was a great satisfaction for me to find that Professor Albright, one of the best present experts in Palestinian pottery, during a visit at Balata, expressed his agreement with my view in this respect." Welter is to be esteemed, Sellin continues, as an archaeologist with great accomplishments in Greek archaeology. It is unfortunate that because of all that happened "the German excavation of Shechem has become the object of mockery among Germans, as well as among non-Germans." Sellin concluded by saying that he did not wish to go into detail as to how this could have developed. He said only that he had privately presented the causes to the administration of the *Notgemeinschaft der Deutschen Wissenschaft* as early as 1928, "but they did not want to listen to me."[12]

Nevertheless, Dr. Sellin indeed has had to bear a good deal

of the blame for the "situation." On the one hand, to archaeological scientists in other fields he was an Old Testament scholar
and member of a theological faculty—therefore a "theologian."
For some in the fields of the social sciences this necessarily involves the implication that such a man as a matter of course
cannot be a "scientist." Yet in Sellin's defense it must be stated
that he had learned a good deal about Palestinian pottery, and
his initial judgments regarding dates are generally to be trusted.
Welter was primarily an architect, and while his relative chronology of the city fortifications is correct, he knew little about
Palestinian ceramics, and his opinions regarding dates, as also
about historical questions, are generally of little value.

On the other hand, while Sellin had the energy and the
interest to inaugurate archaeological programs, he simply did
not have the requisite native ability in "practical" matters ever to
be a really good field archaeologist. Yet the scientific control of
the Shechem excavation was actually under the authority of the
German Archaeological Institute and the *Notgemeinschaft*. Dr.
Welter's assignment was their responsibility. Had they instead
appointed as archaeologist one of the promising men who had
received their training under Koldewey at Babylon in Iraq, for
example, the Shechem excavations would have been a very
different story. It must be remembered that the Sellin and
Watzinger excavations at Jericho between 1907 and 1909 were
the best which had been conducted up to that time in the matter
of architectural recording in Palestine, and its all-around quality
was surpassed only by Harvard University's Reisner at Samaria
in 1909 and 1910. The difference between Sellin at Jericho and
Sellin at Shechem was the difference between Watzinger and
Welter, who were assigned their respective positions because of
their experience in classical archaeology. To this outsider the
matter is as simple—and complex—as that. Hence the final responsibility would appear to have belonged to the German
Archaeological Institute, which failed dismally in the assessment
of the personality and abilities of the archaeologist chosen for
the project.

After the examination of such records as survive and conversation with various persons, including workers in Balâtah who
had labored for Sellin and Welter, the basic difficulties at

Shechem can now perhaps be adjudged as twofold: (1) As in some other excavations of the time, and in the pre-World War I period generally, the staff was too small for the amount of debris removed, and the excavation suffered from the lack of close supervision and control. The most vivid example of this at Shechem is the East Gate. A great hole was dug here in the side of the mound with almost no supervision. The recording of what was dug is meager in the extreme. The gate was schematically planned but the stratigraphy, history and chronology of the structure are unrecorded. Another illustration is contained in a report by the late Danish Dr. Aage Schmidt which he filed with the Department of Antiquities in Jerusalem (unpublished):

> During the first excavation campaign [1926], one of the two grooved stones found on both sides of the temple entrance was considered to have served as a drain, which it certainly did not. Roman stone drains cannot be found in a Middle Bronze Age context, and never were of such enormous size. Most of the time no archaeologist was present during the actual excavations. Professor Sellin once happened to come upon the workmen when they smashed a *mazzeba* [sacred standing stone] which lay on one of the door sills of the temple entrance. The workmen had already cut this *mazzeba* into several pieces but Professor Sellin succeeded in saving the two most valuable pieces, and thus this *mazzeba*, from total destruction. He left the pieces where they had been found (their real nature was not recognized at that time).
>
> Dr. Welter, being a professional archaeologist, and convinced of his superiority, was able to oust Professor Sellin from his excavation. However, Sellin returned the following year (1928) for a brief season of work. One day he sat, by chance, near this stone during a rain. He observed for the first time its groove. This was filled with earth, which in a dry condition could not be distinguished from the stone. Sellin had the groove now cleaned, and put the two fragments of the *mazzeba* into it. One could not but come to the conclusion that the two *mazzebas* belonged in the stone sockets on which or near which they had been found. Although these *mazzebas* were put out of use in ancient times, they were nevertheless left at their places, since they were generally known to be sacred stones belonging to a temple. It is almost certain that a *mazzeba* had also been left on the third stone socket, but that it was destroyed by workmen before Professor Sellin ar-

rived. Also the large *mazzeba* was erected by Professor
Sellin and put into its socket.

A few weeks later Dr. Welter arrived. He had "discovered" that the temple was not a "temple," and was
furious to see the erected *mazzebas*. He had them therefore taken out of their sockets and thrown down the slope
of the fill.

(2) A second main difficulty with the excavations was a
failure to recognize the basic importance of detailed and precise
archaeological recording. Attempts were made actually to dig
the *temenos* and other areas stratigraphically during 1926 and
1927. Yet the digging areas were not divided into different
"rooms" or loci and numbered, so that the objects could be carefully separated and recorded according to their precise find-spots
and levels or strata. Hence the register of objects existing today
in Leiden has no archaeological value, other than the fact that it
is a list which can be studied, each item for its individual significance. There was no understanding that when an object is
separated from its context in the earth and architecture of a
mound's ruins, its historical worth is immediately lessened unless the recording procedures make it possible to reconstruct its
context. The primary purpose of saving pottery in Palestine,
where little of it is anything more than unattractive, is that it
is the key to dating. Thus when vessels or their fragments are
removed from their earth layers, they are of little value unless
their earth contexts have been dated by them.

Such detailed recording methods were not observed at
Shechem. As a result it is impossible to reconstruct the history
of the site with any precision from the surviving records, and it
would still have been impossible had Dr. Sellin's archives survived
the bombing of Berlin.

4

The Drew-McCormick Expedition

In the late summer of 1954 my colleague, Frank M. Cross, Jr., returned from a year in Jerusalem, Jordan, where he had been working as a member of the international team of scholars assigned to publish the Dead Sea Scrolls. Among many other items of news was one which is the genesis of the American excavations at Shechem. Prof. William R. Farmer and Dean Bernhard Anderson of the Theological Seminary of Drew University had been in Jordan that summer looking over possibilities for a modest excavation. Since Dean Anderson needed the association of an archaeologist, my colleague urged me to join forces with him and plan a joint project, sponsored by our respective institutions. Cross and I were teaching at the McCormick Theological Seminary in Chicago at the time, so that the expedition which resulted was named the "Drew-McCormick Archaeological Expedition."

At the beginning of our discussions I suggested that it probably would be no more difficult in the long run to raise money for a large project than for a small one. Of the available sites east of the Israeli-Jordanian boundary line, Shechem was prob-

ably the most challenging to the archaeologist and the best training ground for young scholars in field archaeology. Following
the Arab-Jewish War, the American School of Oriental Research
in Jerusalem, which has been the base and local agent for
American expeditions in the Palestinian area, found itself a short
distance east of no man's land in Jordan. When conditions became fairly well stabilized, it was discovered that we did not
have a sufficient supply of trained archaeological scholars to
staff the school. It was mandatory, therefore, that some young
biblical scholars be trained to carry on the standards set between
the wars by W. F. Albright and Nelson Glueck especially, each
of whom had served long terms as director of the school.
Shechem's maze of exposed rocks and holes was an extraordinary
archaeological puzzle, the perfect archaeological training ground.
Surely, if this maze could be made to make sense, then nothing
would appear insurmountable! In addition, rich literary traditions relating to the site made it ideal for training in historical
method. Archaeology is not an independent or isolated discipline;
it is a research arm of the historian, and the discipline suffers
when it is not treated as such.⌋

Dean Anderson and I secured the commitments of our respective schools to act as sponsors of the project and to invest
money in each of four projected campaigns. We also secured
the co-sponsorship of the American Schools of Oriental Research,
and, beginning in 1957, financial assistance from the Bollingen
Foundation in New York. Application was made to the Jordanian
Department of Antiquities in 'Amman for a digging permit at
Balâṭah, after we had been assured that no one in Germany was
planning to continue the work of Dr. Sellin. Then came the task
of rounding up additional funds wherever we could find them,
and necessary items of equipment. The Webb Manufacturing
Company in Philadelphia, for example, gave us a number of
tents for camp use, and added tent flies, painted with aluminum
paint to reflect the heat. With these as second roofs the tents
were quite livable even in hot summer afternoons. Mr. Nicholas
Lattof of Arlington Heights, Illinois, and the Rev. Douglas Trout,
then a student at McCormick Theological Seminary, were especially helpful in the matter of photographic, surveying, drawing
and camp equipment. Others, too numerous to mention, have

been exceedingly helpful at every stage of our work, including especially the officials of the American Schools of Oriental Research, Dr. Awni Dajani and his staff in the Jordanian Department of Antiquities, Mr. Yusuf Saad, Curator of the Palestine Archaeological Museum, and Père Roland de Vaux of the Dominican École Biblique in Jerusalem.

Work Completed and in Process[1]

Toward the end of July, 1956, Dean Anderson, Professors Lawrence E. Toombs and Robert J. Bull of Drew, and Douglas Trout and I from McCormick made preparations in Jerusalem for our initial campaign. It was to be a brief one, the purpose being to introduce us to the mound and the villagers of Balâṭah who would do the actual digging, and to make the necessary decisions as to how the digging would proceed, preparatory to a major effort the following summer. Within one week, before work could begin, serious illness in his family recalled Lawrence Toombs to the United States. Within two weeks Douglas Trout contracted poliomyelitis, fortunately a mild case but necessitating his return home as soon as he was able to travel. A New York bank, charged with the transfer of our funds to a bank in Jerusalem, sent them to Jerusalem, Israel, instead of to Jerusalem, Jordan. The money was only a few blocks away, but it could better have been in Timbuktu, where we could have had access to it. And, finally, the promised surveyor-architect in Jordan failed to materialize!

While these blows were somewhat distracting, to say the least, those of us remaining were determined. Dean Anderson and I, in order to keep things democratically balanced between our two schools, decreed ourselves Administrative Director and Archaeological Director respectively. Robert Bull, who in his young life appears to have had some experience in almost everything, including a pre-medical education and experience in surveying, was appointed by us as camp doctor and surveyor-architect. Hasan ʿAwad, an experienced archaeological foreman, was loaned to us by the Department of Antiquities. We set up camp at the eastern edge of the mound by the village schoolhouse, and for a period of three weeks between August 6 and

24 we initiated our excavations with the aid of an average of
eighty to eighty-five men and boys from the village.

We began at the East Gate. Welter's plan suggests that the
entire gate had been excavated. We were delighted to discover,
however, that this plan was a reconstruction and that the whole
southern half of the gate still lay underground, untouched. Cal-
culating how much we could do in three weeks, we laid out a
trench 3 m. wide over the top of the unexcavated portion, being
careful as we did so to stay at least a meter from the ragged
edge of the German cutting. We then took the trench down over
the steep bank by a series of earthen steps, and 15 m. eastward
into the plain. Since there was a steep bank there, we reasoned
that the stump of a city wall, which Sellin had discovered running north from the gate, must be present, preventing erosion.
The extension of our trench out into the plain was to make sure
that, if additional fortifications were there, we would be able
to relate them to the gate. The total area dug was about 150
sq. m., divided into Areas 1, 2, 3 and 4.

One of the initial problems was what to do about survey
leveling points, so that we could have figures to use in assessing
the relative heights of the walls and buildings uncovered. We
found a survey stake in the village road as it passed the *Maqam
en-Nebi Yusuf* (Tomb of Joseph), and we identified it as stake
No. 29 on the Nablus survey of Block 24067 (1946). Unfortunately no record of its altitude above sea level is preserved in
the Nablus Department of Lands and Survey. A letter to the
survey department of the Government of Israel, to which the
details of the new survey of the country, completed before the
war, had fallen, also failed to produce any information about
stake No. 29. Nevertheless, we used that stake as our zero point.
Above it the mound rises slightly less than 25 m. at its highest
points. The 500-m. contour line appears to run along the edge
of the street in question, so that the zero point is not far from
that figure, and our excavation levels are actually measurements
of the distance our walls and floors are above the 500-m. line.

The brief campaign in 1956 produced a mass of detailed
information about the history of the East Gate and the relation
between it and the earlier cyclopean wall which is so well preserved on the western side of the mound. The continuation of

this fortification was found deeply buried 11 m. east of the East Gate. As a consequence, we decided to make the complete excavation and re-excavation of the whole structure our main project for the second campaign in 1957.

Actual digging took place between July 4 and August 16, 1957. Twenty-seven people composed the regular staff of the expedition and we were able to hire an average of about 190 workers. Movement of debris was speeded by the use of a hand-operated quarry railroad (Fig. 11), generously loaned to the expedition by Père Roland de Vaux of the École Biblique in Jerusalem. This equipment, composed originally of eight dump cars and 300 m. of track, had been shipped from Germany for use in the summer campaign of 1927. Following the 1934 campaign it was stored in a building of a Balâtah family. By the early 1950s several years had gone by during which no storage charges had been paid nor word heard from Germany. Père de Vaux learned of the situation, paid the charges and took over the railroad for use in his excavations at Tell el-Fârʿah, some five miles northeast. Not knowing how to set up or operate such a railroad, I was bothered about how we were going to learn to use it responsibly. I need not have troubled myself, because our many-sided staff member, Robert J. Bull, our surveyor-architect the year before, had for one period in his life been a railroader! Hence he has been in charge of our use of the equipment ever since, assisted by two elders in Balâtah who had learned to set it up and operate it for Sellin and Welter.

We were very fortunate in having with us in 1957 Dr. Hans H. Steckeweh, who had directed the last prewar excavation there in 1934. His knowledge of the earlier excavations was of great assistance in our attempt to comprehend the meaning of the archaeological remains. Another bit of good fortune was the availability of an experienced archaeological architect in the person of G. R. H. Wright. An Australian in origin, he came to us from archaeological work in Libya. He has absorbed a great store of knowledge and experience from long residence in the Near East. Most recently he has been the archaeologist of the West German government assigned to work with one of the largest construction firms of western Europe in the task of moving a Roman temple in upper Egypt, stone by stone, down the Nile and reconstructing it above the reach of the waters of the Aswan Dam.[2]

Our main effort in 1957 was the complete excavation of the East Gate and its detailed history and plan. Because we had begun to use the term "area" in 1956 for the individual digging plots in a given sector, we adopted the term "field" for the latter. Thus the East Gate sector was designated Field I. While work was under way there we began work in two other sectors. Field II (see Figs. 13 and 20) was an unexcavated plot southeast of the temple along the edge of the deep cut which Dr. Sellin had made in the *temenos* region. The purpose here was to obtain a detailed stratigraphy above the point which Sellin had reached in 1927, so that we could have some knowledge of what had been dug through and the point at which work had stopped.

The purpose was unfulfilled, however, because of Samaritan house-building operations. In the northern half of the sector we found a fine Samaritan house of the third and second centuries erected on an artificially prepared terrace. Its ruins were filled in a great leveling operation, presumably the work of John Hyrcanus. Pottery-packed earth from the second half of the second century B.C. filled the rooms, together with a coin of Antiochus VIII, dated 121–120 B.C., (B 57, Reg. 321). Over that was a layer of black earth with earlier pottery from the first part of the second century together with a Ptolemaic coin (B 57, Reg. 147), probably of Ptolemy I (312–285 B.C.), and other miscellaneous material of still earlier periods. Clearly, someone took the surface earth off a neighboring sector to fill the house ruins. This earth was from the end of the second century and the end of the city's life (Stratum I). By the time the levelers were over the tops of the ruined walls they had dug deeper at the source of their dirt, and had scraped a level of the early second century (Stratum II) containing a mixture from earlier ages.[3] (Fill like this is seldom completely clean or homogeneous as regards the date of objects within it.)

The house showed two architectural phases. At the level of the earliest earthen floor and directly below it there was more black earth containing nothing later than the second half of the third century B.C. (Stratum III). This, then, was the probable time when the house was erected. Below the black earth was what evidently had been the fill used to create a terrace for the house to rest on. The fill was occupational debris mixed with ashes to make it pack hard, with early pottery from the Late Bronze Age and the first part of the Iron Age (ca. fifteenth–twelfth centuries). At first we thought we were within city stratification, but we were puzzled by the alternating layers which sometimes were Iron Age, sometimes Late Bronze Age, and most frequently a mixture of the two. In all there was a depth of about 2.25 m. of this type of debris, with nothing in it of late date, when suddenly near the bottom of it a coin was found. There could be no doubt that it was in place, and not "planted" by a worker, because of the nature of the corrosion on it; furthermore a supervisor witnessed its discovery. It was another Ptolemaic coin (B 57, Reg. 348), probably Ptolemy II (285–246 B.C.), though it was considerably eroded. In any event, it was now clear that this terrace had been positioned by the builders of the house. Its identification as a terrace is confirmed by the sudden drop-off of the mound's surface at the house's southern edge and the discovery of a portion of the terrace wall, deep beneath many feet of Dr. Sellin's dump.

Below the terrace fill we found ourselves almost immediately in a different earth of the same type and from the same level as that within the *temenos* where Dr. Sellin had stopped work. This earth debris was much earlier, from the period MB II B (ca. 1750–1650 B.C.), for the pottery in it was from a stage immediately preceding that in the East Gate (MB II C, ca. 1650–1550 B.C.). One could only conclude that the Samaritan builders, or someone earlier, had removed later earth debris before the terrace fill had been put in place by the builders of the house.

The third main sector of our work in 1957 was Field III, consisting of a trench across the edge of the mound some 50 m. north of the East Gate. The purpose of the trench was to have an independent check on our results at the East Gate in Field I. This was a successful venture, though, as expected, along the edge of the mound most of the Israelite and Samaritan strata had washed away over the stumps of the city fortifications.

As it was apparent that we would finish what we planned to do in the East Gate before the season was over, Professor Bull started running a spur of the railroad from the northern dumping area across to the temple. To prepare a roadway for the cars, fill had to be dumped over the southeastern edges of Sellin's "eastern palace," adjacent to the Northwest Gate (*see* Figs. 9 and 13). Before doing so we re-excavated a part of the sector, labeling it Field IV. Two building levels were found. We could not date the second or later one because all evidence for fixing it had been removed. Sellin was certainly correct, however, in holding the surface rooms here to be later than those southwest of the gate. The earlier of the two phases was the one which was contemporary with the erection of the great western wall and the Northwest Gate.

To provide a nomenclature to distinguish two walls with their respective gates, we decided to call the western one, the first discovered, the Wall A system. The eastern wall with the East Gate was named the Wall B system. We now were becoming more confident. The main outlines of the history of the city and the history of its fortifications were now distinguished. The fog was lifting; the maze of exposed walls and previously excavated ruins was no longer so discouragingly strange. The stones took on an ever more lively aspect as we could fit them into the life of actual people in time.

Our final operation in 1957 was to make a beginning on the temple, which we termed Field V. This work was to be one of the most intricate operations of our whole "dig," because the various building phases were difficult to disentangle, let alone to date, when all earth around the walls had been removed. As men were released from the East Gate, however, a start was made and a few of the building secrets were discovered before we quit for the summer. We now planned that this western sector should be one of two main foci of our work during the third campaign.

Illness of the Archaeological Director caused postponement of the third campaign until the summer of 1960, when we worked again for six weeks, between July 1 and August 13 (cf. Fig. 14). The staff numbered 32 and the average number of laborers was 165. Dean Anderson's pressure of work made it impossible for him to be present. I remained Archaeological Director, but administrative duties were taken over by Lawrence E. Toombs of Drew as Associate Director and by Edward F. Campbell, Jr., of McCormick as Assistant Director. They in turn were aided by Vivian (Mrs. Robert J.) Bull who acted as camp manager and keeper of the books. G. R. H. Wright continued as architect. Paul W. Lapp, assisted by Ovid R. Sellers, was in charge of recording and of the analysis of the Hellenistic pottery, his specialty. Lee C. Ellenberger now became chief photographer, after studying the requirements and problems of archaeological photography. This organization was continued in the fourth campaign in 1962, with Professor Toombs taking over major responsibilities as field director.

In addition to the field techniques required for successful archaeological digging, a certain minimum of technical assistance is imperative. This includes a trained archaeological architect for the preparation of accurate plans, a photographer whose responsibility is the photographic recording of the results of the work, and a system for the cleaning, preliminary study and proper recording of objects found, including particularly the vast amounts of broken pottery fragments which serve as the chief clue to the chronology of the work.

We approached our work in 1960 with somewhat more confidence. Not only had major chronological problems been solved in the preceding campaign, but there was now in existence an experienced core staff steadily improving in organization and knowledge of how to work most effectively. We concentrated on three digging sectors, which continued to occupy our attention during the fourth campaign also. Field V, the temple and what was below it, was committed to Robert J. Bull as supervisor. Field VI was our new designation for Sellin's *temenos*, a complex of ruins that had been covered over to make a courtyard for the temple. Enclosing it to the southeast and northeast were the *temenos* walls, which Sellin had considered contemporary with the temple but which our soundings in 1957 had indicated were earlier. James F. Ross of Drew became field supervisor of this sector.

We now believed that we were in position to begin work on the detailed stratigraphical history of the city. To achieve this goal we chose what we understood to be an unexcavated portion of the mound where private homes and streets should exist in abundance, and where debris disposal would be comparatively simple for our railroad. This was Field VII at K 5–6 (Figs. 13 and 20), where Edward F. Campbell, Jr. was field supervisor. It was a square plot, consisting of nine 5-m. squares with balks 1 m. wide between them—a total area of 289 sq. m. Finally, in the widened portion of Sellin's north-south trench there was a deep pit, 5 to 6 m. deep, left from 1926 and 1927. We obtained the promise of a "Point 4" bulldozer to fill it, at least partially, planning to push into it some remaining piles of debris from Dr. Sellin's digging in the area. Before doing so we decided to seize the opportunity to obtain stratigraphical sections from the south side of the pit and at the same time to sink a sounding from the bottom of it to virgin soil. This was Field VIII, supervised by J. P. Lockwood and Horace D. Hummel.[4]

Areas 7 and 9 in Field V, immediately west and south of the temple and deep below it, were our attempts to probe the earlier fortifications discovered by Welter in order to date them and fit them into the pattern of the stratification emerging below the temple's courtyard. We discovered below and within the temple foundations an earlier fill of major proportions, the latest pottery in it being MB II B (*ca.* 1750–1650 b.c.). In Field VIII, Area 1—the deep pit at the bottom of Sellin's trench—we found the same fill. We dug there 6.20 m. (over 19 ft.) below where Sellin had stopped. One-third of the way down was a fine cobblestone pavement, but above and below it we found almost sterile fill down to virgin soil. Here, then, is further evidence of gigantic efforts to create a strongly fortified city in the era before the erection of the great cyclopean Wall A system. We shall analyze the meaning of this in the next chapter.

Field VIII.3 was the section dug along the southern edge of Sellin's scarp. It was 5 m. long and attained a width of 3 m. The surface layers here had been removed by Steckeweh in 1934. The first 2.25 m. of our digging belonged to the early Israelite period (*ca.* twelfth century), except for a pit and a wall lined with a row of storage jars at its eastern edge, dating from the ninth century. Below this were nearly 3 m. of Late Bronze debris, separated by a series of black striations at mid-point, and all dating from the second half of the fifteenth century through the thirteenth century. The Israelite level was neatly separated from the Late Bronze by a flagstone pavement. That was all; there was no burned layer; there had been no conquest of the city in the thirteenth, or even early twelfth, century.

In 1957 we had found the same situation to exist in the Late Bronze guardrooms of the East Gate: namely, that there was no destruction layer separating the Late Bronze and Iron Age deposits. Below the Late Bronze section of the debris we immediately encountered late MB II C destruction debris in two phases, separated by a floor. Each phase showed eloquent evidence of destruction by fire. That is, during the sixteenth century there had been two destructions of the city, following hard upon each other. We had found the same evidence on an even larger scale in 1957 in both Fields I and III. Adding this to the literary evidence from Egypt, we can say with confidence that we have here attestation to the fury of the Egyptian conquest of Palestine and Syria to create the Egyptian empire of the Eighteenth Dynasty—what is called the New Kingdom.

In Field VII, meanwhile, a very complex stratigraphy was encountered, but it enabled us to count four strata or separate building phases from the surface down, which belonged to the Hellenistic or Samaritan period between the fourth and late second century B.C. (For a definition of "stratum," see below.) Only the third and the fourth of these strata appear generally preserved under the surface. The best-preserved is Stratum III (ca. 250–190 B.C.), though fragments of Stratum II (ca. 190–150 B.C.) were present in Field VII, as well as in Field I. Between Stratum IV (late fourth and early third century) and V there was a lengthy time-gap, filled only with fragmentary evidence of occupation, when we suddenly found ourselves with massive evidence of the destruction of Israel by the Assyrian army in 724–723 B.C. Much more evidence for this event was forthcoming in 1962, however, and the term, "Stratum V," had to be reassigned to the reoccupation period of the sixth century. But more of this in a subsequent chapter.

The fourth campaign extended over a seven-week period, June 25 to August 10, 1962. The staff was even larger than in the third campaign—some thirty-eight in all, representing fifteen different American and Canadian institutions of learning, in addition to the Waldensian Theological Seminary in Rome, the American School in Jerusalem and the Jordanian Department of Antiquities (Fig. 15). The average number of workers employed was between 185 and 190, and the organization and core staff remained basically the same as in 1960.[5]

In Field V Professor Bull was kept busy on two projects. One was the careful study of the portico of the temple in the attempt to determine the history of the towers and entrance of the great structure. The other was the study of the court fill below the altar of the last temple phase in order to learn what surfaces were used in the earliest phases, and then to find out what lay directly below the altar in the pre-temple phases belonging to Field VI. Among the discoveries here was the base of an earlier altar of the great temple, dating about 1600 B.C. and first identified by Lawrence Toombs. It was also learned that the altar area was the pivot of the earlier structures in Field VI where Professor Ross and assistants were attempting to disentangle five strata of construction. This conclusion became one of several factors leading to the deduction that the earlier buildings were part of a large sacred compound, separated from the city by the strong *temenos* wall (Wall 900 in our terminology). Another factor leading to this crucial deduction was the discovery by Prof. D. Arnulf Kuschke of the University of Mainz, in the basement of the Lutheran Church in Jerusalem, of certain of the original plans from Dr. Sellin's expedition. These plans included details which we could now put together with our own plans to give an over-all picture of what once had existed in Field VI during the time between ± 1800 and 1650 B.C. We are deeply indebted to Professor Kuschke for this discovery and for presenting it to our expedition. The attempt to describe what these discoveries now mean will be made in Chapters 6 and 7.

Field VII was enlarged another 119 sq. m. with supervisory oversight now divided between Prof. Campbell and Prof. Siegfried H. Horn of Andrews University. By the end of the season work there had disentangled nine strata and had reached the early part of the ninth century B.C. in the central part of the field. The stratigraphical history of the tell from the surface down can now be summarized and dated approximately as follows:

	Stratum I	the last *city* on the tell
		ca. 150–107 B.C.
	II	.... *ca.* 190–150 B.C.
The City of the	III A .... *ca.* 225–190 B.C.;	
Samaritans	III B .... *ca.* 250–225 B.C.	
	IV A .... *ca.* 300–250 B.C.;	
	IV B .... *ca.* 331–300 B.C.	

Gap ± 475–331 B.C.

Reoccupation	Stratum V .... 6th–early 5th cent. B.C.	
	VI A and B .... late 8th–7th cent. B.C.	

Destruction by the Assyrians, 724/723 B.C.

The City of	Stratum VII .... *ca.* 748–724/723 B.C.	
the State of	VIII .... *ca.* 810–748 B.C.	
(North) Israel	IX A .... *ca.* 860–810 B.C.;	
	IX B .... ends *ca.* 860 B.C.	

These dates are given on the basis of the pottery chronology, the stratification or building periods, combined with the known history from written sources. Round numbers such as 225, 300, sixth century, mean that we are not sure at this time whether or how a change of stratum or phase is to be fitted into known political events. We suspect that Str. X represents the city which was rebuilt after violent destruction by Pharaoh Shishak of Egypt *ca.* 918 B.C. (cf. 1 Kings 14:25–28); further excavation in 1964 confirmed this supposition.

Almost every ancient city shows gaps in its occupation, brought about usually by destruction and killing so violent that the mound lay waste for a period. To be sure that we were not missing one or more periods when people at Shechem did not live as far away from the water supply as Field VII probably was, we decided to open a small area, 11 m. square, within a garden directly behind the first houses of Balâṭah (in squares F–G 10; see Fig. 13). This new work, under the supervision of Prof. Joseph A. Callaway of Southern Baptist Theological Seminary, was planned to be no larger than could be completed in two digging seasons. In 1962 it was taken down to Stratum IX A and was found to possess essentially the same stratification as Field VII. The main difference appears to be that Field VII is where fairly prosperous people lived, while Field IX can probably be designated as a "slum" area.

Wherever a steep bank was left by Dr. Sellin, it has been a temptation to make a fresh cut into the bank to get a fresh section through the debris which the earlier digging had gone through—an inexpensive way to check stratigraphy and sometimes to date exposed ruins. We have already described the one operation of this sort, designated Field VIII in 1960. In 1962 another section was done in Field VI, Area 2, under the direction of Daniel P. Cole (see Figs. 16 and 17). The cut was 3 m. in width along the north bank of Sellin's *temenos* area at a point where major constructions either began or disappeared, deep below which the earliest city wall (Wall D), discovered by Welter south of the temple and under its eastern portico, should be present. The stratigraphic history turned out to be closely parallel to that in Field VIII. The transition from the thirteenth to the twelfth century is marked only by a floor and wall, and there is no evidence of disturbance in the city's life at that time. The greatest disturbance shown in the section is marked by a layer of dark-brown field soil running across the whole section, roughly separating the Middle from the Late Bronze Ages. Since on other grounds we have postulated a 90-to-100-year gap in the city's history between the sixteenth century Egyptian destructions of the Middle Bronze Age city and the Shechem of the Late Bronze Age (that is, between *ca.* 1540 and 1450 B.C.), this layer of field soil suggests that the tell was used for farming during the period of the gap.[6]

Organization and Procedures

The size of the staff in our expedition has been allowed to grow as the core group gained experience in what was being done and in the best methods to do it. Regular staff meetings, the analysis of methods and problems and a self-critical attitude toward our work have meant that each year the quality of our joint effort has markedly improved. Where we have been dissatisfied with results in a given spot, we have decided, where possible, to tackle it again. A good example is the recutting of the balk on the slope of the East Gate in 1962 and 1964 because our knowledge of the pottery of the Hellenistic period had been greatly refined since 1956 and 1957.

Modern excavation is becoming more and more expensive, not only because of rising costs, but because the increasing refinement in method requires slower work, closer supervision and larger staffs. The most important influence on excavation method in recent years has been the work at Jericho directed by the British archaeologist, Kathleen M. Kenyon, between 1952 and 1958. While any method must be adapted to the nature of the site being dug, a visitor to one of Dr. Kenyon's "digs" will be impressed by the elaborate care taken to cut the sides of the trenches or squares being dug (that is, the "balks"—or in England "baulks") with great care and neatness. While the work is in progress, a given balk may have a number of tags attached to it which designate the different layers visible in the debris. Each digging plot will have a trained laborer with small hand-pick, trowel and brush, and a supervisor with the same implements, who cut the balk, clean off stones which appear to be in place and continually scrape and study the earth in the careful search for floors, occupational surfaces and brick walls which can often be very elusive. If one got the impression that the archaeologist spent more time in the study of the dirt and stones in his balks than in the visible walls of an emerging ruined building, he would not be far wrong. The secrets of the mound's history are to be discovered in the way those earth and stone layers got into their present position. Each layer must be labeled in a way to differentiate it from another. The objects found in a layer must be labeled so that the information about their find-spots is precisely recorded. The debris layers that precede, are contemporary with and are later than existing walls must be carefully studied, for in this way walls and floors are associated with the layers and are dated by the artifacts that precede, are contemporary with or are later than the time of construction and the period of use. The supervisor must take careful notes in a field notebook of what he sees, aided by the directors of the expedition. Of especial importance, the balk must be accurately drawn to scale.[7] For examples of section drawings in this book, see Figs. 17, 22, 23, 44, 74, 87, 108 and 110.

Not that all of this is completely new, nor did previous excavators ignore earth divisions entirely. They certainly did not. Indeed, a careful study of Reisner's ideas on the study of debris in his *Harvard Excavations at Samaria* (Cambridge, Massachusetts, 1924) will reveal how much he understood of the issues involved. Certainly his later work in Egypt is masterly and unsurpassed in this regard. Nevertheless, it is still true that Miss Kenyon's focus on the problem in a fresh way has now, and will have in the future, a very important effect on the methods and quality of excavation, at least in Palestine.[8]

In our work at Shechem we have been attempting to dig in accordance with these procedures, methods which are easily learned in theory but difficult to put into practice. "Reading a balk" successfully takes experience. More than that, it calls for a certain "plus," an "artistry" or empathy, which indeed must characterize the work of every historian attempting to comprehend a people who once lived by the study of what they did. If one may oversimplify archaeological method considerably, he might put the matter somewhat as follows:

It has generally been the custom to think of a stratum as including everything between the floor level of one building and that of the next building below. Or if the building below did not have a floor preserved, then one may attempt to calculate where it once had been, or to observe changes in artifacts, as a means of separating the strata. The building in question is then interpreted as the architecture of the stratum. Where something is obviously wrong, the debris is thought to be mixed. If one is thoroughly grounded in the typological history of the artifacts and studies the content of a given stratum carefully, then he obviously will remove items he knows were out of place and will in publishing indicate that they were out of context.

At Shechem it is clear that most of the dirt we have dug is from a variety of fills which have been carried in from elsewhere to level up an area for a new building, a courtyard or street. If, then, we were to publish all the artifacts found in fill between two floor levels or occupation surfaces, what would we use as a basis to date these surfaces? Occasionally there is some dark-colored occupational debris on the floor which is contemporary with the floor's use. Yet most of the dirt above a given floor is clearly a fill carried in for leveling purposes. And such fill is seldom homogeneous. One can never predict in advance what is going to be in it. If one knows his pottery well, then the *latest* fragments in the fill are probably not far removed in time from the date when the building was erected on the fill.

The easiest building to date is one that was destroyed while being used, so that the ceiling and walls collapsed on the floor, crushing vessels that were in use. Subsequent builders, the archaeologist hopes, may have leveled the ruins for new construction without removing the debris down to the floor level. If they did, then a dating problem arises. Other headaches are caused by rebuilding operations which cut through earlier floors. In such cases one is forced to date by the latest material *below* floors. Where in a given place all materials are destroyed, one can only hope that in a second or third cut (or section) they will be found so that an accurate archaeological horizon may de determined for the stratum in question. If no floors are preserved in a given stratum and the fill below is also disturbed, then one must save the artifacts carefully and reserve judgment while the work goes down to the next building level, the debris layers between and against the walls being watched carefully. By this procedure at least a relative chronology can be set up, and coherent ceramic groups can gradually be clarified for the different strata, even though in every case they are mixed.

We at Shechem have attempted to be consistent regarding the use of terms. For us "stratum" is used for a definite architectural horizon in the city as a whole, which may have two or more "phases." That is, if the same walls are used, but are rebuilt or only slightly altered and new floors put in, then it is a second phase of the same stratum. We also use the term "phase" followed by small letter or Arabic number as the temporary stratum indicator in a given field, pending the final numbering of the strata. The term "level" is used either for the surveyor's elevations or for the layers in debris which lack architectural features but have a vertical relationship to one another that is important. It would probably be better if we consistently used the term "layer" for the different types of debris encountered in an earth section.

The term "field" is used for a major digging sector, which in turn is divided into "areas." In freshly laid-out plots an area may be a 5-m. square. In digging areas previously excavated the term may refer to any small digging plot controlled by one supervisor, for there is nothing sacrosanct about the 5-m. square. The point is to have an area in which the stratification can be carefully controlled by balks and which can serve as a coherent subdivision of a field. Each earth layer or consistent and clearly definable small plot which is producing artifacts, and also each architectural feature encountered—a wall or floor, or even a pile of stones—is a "locus" and is given a number.

Thus in our nomenclature the designation "B.56 I.3 Loc. 1" means Balâṭah, the first campaign in 1956, Field I (the East Gate), Area 3, Locus 1. This was a small surviving fragment of an earthen floor which had escaped erosion and the digging or plowing of farmers on the slope of the mound immediately under the surface and over the south tower of the gate. It was covered with charcoal-filled dark earth, indicating burning, and some pottery fragments, including three whole juglets (see Fig. 88). I had occasion to re-examine this pottery following the 1962 campaign when Stratum VI of the seventh century B.C. had been clarified. It is now clear that this locus is to be dated to the seventh century, and is, therefore, a part of Stratum VI.[9]

In 1956 it was my privilege to visit the Rothschild-Hebrew University excavation at Hazor, north of the Sea of Galilee in Israel, directed by Yigael Yadin in four lengthy campaigns between 1955 and 1958. Its staff was composed of forty-five people —the largest ever assembled in one Syro-Palestine expedition— and its procedures were beautifully organized. I learned much from it, though I found myself wishing that Miss Kenyon's methods were more seriously taken. In any event, I was most impressed, and adapted certain things for our use at Shechem— though Professor Yadin might not have recognized them in their attenuated form! Both they and we, in partial contrast to the British, placed an absorbed attention and intensive emphasis on pottery analysis, one that was not casual or postponed, but prompt, immediate and careful. As the primary key to dating, pottery has served us at Shechem as a constant check on our digging procedure, as well as on the problems of stratigraphy and historical reconstruction.

In this regard both the Israelis and we are students of W.

F. Albright, in whose work at Tell Beit Mirsim, southeast of
Hebron on the border between Israel and Jordan, is to be found
the first systematic and empirical presentation of Palestinian
ceramic chronology, the main outlines of which are still basic to
Palestinian archaeological history.[10] Furthermore, Albright has
taught us never to forget that archaeologists are the research
arms of the historian, and without exceedingly great care in matters of chronology the literary and material evidence cannot
properly be put together. As a corollary one must, while digging,
constantly be attempting to push back the frontiers of chronological knowledge, always attempting to introduce more precision into our knowledge of the typological history of ceramic
forms.

The manner in which we have proceeded at Shechem in this
regard is somewhat as follows: each locus, as that term was
defined above, has a reed basket into which all pieces of pottery
are placed as they are found. The basket is quickly replaced with
an empty one as soon as any change in the debris is discerned. As
soon as this is done the basket is labeled and the find-spot of its
pottery is carefully described in a special ceramic notebook kept
in each field. The baskets of each area are numbered consecutively. Each object found, perhaps a metal tool or weapon or
seal, figurine or coin, is also labeled, not solely with its locus
number (that is, where it was found), but also with the pottery-
basket number which refers to the pottery coming from the
locus at the time when the object appeared. This basket number
becomes a permanent part of the object's recording so that its
context can be preserved.

Here, for example, is a typical number on a basket tag:
"B62.VII.8.17" followed by the date dug and perhaps by the
locus number. If the locus number is not on the tag, in any case
it is in the field ceramic notebook. The notations mean "Balâṭah,
the 1962 campaign, Field VII, Area 8." Basket 17 from that area
in 1962 came from Locus 1739 which is described as follows
in the field notebook: "Rusty limed layer sealed beneath 1627
and 1727, associated with Wall 1740. Stratum VIII, sealed by
Stratum VII above, and above the level of 1739 below." While
this pottery was appearing, a whole clay juglet turned up, calling
for special treatment because it would need to be listed in the

object register. The juglet was placed in a special box with the pottery-basket's number on it. Had it been a seal or other small object it would have been placed in an envelope bearing the pottery-basket number and locus number with date.

Both basket and object box are sent off the tell to the camp where a group scrubs the pottery clean with brushes and water. The contents of each basket are then spread on a mat to dry, after which they are given a preliminary sorting, with rims, handles, bases and other distinguishing or unusual features placed in a special box while body sherds are put back into the basket. The box and the special object (the juglet) are placed on top of the basket and the latter is set in a special row with other baskets brought that day from Field VII, Area 8. Had the special object been other than a pottery vessel, it would have gone directly to the recording room where Dr. Sellers would have cleaned it as much as possible and registered it in the object register with the appropriate information. Later that day or the next, Basket VII.8.17 was studied either by myself or Dr. Lapp (had it been from Field VI, it might have been Dr. Toombs), together with a field supervisor referring to his field ceramic notebook. The results of this study are recorded in special notebooks kept by the pottery analysts which list every basket of pottery, together with our notations as to its contents and date.

In the case of Basket VII.8.17, it is a mixed lot with Iron I and Iron II sherds, but nothing *later* than Stratum VIII material appears. Since it is sealed by a floor of Stratum VII above, we can confirm the conclusion reached in the field that Locus 1739 is fill laid over an VIII floor to level up for the VII floor. A number of the latest sherds were saved from the basket, not only as a proof of date, but also in an attempt to define as clearly as possible the nature and typology of VIII pottery. If some pieces earlier than VIII are also saved, this harms nothing, inasmuch as the differences between the pottery of VIII and that of the strata below will be defined as we excavate further.

The whole juglet appears to be a clear VIII form. It, together with the saved sherds, is sent into the recording room where two registers are kept, one for the pottery and one for objects. Whole pottery is in a special category: it may be desired by the Department of Antiquities in the selection of the objects it will choose to be kept in the country after the excavation is concluded. It is, therefore, listed in the object register as well as in the pottery registry. It thus receives two numbers which are written on it in India ink or attached to it on a tag: B62.VII.8.17. O(bject) 425. P(ottery) 1570. Had the special object been a seal, it would have been listed only in the object register.

In the final locus listings from Field VII, Area 8 in 1962, we note that Locus 1739 produced Baskets VII.8, 10, 15, 17, 19, 26 and 32. An accounting of the total time-range of the fill is made (that is, MB II B–C sherds are the earliest present, appearing in Nos. 10 and 19), and it is noted that registered sherds 1561, 1569, 1570–1576, 1581–1583 were saved from their respective baskets. Besides the juglet already noted, the locus also produced Object 415, a small limestone cylinder of indeterminate use, with Basket No. 19.

As regards field procedures, each field has a supervisor over the whole, and generally one assistant supervisor in each area of the field. Each assistant keeps notes and sketches on the work in his area. The field supervisor keeps his own notebook and sketches, and is responsible for the balk sections. In addition, Dr. Toombs as field director in his daily rounds may spend hours with the supervisor and assistants in the study of features difficult to interpret, in the discussion of section drawings or over the problem of how best to dig in order to solve a specific question. He, too, keeps his own notebook of his interpretations. Finally, in my own daily rounds I attempt to ask questions, to obtain a full description of what is going on, a full discussion of problems. I also offer critical comments about certain interpretations, or put forth hypotheses of my own for over-all interpretation in order to provoke discussion. This is not to dictate decisions, but to keep discussions open, to consider various possibilities before decision and to involve the whole staff as far as possible in the decision-making.

At the conclusion of a campaign each field supervisor has as his primary duty before any other commitments—other than supporting his family—to prepare a detailed and full written report on the work in his field during the campaign. Dr. Toombs and I have in our hands a series of manuscripts from three to four hundred pages long which we use, together with our own notes, in the preparation of the official preliminary report of the campaign. This material is prepared while memory is still green, and is now available for editing and rewriting for publication in the light of fuller details subsequently discovered. Meanwhile, staff members are either assigned or are encouraged to take over specific research for the final publication, and to publish preliminary reports as they are moved to do so.

This glimpse into the workings of one expedition may serve to indicate the detailed complexity of archaeological endeavor. More than scientific or procedural "know-how" is necessary. Careful planning and organization are essential. Each staff member must know precisely his duties and how his work fits into that of the organization as a whole. Frequent staff meetings analyze results so that the vision of the whole and the aims of the whole are seen by all. Self-criticism and a striving after excellence assist in maintaining high staff morale, without which the keen edge of curiosity and the continual search for meaning may be lost, the quality of the work suffer. Behind all of this is the importance of great care in the selection of the staff. The higher the quality of mind and heart, the greater the desire for knowledge and the better the historical results to be derived from the work.

5

The Fortification of the City

Wall A and the Northwest Gate

My first visit to the site of Shechem was in September of 1934 after the conclusion of the Bethel excavation. Dr. Albright, the Director, loaned a 1930-model Ford station wagon to four of us students on his staff, and told us to explore the country. My only memory of the visit to Shechem was an impression of the grandeur and strength of that great western Wall A. Welter had dug a trench along the outside of it in 1931 so that one could walk along its base as far as the Northwest Gate.[1] The trench was very deep. The top of the wall towered over one's head to a height of 30 ft.,[2] and one could walk along it for over 200 ft. (Fig. 18). The wall has a batter, that is, a slight slope inward as it rises, so that its top edge is 1.60 m. (over 5 ft.) off the vertical. It was erected on a layer of packed clay which overlay the bedrock and made a level surface for its footing. The stones used in the wall were huge boulders, some of them over 7 ft. in width (2 to 2.20 m.). Because of their uneven size they could be coursed only roughly. The worst of the projections on their faces had been chipped off to make their surfaces fairly flat. Smaller stones filled the spaces left between the larger ones.

According to Sellin, the inner face of the wall was not as well smoothed as the outer; it was not meant to be seen because earth would be piled against it. Here, then, we have a type of fortification that was introduced into Palestine during the second half of the Hyksos period of the seventeenth century B.C., a time when Syria-Palestine was controlled by Asiatic rulers who had been able to conquer Egypt. This type of fortification was erected around the base of mounds, so that if battering-rams attempted to make holes in the wall, they would only be pushing the stones into the earth behind.[3] Above the top of the stone wall, where necessary the earth slope of the mound was filled in, or smoothed off, tamped and plastered in place, so that attackers, if they got above the battered wall, would still have to ascend an open, slippery slope, the advantage remaining with the defenders at the top. During the early part of the Hyksos period more stress had been placed on the earthen bank; in the later period the heavy wall of stone had modified the original concept.

Such was the type and theory of the great Hyksos fortifications. Yet the topography of Shechem required that Wall A be something special and different. Welter's debris sections in 1928 and those of the Drew-McCormick Expedition in 1962 show that Wall A was initially erected as a freestanding structure (see Figs. 22 and 74), some 4 m. (13 ft.) thick. As it was built, masses of earth were thrown in against its inner face, until, when it was finished, the earth was leveled to its top. Fig. 74 shows how the earth was thrown in against Wall A from a previously existing slope, so that initially the earth layers fell against the wall horizontally, and were gradually raised as the builders put on the successive stone layers. At two points along the western face of the wall rectangular drains opened, 1 m. high and 45 cm. wide, from which the water was drained from the surface of the fill above them (Fig. 9). Fig. 19 is a sketch made by Architect Heinz Johannes on June 23, 1926; it shows the mouth of a third drain which led the water of the winter rains from the foundation of the fortress-temple.

As Sellin followed Wall A in its gentle curve to the north-

east in 1913, he was suddenly surprised to find a tower jutting
out from the wall 4.40 m. (nearly 14½ ft.). During the spring
of 1914 it was clear that he had come upon a city gate, completely preserved, including a stone cyclopean socket, 1.80 to
2 m. high, on which there was a superstructure of brick (Fig.
9). In the interval between 1914 and 1926 the villagers used the
gate as a quarry for building stone, thereby destroying many
of the features which would have made sense out of its plan.
This Shechem gate is recognizable, however, as an example of
the most typical Bronze Age gate, possessing three entryways,
one behind the other, or as Sellin put it in 1914, "it has a three-
fold locking device." A detailed description with precise dimensions was never published. We think much of the detail can be
recovered, however, from what exists now, from published general plans and from a notebook of Dr. Praschniker, showing
stone-by-stone sketches and elevations drawn in 1914.[4]

Essentially the gate was a great structure approximately
16 m. (52½ ft.) wide and 18 m. long (59 ft.), set into Wall A
as it turned at the northwest (see the plan in Fig. 9).[5] At each
side are towers running the full length of the gate and about
4.50 m. wide (14¾ ft.). Inside the towers are narrow passages
that undoubtedly once held wooden ladders leading into store-
rooms within the brick superstructure and thence to the roofs
for the use of guards and defending soldiers. In the southern or
left-hand tower as one looks from within the city, the narrow
passage continues, opening into a guardroom or storeroom in
the corner made by the wall and gate tower. It seems that the
passage must have contained a ramp because the level of the
room was much higher than the floor of the gate.

The entryways both in the Northwest and in the East Gate
are constructed in a peculiar way. In each entryway two huge
blocks jut inward from the towers on each side. Between the
outer and inner blocks of each tower is a slot in which a door or
gate must once have been held. The width of the blocks jutting
from each tower is only a little less than the width of the entry.
Hence if a gate were pulled out of its slot, nearly one-half of it
would still be supported by the stone blocks, while the other
half filled one-half of the opening. Then when the door on the
opposite side was pulled to, the whole opening would be closed

by the pair of gates.[6] It is also possible that the gates were let down from the towers above, or that beams were set in place from above. To protect the great doors from being forced by a battering-ram, a long bar between two and three inches in diameter and evidently covered with copper, was placed behind the doors in slots prepared for it. This deduction is drawn from the fact that the top inside edge of the inner stone of the southern tower's entryway at the outermost (northwest) gateway has the circular grooving where the bar was moved back and forth in its tower support. Presumably the other two entries could be blocked in the same way. It must be admitted, however, that the excavation staff has found the problem of the effective use of these gates most puzzling. However the slots were employed, it would not seem as though they would effectively hold a door for long against a vigorous battering-ram.

We cannot at this time state the precise dimensions of those openings. It will not be far wrong, however, if we say that the gate opening was about 2.60 m. wide (8½ ft.), and that the width of each of the stone blocks on either side was nearly the same, making the total width between the towers not less than *ca.* 6.75 to 7 m. (between 22 and 23 ft.). The two inner courts created by the two entries are roughly 6.75 by 3.50 m. (*ca.* 22 by 11½ ft.). The foundations of the tower and of each of the three entries were found to be made of the same kind of huge stones as were used in the wall itself, and set 6 m. deep (over 19½ ft.) to discourage sapping operations.

This interpretation of the nature of the gateway may seem unjustified, and indeed, as far as I am aware, there are no clear parallels to rolling doors elsewhere. City gates, like house doors, were generally hung from a vertical beam which was fixed to turn in a stone socket at the bottom. This beam bore the weight, and when fastened above in the wood and brick superstructure of the gate, the beam would turn satisfactorily on the vertical.[7] Yet the Shechem city gates are not of this type. Though their stone platforms and underpinnings were found beautifully preserved when originally excavated, there were no gate sockets for the doors to turn on. Instead there were these great stone blocks or orthostats, a pair on each side of each entryway. Something obviously fitted between them, and this could only be the gates.

The symmetrical dimensions are also a factor to be considered. Consequently, only one more simple hypothesis is called for: the heavy doors must have moved backward and forward between the stone orthostats on rollers or on wheels of wood.

In Fig. 21 we present a reconstruction of Wall A and its Northwest Gate on the tell's west side. The wall which we here see with its two drain openings is still in existence. The gate and the superstructure of the wall are, of course, reconstructed by hypothesis, based on the ground plan of the gate; the top is pictured in accordance with representations from Egypt of second millennium Syro-Palestinian fortified cities. These do not have the many towers and the stepped, or "crowfoot," battlements of the Assyrian Iron Age representations. Instead, the projecting battlements or fighting platforms were evidently made of brick and beams set over the stone, as is here suggested.[8]

Inside the Northwest Gate and along the wall directly south of it were structures which Sellin believed to be the city's palace. Our evidence, especially from Fields I and III, now suggests that Sellin's is a very doubtful hypothesis. In all probability the rooms built against the city walls were magazines or storage rooms, which aided in supporting the fighting platforms, in places over 10 m. wide, erected over the walls for defense. The row of columns found by Sellin need not at all have been the columns of a hall. Rather, because the row was so long, they could have supported the battlements, leaving either a closed or open area under them (*see* for suggestion, the background behind the temple as reconstructed in Fig. 47).

What is the date and history of this great fortification? This can be established when we examine the fortifications which preceded it and which it replaced, and when we examine the stratification in Field I at the East Gate. One would think that the date could be easily determined by an examination of the fill thrown against it when it was being built. This earth does indeed have sherds in it. They are Chalcolithic of the early fourth millennium B.C., a few Early Bronze (late fourth and third millennia) and Middle Bronze I (twentieth century) pieces, and MB II A to C (nineteenth to mid-seventeenth century B.C.). Hence the strong suggestion is that Wall A and the Northwest Gate were erected during the course of the seventeenth century. This is

what we should expect from its type, and that date will be conclusively confirmed when we look more closely at the whole history of the city's defense.

Fortifications C and D

One of Welter's main objectives in 1928 was to dig trenches
across the whole western side of the tell in order to enable him
to draw a cross-section and show the various features in relation
to one another. Fig. 22 shows a sketch of what he found, and to
it there have been added a number of our own discoveries and
the designations we have given them to facilitate discussion.

Between Wall A at the left in Fig. 22 and Wall 900 at the
right, the latter being Sellin's "*Temenos* Wall," is a distance of
ca. 67 m. (220 ft.). Inside Wall A at a distance from it of just
over 8 m. (26 ft.) is Retaining Wall C. This is a battered wall,
5 m. (*ca.* 16½ ft.) high, erected on the bedrock. Its inner face
was left very rough, indicating that it was built against debris
which was already in place. In this respect, as also in type of
masonry, it is almost an exact duplicate of a comparable wall at
Jericho, built around and against the outer slope of the mound.[9]
Slightly to the right of center in Fig. 22 and directly below the
temple portico is still another city wall, Wall D. What are the
dates and relationship of Walls C and D?

Since D was exposed by Welter for a considerable distance
south of the temple, we attempted to get a debris section against
it in 1960 by a trench, dug under the supervision of H. Neil
Richardson (Field V, Area 9). The earth against the inner face
of the wall had been removed by Welter, and nothing could be
done there. On the outer or western side, below a filled-in German trench which followed the edge of the wall, we encountered
almost sterile layers of brown earth and clay that gave us an
insufficient amount of pottery for any conclusive date determination. Finally, a section was dug straight through the wall, and
the result is shown in Fig. 23. The two faces of the wall are ex-
cellently made of carefully coursed stones, the outside of which
have had the worst projections chipped off so that a vertical
flat surface was obtained. The interior, however, was stone rubble mixed with earth. From this rubble we were able to collect

a sufficient number of sherds to show that the wall could not be earlier than the first part of the developed Middle Bronze Age of the second half of the eighteenth century B.C. There were sharply carinated vessel fragments present of MB II B (*ca.* 1750–1650 B.C.).

On the other hand, the *type* of fortification suggests a pre-Hyksos date, that is, before *ca.* 1700 B.C. It was a freestanding socket of stone, comparatively small in width for city walls. Our measurements showed it to vary between 2.50 and 2.85 m. (between *ca.* 8 and 9 ft.), indicating that the builders were erecting a 6-cubit wall.[10] Welter says that when he discovered it running under the temple's portico it had bricks still preserved on top of the stone socket (see Fig. 22). We discovered it in two places running northeast of the temple. In Field VI.2 we found its top and outer surface well preserved deep in the debris (Figs. 16 and 17). The height of the stone socket was 1.70 m., and its smooth top suggested a pavement, until further digging revealed the nature of the wall and the fact that the flat surface of the stone socket had been carefully prepared for the wall's superstructure of brick. The socket had been laid on an MB II A (*ca.* 1850–1750 B.C.) flagstone-and-cobble paving which surrounded an oven. Here again is the strong suggestion that Wall D belongs to MB II B. In the next chapter it will be noted that D belongs to the second phase of the *temenos* area, and the first of four phases of MB II B.

This evidence suggests that a date in the third quarter of the eighteenth century cannot be far wrong. Three other Palestinian city walls of the same type and general period have been found at Megiddo, Debir (Tell Beit Mirsim) and possibly Jericho. At Megiddo a brick city wall and gateway were found; the wall is only 1.80 m. wide and belongs within the phases of Strata XV–XIII of the MB II A period.[11] Jericho has a 2-m.-wide brick wall which is probably contemporary with Shechem's Wall D.[12] Tell Beit Mirsim G (probably about 1800 B.C.) has a fine stone socket for a brick wall, *ca.* 3.25 m. (*ca.* 10½ ft.) wide.[13] In type all of these follow the Early Bronze tradition of vertical walls, erected around the summit of a mound, without the support of a prepared slope (glacis), fosse or battered wall against the mound's lower sides.

As already indicated, Wall C is simply the outer support and protection for a great pile of earth behind it. As a result of his trenching in the sector in 1928, Welter stated his conclusions as follows:

> The battered wall [our Wall C] is older than the cyclopean city wall [Wall A]. It "comprises a sloping stone socket and a high sloping fill of packed marl. . . . Several trenches . . . were dug. In this way the length of the slope was found to be 40 m. The western [southwestern] end of the slope has been excavated . . . where it forms an angle of 90 degrees and disappears in a southerly [southeasterly] direction. It has been established that it represented a truncated pyramid built on a sloping stone socket of a height of about 5 m. Its socket, being a retaining wall, consisted of large unhewn stones laid on bedrock. The fill is, for the greatest part, composed of calcareous marl interspersed with occasional layers of ordinary soil from Mt. Ebal, containing ferric oxide. The surface of the pyramid is covered with a layer of sifted white marl, well packed."[14]

In other words, the fill retained by and rising over Wall C is artificial fill from the slopes of Ebal. Our own investigations sustain this conclusion. Between Wall C and Wall D there is a great mound of marly soil, the darker layers increasing in extent as one descends within it. Welter traced it as far as the Northwest Gate and believed that he had found the ends of the fill. Hence he suggested that it was a great pyramid, 40 m. square, erected as the base of a fortification tower which has disappeared, its place being taken by a later tower, the building both Sellin and we claim to have been a temple.

The evidence for this so-called "pyramid" is most tenuous, and by 1932 Welter seems quietly to have given it up. Instead, he speaks of "a rampart of white, packed clay." Above "the steeply sloping socket of crudely-cut, large rocks" (Wall C), he says that "the surface of the slope had originally been overlaid with fist-sized stones, in order to give it more stability."[15] In any event, it is to be hoped that the pyramid idea will not be continued in the literature.

Since Wall D was used as the inner revetment for the great earthen rampart, we must agree with Welter, therefore, that D is the earliest city wall known at Shechem. Shortly after it was erected, Shechem was given massive protection by the C earthen fortification, which at the bottom of its exterior face was buttressed by the C battered wall, 5 m. in height. At the north of the tell in our Field VIII we dug to the bottom of the C earthern fortification, which was over 6 m. below where Sellin's deep pit in his north-south Trench L had gone. That is, there is clear evidence for the C Embankment on the north as well as on the west and northwest. On the east, at least one debris section left by the German expeditions, though unrecorded, shows clear evidence of the same embankment a short distance north of the East Gate.

Under the temple at the west the width of the C Embankment between retaining Wall C and Wall D is approximately 30 m. (*ca.* 100 ft.). How high it once was is unknown, though it was at least 10 m. (*ca.* 32 ft.), and was probably much more. In any event, it was the existence of this artificial embankment that led to the type of structure represented by Wall A when it was deemed necessary to strengthen further the defenses. The C Embankment was also a major factor in the height to which Wall A was built, as well as the position of the temple on top of it. On the other hand, the leveling of the top of the C Embankment for the temple may well have provided a good part of the fill thrown in against Wall A when it was erected, at least in the sections made through it (cf. Figs. 22 and 74). Welter found a limestone pavement 4 m. below the level of the Northwest Gate, and suggests that the city gate of the C Embankment period had been located there. It will be recalled, however, that in 1960 we also found a fine stone pavement in the midst of the embankment fill, but at so deep a level, with fill of the same age both below and above it, that it is dangerous to theorize about its purpose. For this reason we must remain doubtful that Welter actually found evidence of the C gateway.

Great earthen fortifications like the one at Shechem are known to have been introduced into Syria and Palestine at the beginning of the Hyksos period. The best known examples are those at Hazor (and perhaps Jericho) in Palestine; at Qatna on the Orontes River and at Carchemish on the Euphrates in Syria; and at Tell el-Yehudiyeh in the Egyptian Delta.[16] One must suppose that the earthen embankments were thrown up where needed by a great army, which mobilized the local populations for a maximal and quickly completed effort in fortification. Existing slopes were used where possible, but where they did not exist, they were literally created.

The following, then, is a summary of our evidence for Shechem's fortifications on the mound's western side:

(1) Wall D—a vertical-standing wall of brick on a stone socket, *ca.* 2.50 to 2.85 m. (or 6 cubits) thick. Date: *ca.* 1750–1725 B.C. (Pre-Hyksos).

(2) The great earthen embankment with revetment Wall C on its exterior face and employing Wall D to retain it within the city. Date: *ca.* 1725–1700 B.C. (Early Hyksos).

(3) The cyclopean Wall A and the Northwest Gate. Date: *ca.* 1650 B.C. (Late Hyksos).

Needless to say, these dates are only approximations, but the evidence for them will mount as we consider now and in the chapter which follows the stratification that can be related to them.

Wall B and Its Relation to Wall A

During 1956 and 1957 the eastern slope outside the East Gate in Field I proved to be most interesting, complex and important. Preserved are two main periods of intense activity on that slope. The latest was Hellenistic (or Samaritan) during the time between *ca.* 331 B.C. and 190 B.C. At this time the Samaritans cleared away all debris down to the Middle Bronze levels, filled in the slope with deep layers of earth, covered older defenses, and then plastered or cemented the whole slope up to the gate so that it would not erode. The earliest layers of cement dropped away so rapidly, deep within the earth of the orchard outside our digging area, that one may suppose that a dry fosse was created at the foot of the slope (see Fig. 108). In other words, the Samaritans created a glacis and fosse for defensive purposes. The gate towers were rebuilt and curb walls were installed to hold the steep piles of debris from filling in the now sunken roadway of the gate. Within a short time, however, still within the earliest Samaritan period (Stratum IV, *ca.* 331–250 B.C.), the fosse was filled in and evidence of houses there appeared. Toward the end of the third century or early in the second century, another disturbance caused the Samaritans to abandon the gate and Wall B entirely. In its place a tower and screening walls were erected which could not have offered a serious defense to a determined army (Stratum II, *ca.* 190–150 B.C.).

We shall return to the Samaritan story for more detail in our final chapter. Of particular interest at this point is that the Samaritan glacis or cemented slope was laid upon an earlier one, precisely like it, of the Middle Bronze Age, though the actual cement was preserved only for a short distance beside the south tower of the gate. (See Fig. 108, Section B–B below the "H[el-lenistic] Striated Make-up.") So unexpected was the Hellenistic glacis that when we first encountered it in 1956 I was certain that it was Middle Bronze Age, and this conclusion was but-tressed by the fact that a dark layer of earth fill over it contained nothing but Middle Bronze Age sherds.[17] In 1957 excavation below the late glacis turned up Hellenistic pottery. This was the first dramatic warning to me about earth fills: be extremely care-ful in the trust you place in an archaeological fill; it can so easily betray you!

The matter was clarified in 1957, however, by the discovery of the remnant of the Middle Bronze Age glacis below the Hel-lenistic. Below that two heavy walls appeared, roughly parallel to each other and *ca.* 4.90 to 4.95 m. (16 ft.) apart. In 1956 we called them Middle Bronze "revetments," thinking that they were in place to hold back erosion.[18] In 1957, however, we found that the outer one went down and down, and the stones in it became larger and larger as we descended along its outer face. We dug in front of it to a depth of 6.30 m. (just over 20½ ft.) before we had to quit for fear that the stones of the Stratum II tower above would topple in on the workers. Large stones measuring up to 90 by 120 cm. had at that depth become common. The cyclopean building technique was identical with that of Wall A on the west, so that there was only one conclusion: Wall A exists on the east in front of the East Gate (see Figs. 24 and 108). This con-clusion was confirmed by the following further considerations:

(1) The position of Wall A was also discovered in Field III, precisely 11 m. (36 ft.) in front of Wall B, the space between the two having also been filled by a glacis at the end of the

Middle Bronze Age. In Field I Wall A is also 11 m. from Wall B as the latter leaves the East Gate and continues on south.

(2) In Field III the footing for Wall A is at a surprisingly high level, and only three or four courses of large stones remain of it, though what we found may have been a reconstruction of the original. In Field I the depth to which Wall A was buried indicates that there was originally a valley at this point which Wall A crosses (cf. Fig. 31). The filling in of this valley behind the fortification created the platform on which the East Gate was erected. Here, then, is another dramatic example of the vast leveling and filling that went on to create a powerful city-state center at Middle Bronze Shechem.

(3) The street leading to the East Gate seems never to have come from the east, but always from the south along the edge of the gate's southeast tower. The strong suggestion implicit in this fact is that an obstruction existed to the east which prevented the road from climbing the bank. That is, Wall A is, therefore, presupposed; and in the Samaritan period the glacis and fosse were part of the fortification and not a road. The road at the foot of the gate tower would thus have been under the direct protection of those guarding the gate from the tower above.

The proof that Wall A was erected some time before Wall B and the East Gate were built is to be found in the Rooms 362, 365 and 366 (Building 110) between Walls A and A 2 (Fig. 24). The latter is a heavy wall, *ca.* 1 m. thick, and preserved to a height of over 2.50 m. A door in it gave access to a court, Locus 362, and from the court another door opened to Rooms 366 and 365. The northern wall was incompletely preserved and in any case showed signs of reconstruction. Most important is the fact that two living surfaces were preserved here. The original court had a cobblestone floor, Locus 364. Forty centimeters above it was an earth floor, Locus 362. Each surface had considerable charcoal in the debris upon it, and one could presume, therefore, that the city had seen fighting and destruction, or else there was at this point local burning, during the time when Wall A was the sole fortification.

There were, therefore, two phases of the use of Building 110 and its Court 362–364, after Wall A was in existence. Only in the third main phase was the door into Court 362 blocked up, perhaps gradually, and a series of cobblestone streets, Loci 310–314, one a repaving of the other, passed outside Wall A 2, at levels high above Court 362 (Fig. 25). The streets abut directly on the southeast tower of the gate (Fig. 24). The blocking of the door into Court 362 was done, therefore, when the East Gate was erected and the street placed between Wall A 2 and the gate's southeast tower in Loci 310–314.

Figure 26 shows an isometric drawing of the earliest phase of the East Gate, corresponding to the third phase in the story of Wall A 2 when its door was being blocked up. Whether Court 362 was still in use at this time is not known, though perhaps doubtful. The street levels are so high comparatively that Building 110 may not have been occupied. What was the purpose of this building? The size and strength of Wall A 2 suggests that it may not have been unrelated to the Wall A defense system. While Court 362 is too wide to have been roofed, since beams longer than about 12 ft. would have been rare, nevertheless Rooms 365 and 366 undoubtedly were, and these roofs may well have been related to Wall A's battlements and fighting platform, just as was probably the case southwest of the Northwest Gate (cf. Figs. 21 and 47). All Bronze Age fortification walls at Shechem appear to have had parallel walls inside them, which are subdivided into rooms and courts. The latter in a different type of fortifications would be called "casemates." That is the reason at any rate for the use of the term "MB Casemate" in Fig. 24.

The pottery from Building 110, certainly that sealed in Locus 363 between surfaces 362 and 364, should date from a time *after* Wall A had been erected but *before* the East Gate and Wall B were built (*see* Appendix 6). This pottery belongs to the period of MB II C (*ca.* 1650–1550 B.C.): that is, from the same period as the masses of pottery recovered from the successive destructions of the East Gate, but succeeding the quantities of MB II B pottery (*ca.* 1750–1650 B.C.) from Field VI which precede Wall A and are contemporary with fortifications C and D. Hence the Wall A system belongs to MB II C, but during the course of the same period it was strengthened on the east and north by the Wall B system.

Turning now to Wall B, Sellin followed it from the East

Gate to his east-west trench; it crossed our Field III (*see* Fig. 20) at a distance of over 50 m. (i.e. over 164 ft.). An entirely different type of fortification from that of Wall A, it was not built against the mound's sides, but like Wall D was meant to stand vertically on the edge of the mound's summit. Today it exists as a stone socket which varies between 3.25 and 3.75 m. The average between these extremes indicates that the builders were building an 8-cubit-wide structure (*ca.* 11 ft. 8 in.), the variation being caused by the size of the stones and the manner in which they were laid together. In size these stones are medium to small, roughly coursed. On top of the socket the main part of the fortification was of brick interlaced with beams, and probably with brick and wooden battlements above that. When it was first destroyed, evidently by the Egyptian army between *ca.* 1550 and 1540 B.C. (*see below*), the Egyptians were able to set fire to the wall because there was so much wood in it and in battlements upon it, and to pull sufficient brick from its lower part as to cause it to fall inward, instead of outward down the slope. The great quantity of charcoal remains of the wooden beams indicates an exceedingly hot fire. The distance the fallen debris spread within the city from the wall base was at least 14 to 15 m. (46 to 49 ft.) in Field III. This suggests that the height of the brick above the stone base was surely a minimum of 10 m. (*ca.* 33 ft.).

Wall B furthermore was an "offsets and insets" structure. That is, it was evidently built in straight sections, each *ca.* 15 m. (49 ft.) long. The next section would either jut back or forward as the case may be, *ca.* 50 cm. (or perhaps about 1 cubit, 17½ in.); see Fig. 20. This type of building gave added strength, and it also enabled the builders to follow the curve of the mound's summit by simply altering the angle by which the straight sections were joined to one another.

One of the major unsolved questions of Dr. Sellin, as also of Welter, was the relation of Walls A and B. One theory was that Wall B was simply the eastern fortification, while Wall A was the western. What Sellin found in his various trenches and pits on the mound's north and northeast sides was never completely drawn on plans by an architect. At one point he believed he had found a jog in Wall A at the north which connected it with B. Welter believed that Wall A was a fortification for the "acropolis" (west and northwest sectors) alone, while Wall B took care of "the lower city." In cutting a trench across the threshold of the East Gate he seems to have found Wall A, as we did, but he did not dig down far enough to discover its true nature. Instead, he considered it a retaining wall or revetment to protect the foundations of the gate and Wall B from slipping.[19] In 1956 I had the same theory about our "Revetments 1 and 2," which only in 1957 were renamed Wall A and Wall A 2.

In a trench dug in the spring of 1928, Sellin followed ruined masses of brick work from Wall B around the northeast and northern sectors, Fig. 20, H–M 3–4. How much of the actual stone socket of Wall B he discovered is today not clear from the surviving trench. A large section of it, however, was exposed in H–3, and its location indicated in Fig. 20. This means without question that it circled the whole eastern and northern portions of the tell and joined the Northwest Gate at the inner side of the northeast tower, below the upper building[20] shown on the drawing in Field IV, Figs. 9 and 20.

The nature of this fortification system and the fact that in both Fields III and I it is above and just 11 m. (36 ft.) inside Wall A, proves that it was built as a means of strengthening the Wall A system from the Northwest Gate around to the East Gate, and on south beyond the limit of excavations. The fact that the bank between the two in Field III was a cemented glacis is a further support to this conclusion. Consequently, the reconstruction of the relation between the two in Figs. 21, 26 and 31 has its justification. One would think that this intensive effort would indeed have made an impregnable city. Wall A south of the Northwest Gate (Fig. 21) was so high that Wall B was not needed in that sector.

The East Gate

The plan of the gate as it was originally built is shown in Figs. 24 and 26. One approached it from the south along the cobbled street and then turned left into the gate and thence into the city. To the south, therefore, somewhere underneath modern Balâtah village, there existed another gate in Wall A, in addition to that at the northwest. In type the East Gate is a slightly simplified version of the latter, with only two entries instead of three. These are wider than those in the Northwest Gate and spaced farther apart. The northern and southern tower blocks in over-all dimensions were *ca.* 13.30 m. in depth (43½ ft.) and 4.70 m. in width (15½ ft.). Within each was a guardroom and stairwell to upper stories, 6.55 m. long by 1.80 m. wide (21½ by 6 ft.). The rectangular court between the two entryways is sizable, being approximately 8 m. wide by 6.55 m. in depth between the entries (*ca.* 26 ft. by 21½ ft.). The width of the entries is *ca.* 3.40 m. between piers jutting out from the towers on each side (cf. Fig. 27).

Wall B leads off from the north tower, 2.50 m. from its outer edge. Parallel to it is a thin 90-cm. wall, the space between them being 1.75 m. If this were a structure to support a fighting platform above, the total width of the platform, including the width of the B wall itself, would have been 6 m. at this point (just under 20 ft.). South of the gate the platform would have been slightly wider because the inner wall is a bit farther away from Wall B. In Field III, on the other hand, the inner wall is 8.30 m. (27 ft.) distant from B. A brick cross-wall helped support the upper story, and three stone steps remained beside Wall B, a portion of a stairway to the second floor of the battlement structures.

It was characteristic of all Middle Bronze Age fortifications at Shechem to have inner walls running parallel to the main walls. The cross-walls between the two created rooms, casemates, or sometimes courts (in the case of Building 110 in Field I). There was no fixed rule, however, as to how far away from the main wall the inner one would be. Perhaps the determinant in each sector was the nature of the fortified superstructure which a given area was believed to need or the size of the building beside the wall which was desired. In the case of Walls A and A 2 at the East Gate, the distance between the two was 4.90 m., but to the south of the Northwest Gate a comparable distance was 10 m. It might be argued that the rooms along the city walls were simply dwellings of one sort or another without any particular architectural form. Yet the size of Walls A 2 and B 2 in Fields I and III, as well as of B 2 leading north in Field I, makes no sense unless these walls are related to the fortifications.

The quantities of pottery and objects found in the ruins of the earliest phases of the East Gate make the date of its construction quite certain. Though stratigraphy proves that it was erected some time after Wall A had been in existence, the pottery shows it to have been built in the same period, MB II C (*ca.* 1650–1550 B.C.). Only detailed ceramic study now under way will be able to discern differences between the earlier and later phases of this century.

It appears evident that the East Gate suffered destruction some time after it was erected, but, still within the MB II C period, it was reconstructed. The road surface was raised *ca.* 1.70 to 2 m. higher than it had been. Heavy threshold footings crossing under the gate openings were raised to prevent sapping. The south wall along the court, enclosing the guardroom stairwell, was reconstructed and its stone socket raised. Whether the same was done on the north side is unknown because of later stone removal. Most clearly evident is the installation of large, carefully cut, basalt blocks or orthostats on the stone thresholds, a pair on each side of each entryway (see Fig. 27). Their top edges are carefully prepared to receive wooden beams averaging 30 to 35 cm. (just under and over 1 ft.) in width. Their arrangement and dimensions are shown in Fig. 28. Stones 2 and 5 had recessed areas on their inner faces as though worn by something pushed in and out between them and their mates. Sliding doors may be argued for these gate entries as for those in the Northwest Gate, but, as indicated above, the question of the effective use of the doors in these gates is by no means settled.

The raising of the threshold level of the gate also raised the street level in the gate; in order to enter the city, a flight of five steps had to be installed descending to the court immediately before the gate's entrance (see Fig. 27). This entrance must have originally been well done, as the arrangement of orthostats 4a, 4b and 5a indicate (Figs. 28 and 29); 5b, corresponding to 4b, had been removed some time between the fifthteenth and twelfth centuries B.C. Fine masonry represented by these stones is far more common in Lebanon, Syria and Anatolia than in Palestine. It was even more frequently used at the magnificent site of Hazor, north of the Sea of Galilee. Shechem, for all its power and strength, evidently did not care to spend much of its resources on artistic endeavor for the sake of "show."

The steps show little evidence of wear. They are so rough that they were probably covered with a marly earth cement originally, just as is done in Balâṭah today with uneven stone surfaces. But in any case they cannot have been long in use when they were completely covered by fallen brick debris from the towers above. A fierce battle had taken place and the towers were burned and at least partially destroyed. Rebuilding was evidently rapid. The debris of the gate, including the disarticulated fragments of at least six human bodies, was swept into the step area until its level was raised nearly to the threshold level. A new street was created with brown field earth mixed with marl. Then came a second destruction of much greater violence. It filled the south guardroom stairwell with 2 m. of brick debris which spilled out through the door into the gate's court. Some of it remained through the centuries against the south wall of the court. Outside to the south, a pocket created by Wall B and the tower was filled with brick to a depth of over 3 m.; this debris was simply leveled over by later builders and never removed. Thick masses of brick and carbonized wood from the large timbers which reinforced the brick fell inside the city when Wall B was destroyed along its entire length. As suggested above, apparently an enemy had pulled out enough brick and beams from the inside foundations to make the whole mass fall inward on the city, instead of outward down the slope.

The sixteenth-century defenses of the city, after the erection of the B fortification system, would seem to have been impregnable. The undiscovered southern gate through Wall A must have been forced to allow the attackers to get a large battering-ram at work on the East Gate. This, too, proved vulnerable to a determined enemy and was forced. The southern set of orthostats at the inner entryway shows the evidence. One of the stones was dislodged and its corner broken off by a battering-ram. It was never again straightened (Fig. 29).

In both Fields III and VIII we encountered the same evidence of two violent destructions of the city within the final years of the Middle Bronze Age. A glance at the recorded his-

tory of the period quickly provides the cause. The Theban native
Egyptian monarchs of the Seventeenth Dynasty (*ca.* 1600–1570
B.C.) began the slow process of accumulating the resources to
throw the Hyksos foreigners out of their country. The founder
of the Eighteenth Dynasty, Ahmose (*ca.* 1570–1545 B.C.), finally
succeeded in capturing their capital, Avaris, in the Delta. Then
began the conquest of Palestine, Lebanon and Syria. Sharuhen
(Tell el-Fara, southeast of Gaza) on the Palestinian frontier fell
after a three-year siege. Every excavated city of the time in
Palestine shows evidence of destruction in the same era.[21] How
far north this Pharaoh managed to go in his conquest of the
Mediterranean coastland is unknown and consequently debated.
The Palestinian evidence suggests that a positive appraisal of
his achievement is probably in order. In any event, we may with
fair probability attribute the first of the last two Middle Bronze
Age destructions of the Wall B system to Ahmose in the final
years of his life (perhaps *ca.* 1550–1545 B.C.).

The son and successor of Ahmose was Amenophis I (*ca.*
1545–1525 B.C.). In the early years of his reign he claims to have
reached the Euphrates in Northern Syria. To him, then, we may
probably attribute the second destruction of the Wall B system
at Shechem. To assume it was an accomplishment of one of his
successors, Thutmose I (1525–1508 B.C.) or Thutmose II (1508–
1490 B.C.), is too late for the pottery chronology. The evidence is
best satisfied with the two destructions as suggested above in
the decade between 1550 and 1540 B.C.

To summarize the history of Shechem's fortification systems
so far described, we obtain the following:

(1) Wall D, the first known city wall, *ca.* 1750–1725 B.C.
(Pre-Hyksos)

(2) The great C Earthern Embankment, *ca.* 1725–1700 B.C.
(Early Hyksos)

(3) The cyclopean Wall A and the Northwest Gate, erected
ca. 1650 B.C. (Fifteenth Dynasty period)

(4) Wall B and the East Gate—First or Cobbled-Street
Phase, *ca.* 1625–1575 (?)

(5) The East Gate rebuilt—Second or Orthostat Phase, *ca.*
1575 (?) (cf. Figs. 27, 29 and 30). First Egyptian destruction,
ca. 1550 B.C.; second Egyptian destruction, *ca.* 1540 B.C.

(6) The East Gate of Lab'ayu and Abimelech, *ca.* 1550–1100 B.C.

The violence of the Egyptian conquest of Palestine was so terrible that the country made a slow recovery. I do not believe that we can point to a single stratum or deposit in any excavated site within the country which can be considered as dating with certainty within the period *ca.* 1540–1500 B.C. The most characteristic feature of the first half of the fifteenth century is encountered in strata at Megiddo in the north and at Tell el-'Ajjul in the south: an interesting and beautiful type of pottery bearing a bichrome decoration and amusing representations of a bird and a fish on large and small jugs. We have found the ancestor of this pottery in the leveling fill at the East Gate for the last Middle Bronze or Orthostat Phase (*see above*). Its ware is much like that of the bichrome ware, but the painted decoration is a monochrome red, the color varying from a slightly purplish red to orange-red and reddish brown.[22] In addition, we have found the immediate successor of the bichrome ware in stratified contexts following the Egyptian destructions. This also has a bichrome decoration, but the ware is much different and there are no birds or fish.

This, then, is the basis for our suggestion that a gap exists in the occupation of Shechem. The city was so violently ruined, and so many people were killed by the Egyptians, that nearly a century goes by before the city begins to flourish again. After that the great age of Shechem continues in two phases before it is brought to an abrupt halt: the Late Bronze phase, *ca.* 1450–1200 B.C., which for convenience we shall call "The Lab'ayu phase," though this gentleman was king in the early fourteenth century only; and an early Iron Age phase, dating from the twelfth century, which for convenience we shall name "The Abimelech phase."

The normal course of erosion and later building has done away with all direct evidence for the rebuilding of fortifications A and B. However, we have the following evidence that they were repaired and rebuilt:

(1) Wall A in Field III evidently needed repair and strengthening. Hence another strip of heavy buttressing wall was erected inside it, leaving a pocket between the two which had

been used as a pottery dump. It was full of the worst kind of
Late Bronze Age pottery which we dubbed "sewer" ware, because it was so crude, unpleasant to handle, and frequently covered with a greenish patina as though it had been sitting in a
dirty, damp area for a long time. I heard Dr. Albright once say
that the worst of the Late Bronze Age pottery was some of the
most terrible ever made in Palestine. This was the first time I
had encountered it, and there was no question about the correctness of Dr. Albright's judgment. Fine wares could be made and
imported, but the gap between good and poor had now been
vastly accentuated. One can only suggest that the rapacity of
the Egyptian overlords had created poverty at a more terrible
level than that of the preceding Middle Bronze or Early Bronze
Ages. At any rate, this mass of pottery by Wall A suggests that
the Wall A system may have been repaired and reused.

(2) Inside Wall B in Field III the casemate fortification
was rebuilt precisely along Middle Bronze Age lines. Wall B 2
had Late Bronze Age B 3 built over it. This was a 1.50-m.-wide
stone socket for a brick superstructure. Between Wall B 2 and
Wall B in the Middle Bronze period there was a brick cross-wall,
made of square, kiln-fired bricks, 35 by 35 by 15 cm. in size. This
brick wall was simply built higher in the Late Bronze Age, since
the level of occupation had to be raised over the earlier ruins
some 2 m. Late Bronze bricks, however, were rectangular, 55
by 35 by 15 cm. in size. The main point, is, however, that this
rebuilding of the casemates would have made no sense had
Wall B not also been rebuilt (see Fig. 32).

(3) Finally, we know that the East Gate was rebuilt, but
on a new plan. The south guardroom stairwell was left filled with
debris. Brick debris was left between the piers or orthostats and
the southwest or inner pair we know to have been almost covered. What seems to have happened was that curb walls were
installed within the gate to hold back the debris, and from this
time on the roadway in the gate must have been a kind of
sunken passageway.

Most important, however, is the fact that a new guardroom
and a new fortification wall were erected immediately behind
(west) of the gate's south tower (see Fig. 24: Walls 118, 126–
128). As one entered the East Gate in the time of Lab'ayu, then,

one passed through the inner entry, turned left and climbed a
few steps over the Middle Bronze brick debris to find himself
in a small paved courtyard, facing a door which led into the
new guardroom. The walls of court and guardroom were very
heavy and well built. The southeast corner had two buttresses
to prevent it from crumbling in the unstable brick debris below.
The west wall of the guardroom appears to have been a new
fortification wall which ran southward, probably to connect with
a newly constructed Wall B not far away.

The stratification of court and guardroom was most interesting. In the guardroom, for example, there were at least five
resurfacings of the earth floor in the Late Bronze era. On the
uppermost there was the skeleton of a young animal, evidently
a colt (Fig. 33), buried in some 30 cm. of gray clay fill flecked
with bits of charcoal, plaster and brick. Above this there were
fourteen resurfacings of the Abimelech phase (ca. twelfth century). Each floor consisted of a layer of hard-packed earth covered by a very thin layer of cement, and separated from the
next floor below by one or two centimeters of brown occupational debris. The floors represent the successive repairs and
leveling of the occupational level by simply laying on a mixture
of sifted earth and a small amount of marl or crushed lime. In
the Iron Age a slight alteration of plan enclosed the court with
a rather poorly constructed wall (Fig. 24; Wall 133). In Figs.
34 and 35 the different phases in the gate's history are presented
graphically, both as regards their elevation and surface plan.

The main historical point to this stratification is that there
is no evidence of sharp conflict, separation or destruction between the thirteenth- and twelfth-century phases, such as one
would expect to find to the south of Jerusalem and at Hazor,
north of the Sea of Galilee. As is the case at Megiddo, the
twelfth century witnesses the continued use and repair of the
Late Bronze Age fortifications. Shechem has no evidence of a
radical disturbance when Israel arrives in its area. Instead, at
Shechem as at Megiddo, the end of the great Bronze Age city
comes evidently during the second half of the twelfth century.
As indicated in a preceding chapter, this accords well with the
biblical traditions of Joshua at Shechem (Joshua 24) and the
story of Shechem's destruction by Abimelech (Judges 9).

The story of the fortifications of Shechem during the subsequent Israelite and Samaritan periods is shrouded with many obscurities. The implications of short stretches of casemate walls on the north and northwest sectors, erected during the ninth century, and additional evidence from Fields I and III will be summarized in Chapters 9 and 10.

6

The Temple of El-berith

In the preliminary report of his summer campaign in 1926, Dr. Sellin wrote: "Starting at the western [actually southwestern] wing of the palace we dug a wide area towards the south [southeast] and, about 10 m. south of it, made the most significant discovery of the whole campaign. We hit a tremendous mass of stones which, when pursued, proved to be the 5.30-m.-thick foundation of a rectangular building, 21 m. wide and 26 m. long." After describing the work on it, he concluded:

> Every student of the Bible knows that the Temple of Shechem, "The house of the covenant God," had a great importance for the Canaanites and, also, for the history of Israel. It is known that it was destroyed by King Abimelech of Manasseh (cf. Judges 9). Hence, the discovery of this temple is, in spite of some missing evidence, of utmost importance, since it is, except for the smaller one of Besan [*sic;* Beth-shan], the first Canaanite temple so far recovered.[1]

Temple or Fortress?

A large number of Canaanite temples has been excavated since 1926. But was Sellin correct? Did he actually find "The

House of El-berith," (or Baal-berith) mentioned in Judg. 9:4 and 46? Dr. Welter for one did not believe it, as already indicated. In 1932 he wrote:

> The main building of the acropolis is a structure of 21 m. width and 25 m. depth [*sic!* See below for precise dimensions], containing two towers at the front side. It has one single room (11 by 13 m.) with two rows of three bases, each serving for the support of the roof. The walls are 5 m. thick. . . . The thickness of the wall is an indication that the building consisted of more than one story. The brick walls of the upper story must have been of decreasing thickness. Whether the building had the character of a pure fortification or of a sanctuary cannot be clearly ascertained—certainly not on the basis of an apparent "base for a divine image" which turned out to be a roof-roller, and of similar things.[2]

Confidence in Dr. Welter's opinions is not strengthened by his inaccurate citation of dimensions in his first publication of his own plans of the structure. Nor is one's respect heightened by the final remark about the "roof-roller." Whatever the function of the stone in the building's main room, what Dr. Sellin shows is a flat stone. I, too, doubt the function assigned by Sellin, but —a roof-roller![3]

In Welter's plan of the great building (Fig. 12) it will be noted that there is a later structure on top of it. We will return later to the problem of this structure, its nature, purpose and date. Sellin says that both he and Welter were agreed that it was a temple belonging to the Early Iron Age. But as for the huge structure below it, Sellin continues:

> Welter puts it—really without giving reasons—into the fourteenth century. . . . Sellin, on the other hand, defends emphatically his view that it belongs either to the seventeenth century or to the beginning of the sixteenth century, just as do the other structures of the acropolis. . . . The deciding factor in this matter is the pottery: on the floor of the main room, as well as in the votive pit (or *favissa?*) lying underneath it, so many potsherds of the Middle Bronze Age were found—no pottery of a later age was found—that there can be no doubt in this respect (cf. ZDPV 50, 1927, p. 207). One is amazed that an archaeologist of the caliber of Welter, being in many respects sharp-sighted, completely ignores in his report the very

clear evidence of the pottery for the dating of this structure.[4]

In the matter of date Sellin has been proved precisely correct, and I share his amazement at Welter's dating methods, or lack of them!

The man who first identified Tell Balâtah as Shechem, Prof. Hermann Thiersch, in 1932 wrote a brief article in which he accepted Sellin's identification of the building as a temple. To be sure, Welter is correct in pointing to its character as a fortification, though this "can probably be explained by pointing out that it lay in a dangerous spot—like a watchtower in a pass." Thiersch was impressed with the building as "a structure with three wide naves," an enclosure wall of tremendous thickness which contained an antechamber "built like a niche," objects of a sacred nature found within and in the vicinity of the structure, the altar, the fragment of a bowl with a snake attached to it in relief, and the beehive pit or *favissa* (crypt) "exactly underneath the center of the central nave," which was filled with black earth, animal bones and Middle Bronze Age pottery. The last-mentioned, he thought, was a container for the refuse of sacrifices and for the ashes and cinders of the sacrificial fire.[5]

In the following May (1933), Prof. Johannes Hempel, in a lengthy review of the Shechem problems, avoided committing himself as to either temple or fortress.[6] Somewhat later Prof. Kurt Galling, very judicious in his statements, appears to follow the views of Welter: toward the end of the building's existence it may have been used for sacred purposes, though not originally erected for such purposes.[7] By 1949 Dr. Albright was able to be quite positive that the structure is a temple and that its exceptionally thick walls and ground plan are comparable to buildings found at Megiddo and also at Ugarit in Syria.[8] On the basis of the Megiddo parallel it was by then generally assumed to be Late Bronze Age—but see below.

On top of the deep layers of fill in front of the building the German excavators discerned four important features:

(1) Flanking the entrance were two stones with deep grooves or troughs in them. The one to the south, or left as one faces the entrance, had a slot or trough cut out of a large stone base, the slot being 1.35 m. long by 42 cm. wide by 25 cm. deep (*ca.* 53¼ by 16½ by 9¾ in.). According to a report filed with the

Department of Antiquities by Dr. Aage Schmidt, the Danish archaeologist, it appears likely that a stone slab which once stood upright in this trough was found in 1926, but that workmen broke it into pieces in Dr. Sellin's absence. Sellin was able to recover two of the pieces. In the spring of 1928 he found that they constituted the original base of the slab and that they fitted into the niche of the stone exactly. The stone upright thus had been 1.30 m. wide by 37 cm. thick (51¼ by 14½ in.). In 1956 we found the larger of these two pieces, but not the other, and we also found a piece of the base down in the deep cut made by Welter in his search for fortification Wall D. In 1957 we cemented the whole back together so that today it appears as in Fig. 36. We shall label this *Maṣṣēbāh* 2.

(2) On the other side of the entrance there is a stone with another slot, open at both ends, the slot being 1.56 m. long and 28 cm. wide by 20 cm. deep (61½ by 11 by 8 in.). Neither Sellin nor we were able to find the stone which once stood in it, though Dr. Schmidt is sure it once existed but "was destroyed by workmen in Sellin's absence." We shall call what remains the socket for *Maṣṣēbāh* 3 (Fig. 37).

(3) On an original surface, 6.55 m. (21½ ft.) away from the entrance, Sellin uncovered the platform for an altar, if not indeed the altar itself.[9] In was made out of earth and stones which had been flattened on top (*see* Figs. 10 and 72). Its dimensions are given as 2.20 m. long by 1.65 m. wide by 35 cm. high (*ca.* 7 ft. 2 in. by 5 ft. 5 in. by 13¾ in.).

Welter, in digging a trench through the area in 1928, had left matters so that by the time we started work in 1956 only an irregular outline of stones, *ca.* 1.50 by 1.00 m., remained in place above the edge of the trench. The cut stones were *ca.* 30 by 20 by 20 cm. in size (just under 12 by 8 by 8 in.), and they were carefully laid in a white, compact earth: that is, in a marl cement.

Under these stones and their cement was a layer of black earth, *ca.* 20 cm. thick above a sterile fill. This black layer was apparently put there to level the surface when the altar stones were laid. The earth was a fill taken from occupation debris in the city. Any objects in this earth, then, can theoretically belong to any period earlier than the time when the altar was put there: that is, from a few days to centuries or millennia.

Great care was taken by Robert Bull, Field V Supervisor, in

1960 and again in 1962 in the inspection of this small pocket of black earth held in place by the altar stones. (If this same earth ever was present elsewhere in the courtyard fill, it had now disappeared through the processes of excavation and erosion.) Several pottery fragments were found and saved. Represented were Chalcolithic from the early part of the fourth millennium B.C., Middle Bronze II of the eighteenth to seventeenth centuries B.C., and—most significant—several Late Bronze Age pieces from somewhere in the period 1500 to 1200 B.C. One piece could possibly have been Iron I of about the twelfth century, but it may also have been somewhat earlier. Would that we could fix the date of these sherds with more precision, but they are small, few in number, and not sufficiently distinguished to tell us very much more than their period![10] (*See* Appendix 5). But note what this means: the altar and the occupation surface around it date either from the time of the latest sherds—that is, well along in the Late Bronze Age—or else in the early part of Iron I. From the history of the great building's use this court surface belongs to its third period, and probably to its second phase (Temple 2b; *see below*).[11]

(4) Southeast of the altar, 2.50 m. (just over 8 ft.) farther out in the court, Sellin says that he found "a water trough cut out of a gigantic rock . . . In it lay transversally a monolith . . . Bones surrounded it in quantity" (Fig. 72). By 1927 he had become doubtful about his interpretation of the rock as a water trough, or laver. In the spring of 1928 he found that the monolith fitted precisely into the trough, so that he now had no doubt that this was the main cultic symbol of the temple.[12] We shall refer to this stone as *Maṣṣēbāh* 1.

In a previous chapter Dr. Aage Schmidt was quoted from his report on what happened when Welter arrived to take over direction of the dig in the summer of 1928. In complete disgust with Sellin—because to him the temple was not a temple!—Welter had the stones "taken out of their sockets and thrown down the slope of the fill."[13] And that was where we found them in 1956.

During the summer of 1960 we filled in Welter's trench across the court, and with great difficulty and rented equipment managed to drag *Maṣṣēbāh* 1 and its socket back on top of the

reconstructed court. We set them up again, and then built a
wall around the elevated area to prevent erosion. The socket is
now within a meter of its original position (Fig. 38). It should
have been placed a short distance farther north, but the condition of the debris made this impractical for a permanent installation. According to our measurements the base is 2.40 m. long
by 1.40 m. wide by 80 cm. in height (7 ft. 10½ in. by 4 ft. 7 in.
by 2 ft. 7½ in.). One end is broken off, however; and whereas
Sellin reports the niche or groove as 1.65 m. long (5 ft. 5 in.),
it is now open-ended, 1.35 m. long (4 ft. 5 in.). That is, Welter's
petulant act broke off a one-foot piece which we have been
unable to find. The other dimensions of the groove are 45 cm.
wide and 40 cm. deep (ca. 17¾ in. by 15¾ in.).

The white stone monolith which fits into the groove is
broken irregularly across the top. It is 1.48 m. wide and 42 cm.
thick (58¼ in. by 16½ in.); the width of the groove in the
socket is 3 cm. more than the stone is thick, showing careful
measurement. The height of the surviving fragment is 1.45 m.
(57 in.) on one side and 62 cm. (24¼ in.) on the other. There is
no indication of what the original height may have been. The
stone is nicely worked, the edges rounded and the surface ground
smooth. It is located 10.70 m. (35 ft.) away from (to the southeast of) the entrance of the temple. Because of the broken base
we were forced to use small stones and considerable cement to
be sure that the stone would now stay in place. The upper edges
of the base socket stone, however, were left visible on each side
(see Figs. 38 and 39).

In 1957 Dr. Hans Steckeweh, who had directed the last German digging at Shechem in 1934, was good enough to join our
staff for the second campaign, to share with us what he knew
and thus to furnish at least some liaison between our work and
that of the former expedition. He paid a courtesy visit to the
then aged and distinguished patriarch of Palestinian archaeology
who had witnessed every archaeological endeavor in the country since 1891, the great Père L.-H. Vincent. During the course
of this visit Père Vincent with his usual wit and humor recounted
his views about the Shechem stones. He still believed Welter's
version that the stones were fakes, that the sockets were for
water, and that *Maṣṣēbāh* 1 had been cut to fit the trough and

cemented in place by Sellin's foreman[14] in order to please the old gentleman!

The next day, on Dr. Steckeweh's return to the camp with this story, we went together to inspect the stones and then to go over what Sellin said about them. We concluded that the following observations were in order: (1) the grooved Stones 2 and 3 were *in situ;* (2) any attempt to explain the grooves in the three socketed stone bases as water-containers was impossible; (3) *Maṣṣēbāh* 1 was so huge that it could not have been moved very far by anyone without major preparation and special equipment; (4) it was a specially fine piece of hard white limestone unlike the other stone used in the great building; (5) great care had been used to cut it and then to smooth it off by polishing, thus doing away with the chisel marks; (6) this cutting and smoothing was surely ancient, with a patina that did not appear to be modern; (7) there was no reason to doubt the reliability of Sellin's photographs showing the stone as he found it and again after it had been set upright in its base—*without being chipped to make it fit* (cf. Fig. 72); and, finally, (8) we have an independent witness in Dr. Böhl of Leiden who was present when the stone and trough were uncovered. His description and his own photography confirm Sellin's statement to the effect that the great stone was found leaning against and over the trough.[15]

There can be no question whatsoever that the building had once had two smaller stones standing on either side of the door and a large one standing in the court. These were what is known in Hebrew as *maṣṣēbôt* (pillars), and all such objects had a sacred or "cultic" function. Consequently, the stone platform between *Maṣṣēbāh* 1 and the building is with the highest probability an altar. Accordingly, then, the building must indeed have served as a temple during the period when these objects were in use. We have already indicated the strong probability that the stone altar derives from the end of the Late Bronze Age or very shortly thereafter. *Maṣṣēbāh* 1 had its base sunk in the sterile marl layer that runs below the altar, which stratigraphically should be Late Bronze in date. Consequently, it was installed either at about the same time as the altar, or else earlier in the Late Bronze Age. We cannot be more precise from the standpoint of archaeological evidence. The courtyard, however, was used for religious purposes much earlier.

We shall point out below that there appears to be evidence for two earlier brick altars below the stone one. The earliest dates from the end of the Middle Bronze Age and rests on the surface "ramp" which led to the first period of the original building. In addition, we shall point to evidence which suggests strongly that *Maṣṣēbôt* 2 and 3 also date from the second phase of the building's use in the Middle Bronze Age.

Consequently, there seems to be no need for further quibbling. The evidence from the court shows that two sacred standing stones and an altar are almost as old as the building itself. It is therefore a temple, and was originally built as a temple. Let us now examine its architecture, and the evidence we have secured for its history.

The Story of the Temple

We shall first describe the two main architectural periods of the building, together with the two sub-phases of each. Let us name the phases Temple 1a, 1b, 2a and 2b. Together with the description, we shall present the sections and stratigraphy of the debris with drawings and photographs in order to point out the evidence on which both description and date rest. Interpretation and suggested reconstruction will not be separated from the description.

Fortress-Temple 1a

This is the largest extant temple-ruin in Palestine—a huge mass of stone masonry which was carefully put together as a stone base for the brick superstructure (Fig. 40). Its exterior dimensions according to our measurements are 26.30 m. long by 21.20 m. wide (*ca.* 86 ft. 3½ in. by 69 ft. 6½ in.). The side and rear walls of the cella, or sacred room, are *ca.* 5.10 m. thick (*ca.* 16 ft. 8¾ in.). The masonry was so carefully laid that wall thickness does not vary more than 20 cm. (8 in.). The orientation of the building is 28 degrees south of east; that is, both walls and entrance point the building in that direction.

Prof. R. B. Y. Scott of Princeton University, who has recently

accomplished much in bringing the study of ancient measurements up to date with actual discovery, wrote me in January
of 1960 that the dimensions for our temple do not come out right
if we assume that the common cubit was used as the unit of
measurement in the building. On the other hand, if the long, or
"sacred," cubit, which Ezekiel says was used in the Jerusalem
temple, were used in this building, then the architects had
planned the structure to be 50 by 40 long cubits.[16] The thickness
of the side walls was meant to be 10 long cubits. When Wall A
was in place with its inner face covered by fill, there was no
special restriction on the temple's size, and one would therefore
suppose that the architects would use round figures, which seems
to be the case.

The masonry base for the temple was carefully made of
roughly cut stones which were laid in courses. Some of the stones
were rather large, but there seems to have been a bit more care
taken in coursing them than was necessary in Wall A. The
foundations are laid in trenches dug for them in the earth-and-
marl fill of the great earthen embankment of fortification Wall C.
That the top of the embankment was cut off and used as fill
against Wall A is quite possible, and the pottery in the fill, particularly in the lower layers, is very like the early mixture found
in the embankment. A trench which we dug against the north
wall outside the temple in 1957 revealed the foundation trench
dug for it.

The entrance hall to the temple passed between great blocks
of masonry supporting high flanking towers in which there were
stairwells (Fig. 41). These towers and the foundations for the
entrance had to be supported on new fill. This fill was largely
occupation debris, and is very different from that of the embankment. The southeastern tower, for example, rests on dark gray
occupation debris filled with MB II B–C sherds. A deep fill with
layers of similar material alternating with reddish field clay was
thrown in for the support of the threshold. This means that the
main walls of the cella were firmly footed on the marl fill of the
C Embankment. The towers, however, extended out beyond the
embankment over the line of Wall D, which was below them.
Hence they had to be supported with new fill. And to hold that
new fill in place a deeply set revetment wall had to be erected,

one we have named Wall 914 (see Figs. 22, 41, and 71). The lower part of this wall may have been quite old, and only the upper part added to prevent shifting of the new earth under the portico: *see* Appendix 5.

It has always seemed peculiar to us that this revetment does not run parallel to the front supports of the temple. Robert Bull, supervisor of the temple excavations, labored hard to prove to himself, Lawrence Toombs and me that it was later than the initial phase of the temple, precisely because of its peculiar angle. Debris sections on both sides of it in 1962, however, proved definitely that its date was Middle Bronze and contemporary with Temple 1a; that is, it was put in by the builders to hold the fill in place for the towers before, or without reference to, the determination of the temple's precise orientation.

The entrance hall to the temple is 7 m. wide and 5 m. deep (*ca.* 23 by 16½ ft.; that is, *ca.* 14 by 10 long cubits). At the outer edge of the 3.25-m.-wide threshold, and exactly in its center, a huge boulder had been carefully dressed and provided with a circular depression 76 to 78 cm. in diameter, and surrounded by a rim. That is, the large entrance had a single column within it, because 23 ft. is too wide for a single wooden beam of that day, usually limited to 11 to 12 ft. There is no doubt that the column which stood on this base was of stone and that it was carefully cut from white limestone. We cannot be absolutely certain that the fragment which we cemented on to the base in Fig. 42 is a portion of the original from Temple 1a. That it is probable, however, is indicated by its size (diameter 72 to 74 cm.), which is just right for the base, considering the fact that the base of the column is not preserved. On the other hand, the diameter of the column is too large for any of the column bases found in the cella or cultic room of the temple.

From the wide entrance or portico with its single column, one entered the cella of the building by a corridor 3.25 by 3.25 m. (*ca.* 10⅔ ft. square; or 6 long cubits). The length of this hall is determined by the width of the second threshold wall, which is the same as the first on which the column rests. The cella is a rectangular room 13.50 m. long by 11 m. wide (*ca.* 44 ft. 3 in. by 36 ft. 1 in.; or *ca.* 25½ by 21 long cubits). Sellin and Welter found column bases which indicated that the roof of the room

was held up by columns, and they posit six of them (*see* Fig.
41). We cannot check this supposition now because we can no
longer be certain as to which column bases belonged to the
Temple 1a floor. One base for a Temple 2 floor remains *in situ*,
and the location for another is clearly visible (Fig. 43), but we
can say nothing about earlier bases.

The floor of Temple 1a is called by us Locus 5010 (*see* Figs.
44 and 45). It is a cement floor, 3 to 6 mm. thick. Above it is
dark-gray Layer 5009, 23 to 30 cm. thick, containing a considerable amount of carbon, bone and sherds, and in the first 10 cm.
a high index of plaster. This is occupational debris, MB II B–C
in date, the significance of which will be mentioned in the next
section. Below the floor (5010) there were nearly 4 m. of fill,
below which were some five successive hard earth surfaces, evidently MB II A–B in date (that is, late nineteenth and eighteenth
centuries): *see* Fig. 44. There was no evidence of any architecture, however, in any of our deep pits below the Temple 1a floor.
The irregular outlines of bedrock began to appear at 5.50 m.
(18 ft.) below the floor. Just above the rock was evidence of a
Chalcolithic encampment from the early fourth millennium B.C.
Part of a basin-shaped pit (Locus 5052; 4.95 m. below Floor
5010) with convex sides, 4 to 5 cm. thick, was found. It was 35
cm. deep at the sides and 45 cm. deep in its center, circular in
shape, from 1.02 to 1.25 m. in diameter. The dirt within it was
moist brown clay with many flecks of carbon and small lumps
of charcoal. These pits of the "Yarmukian," or "Jericho VIII," or
"Jericho Pottery Neolithic B," as the culture is variously called,
are well known from Tirzah and Jericho especially. Ours may
have been a fire pit or hearth.

In the southeast quadrant of the cella there was a bottle-
shaped cistern (Locus 5099A). This was 2.50 m. deep, 1.85 m.
in diameter at its widest point and 1.65 m. in diameter at its
base. Its neck was 50 cm. in diameter, and at its top clay lips
flared out and up to join Floor 5010, forming an opening in that
floor of *ca.* 1.00 m. in diameter, apparently designed to take a
flat stone lid. At the bottom was a small bottle-shaped sump,
55 cm. deep, 73 cm. in diameter at the base and 38 cm. wide at
the mouth on the cistern's floor. The walls of both were lined
with a plaster containing small stones. Here, then, was the con-

tainer for the water needed for ablutions and washings in the temple. Sellin found another similar cistern, or perhaps silo for grain, nearby in the center of the cella. His was 2.25 m. deep and 2.50 m. in diameter with a narrow neck. This is what Thiersch called a *favissa* or crypt in the article quoted above (p. 81).

The stone walls of the cella were carefully prepared for the brick above them. The inner and outer faces were made of large hewn stones (up to 90 by 50 by 40 cm. in size), nicely fitted together. The center was filled with smaller unhewn stones. A flat surface of larger stones was put in place; and this was leveled by a layer of smaller stones and earth. That prepared surface was then plastered over and the bricks set upon it. Some of the original Middle Bronze Age bricks appeared to be still in place under the stones of the later Iron Age building in the northwest corner (Fig. 46).

In the courtyard a deep fill had to be thrown over the ruins of the earlier series of courtyard temples which we shall describe in the next chapter. The earlier *temenos* wall (Wall 900) which separated those structures from the rest of the city was used as retainer for the fill. A cross-section by Welter suggests that there was a pavement, evidently a street, at the level of the top of this wall. From this level a plastered walkway over small stones ascended gradually to the top of retaining Wall 914. Then one step up would have led one on to the threshold at the level of Floor 5010 (*see* Figs. 22 and 49).

The reconstruction of Temple 1a in Fig. 47 with the battlements of Wall A in the background is an attempt to give an impression of the mass and proportions. We do not know how the superstructure actually looked, though what is here shown is not out of keeping with ancient architecture. The narrowing of the side walls by stages would permit light to enter the cella through slits at the top. The upper parts of the towers probably had larger storage rooms and the brick need not have been as thick there.

Temple 1b

It was fortunate for us that Dr. Sellin had not removed the large stone walls of the Israelite building erected on top of the temple's stone foundations. Under two east-west room walls and under a north-south corridor wall of the later structure, columns of earth which we could investigate had been left standing. The evidence indicates that there had been repair and reconstruction of Temple 1 but no basic altering of the building's architectural form. It is reasonable to assume that this reconstruction of Temple 1 represents the rebuilding and strengthening of the city in the second part of MB II C which also saw the erection of Wall B and the East Gate. The evidence in the temple, including evidence for the date of both phases, can be summarized as follows:

(1) A new floor was laid, 74 to 75 cm. (*ca.* 2 ft. 5½ in.) above the first. This was found by Sellin also; it is labeled by us Layer 5005 in the fill within the cella (see Figs. 44 and 45). It is a thin layer of plaster or "cement," only 1 to 2 cm. in thickness, laid on 2 to 3 cm. of red clay (Layer 5006). The fill put in for this floor was carefully laid. Above the earlier Floor 5010, as already stated, there was a 23 to 30 cm. layer (5009) of occupational debris, gray earth filled with carbon, bone and sherds—perhaps debris from a fire in the cella. Above that was a layer of more gray earth but mixed with dark-brown field soil and marl (Layer 5008), 15 to 25 cm. thick. Then as a hard base for the floor a layer (5007) of marl, 25 to 30 cm. thick, was laid.

The fragments of pottery from this fill were very few in number except from the gray earth Layer 5009. Nevertheless, some sherds were contained in each of the other layers. The date of this pottery is consistently MB II C with some earlier admixture. There was nothing later. This, of course, proves that Temple 1a, the floor of which was sealed over by this material, was erected *not later than* MB II C (*ca.* 1650–1550 B.C.). On top of Floor 5005 was a gray earth level of occupational debris (5004), and this shows pottery of the same general period, though because of later disturbances we were not able to clear much of it which had not been previously touched. In any event, Temple 1b with the new Floor 5005 is merely a reconstruction of Temple 1a, and such evidence as we have points to the same Middle Bronze Age as its period.

(2) Since the floor was raised between 63 and 75 cm., the thresholds of the entrance portico and hall were also raised. The great stone used as a column base in the portico was not reused,

however, but rolled off the threshold, top down, into the space between the threshold and retaining Wall 914. There it remained wedged and covered, until Sellin first noticed it in the spring of 1928, and until we raised it on to the threshold in 1960 (Fig. 42). The wide portico was now partly walled up, so that the temple had a smaller and indirect entrance. The doorway comprised only the southern part of the former portico. Presumably, since the level of the threshold was raised, steps had now to be placed against it, leading up from the court, though as far as we know Sellin found no evidence of them (*see* Fig. 48).

(3) The sacred standing stones, Maṣṣēbôt 2 and 3, were now installed, flanking the new doorway. We were led to this conclusion because their spacing and socket-heights are just right for the new arrangements, but not for Temple 1a. The center of the new doorway is precisely equidistant between them. The later Temple 2 has a new orientation, as we shall see, but these two stones are set squarely against the front wall of the temple on the original orientation (cf. Fig. 48). Whether they had been used in Temple 1a and then raised to their new positions in Temple 1b, or were especially created for the latter, we have no way of knowing.

(4) In the courtyard under the later stone altar there is evidence of two earlier brick altars. The lowest one was erected above the ramp which passed under it and rose gradually over retaining Wall 914 (Fig. 49). In size its reddish bricks were 35 to 43 cm. square, and these were evidently surmounted by a low curb made of white marl bricks, *ca.* 35 cm. square (*see* Fig. 50). Bricks of this size are typical Middle Bronze Age bricks, the same size as those used on city Wall B; their thickness is always about 15 to 16 cm. Welter evidently dug through the altar bricks without recognizing them. Hence the only bricks that remained were on the structure's north side, where the nearly complete stretch of marl edging or curbing was preserved. This is *ca.* 3.50 m. (11½ ft.) long, but it may have been a brick or two longer. If two bricks longer, then the altar's length would have been *ca.* 4.20 m. (13¾ ft.), or 8 sacred cubits. Assuming a square altar, that figure may be taken as the approximate dimension of each side: *see* Appendix 5.

Temple 1—a Migdāl Temple

Only one other temple precisely like Temple 1 of Shechem has been found. This was excavated between 1936 and 1939 in a sacred area at Megiddo above three temples of the late nineteenth to early eighteenth century B.C. It is not as large or massive as the Shechem building, but it is nevertheless a very heavy-walled, rectangular structure with towers flanking the entrance (Fig. 51). The Megiddo excavators thought the temple was erected in that city's Stratum VIII, which is probably to be dated *ca.* 1350–1250 B.C. It had two phases of rebuilding and was destroyed finally with the destruction of the Bronze Age city during the last third of the twelfth century.[17] Since its excavation, given the similarity, one assumed that it also dated the Shechem temple.

When one examines the Megiddo building more closely, however, one notes that beneath its foundations there is practically no evidence from the seventeenth to sixteenth centuries. The first discernible architecture under it is from the eighteenth century (Strata XIV–XIII). Consequently, it is difficult to discover any reason why this temple was not erected as early as Stratum X, if not XI, which would make it contemporary with the Shechem building.[18] Both would thus have been erected in the same period, just as they were destroyed in the same period. Indeed, buildings east of the Megiddo temple were rebuilt with the same general orientation from Stratum XII (second half of the eighteenth century) through Stratum VII of the late thirteenth and twelfth centuries. In other words, the stratification of the Megiddo temple is by no means certain. It now must probably be dated from the Shechem evidence, rather than the other way around.

Though these two buildings are unlike any other temples in Syria-Palestine, it is very probable that there were once many others like them. Professor Benjamin Mazar of Hebrew University has suggested to me that a study of place names makes it highly probable that the Megiddo and Shechem temples belonged to a special type of structure, known as a *Migdāl* or fortress-temple. There was a town named Migdal-el in the tribal area of Naphtali in Galilee (Josh. 19:38). This name makes sense only if the town derived its name from a fortress of the god El within it. It is also difficult to understand what it could mean unless the fortress were also a temple. Similarly, the town of Migdal-gad in the Judean lowlands (Josh. 15:37), and Migdol on the northeastern border of Egypt (Exod. 14:2; Jer. 44:1; Ezek. 29:10), evidently were distinguished by the particular type of temple within them. If so, then it is Megiddo and Shechem which provide the only clear archaeological evidence for the type in question. Both were erected in the seventeenth century, and their areas were soon secularized after their destruction in the twelfth century B.C.

Professor Mazar has also pointed to the fact that a town named Penuel, deemed sacred like Shechem by Patriarchal tradition (Gen. 32:30–32), also had a *Migdāl* in it. And it was one which was destroyed only a short time before those of Shechem and Megiddo (Judg. 8:8, 9, 17).

The *Migdāl* or fortress-temple of Shechem, therefore, like Wall A, is a special structure with its own traditions. Its type appeared in the seventeenth century during the second part of the Hyksos age. Since that is the period of Indo-European migrations into the Fertile Crescent of the Near East,[19] it may be that the temple-type was brought with them. Yet of this we have no certain knowledge.

Temple 2

It was noted in the preceding chapter that Shechem has a gap in its history as a city of nearly a century's duration, between ca. 1540 and 1450 B.C. That Temple 1 was completely destroyed in the destruction of the city by the Egyptians is indicated by the fact that the rebuilding in the Late Bronze Age, perhaps by a father or grandfather of Lab'ayu, is quite different from the original structure. The following is the evidence:

(1) Temple 2 was not discerned by Sellin or Welter. We discovered it only because we had to excavate below the walls of the later Israelite building on top in order to find undisturbed debris which might provide us with stratification and dates. During the 1960 campaign Robert Bull began the investigation of the eastern (actually southeastern) wall of the Israelite government building which runs across the cella of the temple. It

soon became apparent that there were two walls here, one on top of the other. The top one, Wall 5904, is like the others of the Israelite warehouse. It consists of two parallel lines of unhewn boulders, probably robbed out of Wall A, the interstices of which were filled with earth and smaller stones. It varied between 1.30 and 1.60 m. in width, the smaller dimension being the usual one. Below it the earlier Wall 5704 was very different. It was between 2 and 2.30 m. (6½ to 7½ ft.) in width, with facings on both sides of the wall carefully formed and evenly laid in line. Only one course of stones was preserved; its builders had cut through the second Temple 1 floor (5005) to place their new wall on 20 cm. of earth directly above Floor 5010 of Temple 1a. Wall 5704 was preserved for a length of 11.80 m. (38¾ ft.) as it angled across the cella between the north and south walls of Temple 1.

Dismantling the later Wall 5904 produced sherds of the late ninth century (or early eighth century at the latest) sealed in the earth between and beneath the stones. This was as expected, because the Israelite building was well dated from other loci. Then came the removal of portions of the lower Wall 5704. In the earth sealed below it and on top of temple Floor 5010 there were clear Late Bronze Age sherds mixed with those of Middle Bronze II and some Chalcolithic (early fourth millennium).[20] With the Middle Bronze Age material there was one scarab, dating between the Thirteenth Dynasty and the early Hyksos period (B60, Reg. 659; cf. Fig. 52).[21] Wall 5704, then, was probably erected in the Late Bronze Age, since other evidence suggests that it is not later.

(2) Wall 5704 in orientation and type was now seen to belong with a strip of unconnected wall (5703) resting on the south cella wall of Temple 1 (Fig. 55). This had been considered by Sellin and Welter to belong to the Israelite warehouse, but it had been puzzling because it was distinctly different in type from the warehouse walls.

It is clear now that the Israelite structure's exterior walls had simply followed the outline of what remained of the Late Bronze Age Temple 2. Yet the first and inexplicable fact about Temple 2 is that the axis was shifted. Whereas Temple 1 was oriented 28 degrees south of east, Temple 2 was oriented 33 degrees south of east. By projecting the walls that remain, while still using the wide walls of Temple 1 as foundations, we discover that Temple 2 had a rectangular room, the entrance to which had to be on the long side in Wall 5704. The dimensions of the new room can only be estimated roughly at *ca.* 16 m. wide by 12.5 m. long (*ca.* 52½ by 41 ft., which would also be *ca.* 30 by 24 long cubits): *see* Figs. 56 and 73.

A large number of Canaanite temples have been found at other sites, and nearly all belong to the broad-room type: they are rectangular (sometimes almost square) with entrance on the long side opposite the podium for the statue of the deity. At Megiddo there is one dating from *ca.* 3000 B.C., and three others from *ca.* 1800 B.C. At Ai a magnificent example was erected *ca.* 2800–2700 B.C. At Alalakh in northern Syria a fine series dates between *ca.* 1900 and 1550 B.C., and another between *ca.* 1400 and 1200 B.C. Two temples from Ugarit also date from the latter period. At Lachish in Palestine a small temple was rebuilt twice between the fifteenth and thirteenth centuries. At Beth-shan in the Jordan valley a fine succession in Strata VII, VI and V date between the thirteenth and early tenth centuries. At Hazor, north of the Sea of Galilee, a fine Middle Bronze temple was discovered, to which towers and portico were added in the Late Bronze Age.

The point of this listing is to suggest that Temple 2 of Shechem was rebuilt as a more typical Canaanite temple-type in the Late Bronze Age. Why the axis was shifted 5 degrees farther south is an unsolved mystery. The simplest explanation is that it had something to do with a change in calendar, and the axis was shifted with the change so that the rising sun would shine squarely into the cella at the New Year. Unfortunately for this hypothesis the orientation faces the rising sun at the time of the winter solstice, which represents neither the spring nor fall New Year's used in ancient Canaan and Israel.

A rather striking parallel to the structures unearthed at Shechem is found in Level VII of Alalakh in northern Syria, dating from the seventeenth or early sixteenth century.[22] A gate in the city wall has three entries like the Northwest Gate of Shechem. Contiguous to this is a temple and palace. Interestingly, between Alalakh VIII and VII there was a shift in temple orientation to the south of the earlier axis, though the extent and nature of the shift are not fully described in the report. Yet what all this means is uncertain because no consistent pattern of orientation in Syro-Palestinian temples can be perceived, except that they generally range from northeast to southeast. The *Migdāl* temple of Megiddo faces northeast.

(3) A floor for Temple 2 was raised 65 to 70 cm. above Floor 5005 of Temple 1a. It is preserved in only a few places because the construction of the Israelite building cleared the whole area to its level. We numbered it 5002A; it was a layer of thin cement (5 to 8 mm. thick) which in a few places had a thin layer of gray earth on it. The foundation for the floor was a thick layer (5003) of red field earth found throughout the area. Below that was the gray layer (5004) of occupation debris, mostly from the destruction of Temple 1b (*see* Fig. 44).

The new floor (5002A) was now 70 to 80 cm. above the level of the rear or original western stone platform for the brick wall of Temple 1. For some time an area about the width of the unused portion of the original wall had been employed as a podium, which evidently had been built and rebuilt more than once. A narrow curb (5802A) was erected above the inner edge of the Temple 1 rear wall, and a cemented platform created there. The level of this cemented podium behind the curb appears continuous with Floor 5002A. Between it and another such curb wall below (5802B) was some 70 cm. of fill (Locus 5060) which contained a large amount of pottery and artifacts, Late Bronze II of the fourteenth to thirteenth centuries for the most part. In this occupation debris there was a small mortar and pestle for grinding a pink cosmetic rouge (B60, Reg. 602). The color is still as fresh as the day on which the last pigment was ground in it over 3200 years ago. A fine alabaster mace head (B60, Reg. 517) and a faience seal (B60, Reg. 432) showing the "tree of life" came from the same locus.

If podium, curb Wall 5802A, and the new Floor 5002A belong together, then they are surely as late as, or later than, the pottery and objects directly under the first two in Locus 5060. This sounds as though Temple 2 cannot be any earlier than the second half of the thirteenth century. Floor 5002A, then, and the final stone altar in the court are probably from the same building phase and era. Certain additional evidence, however, forces us to label this phase as Temple 2b, and assert that an earlier Late Bronze phase, Temple 2a, once existed. This evidence is as follows:

(1) Directly beside and on top of the socket of the original west wall of Temple 1 was curb Wall 5802B and another plastered podium surface. Beneath it Late Bronze sherds appeared, and on top of it was the fill of Locus 5060 described above. In other words, there are two curb and podium installations. The first one probably was erected some time between 1450 and 1400 B.C., though we have no positive evidence of the precise time except that it was Late Bronze. Steps installed in the north and south corners lead up to the podium from a floor level that is no longer preserved (Fig. 57). The gray earth still in place against the northern steps in 1957 contained Late Bronze pottery. This is the only clear evidence in the cella area for a Temple 2a to be distinguished from the Temple 2b podium and Floor 5002A, which was high above the level of the steps.

(2) Out in the court, however, we know that the last altar, the one of hewn stone, cannot date earlier than the end of the Late Bronze Age, while an earlier one of gray brick with white marl curbing was dated at the end of the Middle Bronze Age and assigned to Temple 1b. In between the two, Sellin claims to have distinguished still another altar, this one made of mud bricks, its extent from northwest to southeast being 5.20 m., its breadth 7 m., and its thickness 27 cm.[23] Sellin says that he found it only 10 cm. below the stone altar. Since it did not exist in the small section we dug in 1962, this altar must have been a short distance south of our cut, where its remains were destroyed by the deep trenches of both Sellin and Welter. The Temple 1b altar bricks as shown in Figs. 49 and 50 are from 65 to 70 cm. below the level of the stone altar.

We do not know how the front tower areas over the stone sockets of Temple 1 were used in Temple 2. From the level of the altars one would assume that steps were used to gain the level of the door, which seems to have remained indirect as in Temple 1b. The sacred *Maṣṣēbôt* 2 and 3 were left standing and visible. While speculation is of little use without solid evidence, I would judge that the guardian towers of Temple 2 were quite sizable, and that the solid stone base left from Temple 1 was well used.

Summary and Correlation

Let us now put our findings described in this chapter together with those given in the last chapter. There is no question but that Wall A and Fortress-temple 1a belong to the same period. This was during the second part of the Hyksos period when Syria and Palestine were filled with city-states controlled by a foreign element from their capital of Avaris (later Tanis) in the Egyptian Delta. In the archaeological period, MB II C (*ca.* 1650–1550 B.C.), Hyksos power came to its height in the Fifteenth Dynasty. After 1600 it began to decline as Theban princes in upper Egypt gradually regained control of their country, expelled the invaders and between 1550 and 1450 B.C. quickly seized control of Palestine and Syria.

Wall A and Fortress-temple 1a were erected about 1650 B.C., during the period of the Fifteenth Dynasty, when concentration of power was great. Yet it was also a time when *security* was the paramount concern, and the people of Shechem, as elsewhere, were willing to exert themselves to unparalleled efforts in fortification for self-defense. Even their new temple was a magnificent fortress of a new type. As Professor Mazar first suggested, all this happened while the population was being enriched by new blood and new ideas from Indo-European and Hurrian (Horite) incursions which began to come in waves during the seventeenth century. This fact would account for the fortress-temple as a new type of religious architecture which was erected at various places in Syria, Palestine and Lower Egypt, judging from place names.

Wall A was soon found to be insufficient on the east and north sides of Shechem, however, and Wall B was added in those sectors. Some event, no doubt, forced this change in the defenses, perhaps during the last quarter of the seventeenth century. Temple 1b was erected either contemporaneously with Wall B and the East Gate, or when the East Gate had to be rebuilt in its second or Orthostat phase. Temple 1b was then in its turn destroyed by the Egyptians—whether in their first attack about 1550 B.C. or in their second about 1540 B.C. we do not know.

Temple 2a, the broad-roomed Late Bronze structure, was probably erected in the second half of the fifteenth century, during the rebuilding and refortification of the city which we identified in both Fields I and III.

Temple 2b, on the other hand, seems to represent a repair of Temple 2 which involved a new floor and a new altar about 1200 B.C., or somewhat earlier. The repair may perhaps be correlated with the repair and slight altering of the East Gate guardrooms, and with the flagstone pavement which in Field III separated the thirteenth- from the twelfth-century deposits.

The Destruction of Bronze Age Shechem

When was Temple 2 finally destroyed so that it was never rebuilt? When did the great installations of Middle Bronze Age Shechem, repeatedly repaired, suffer a final destruction so severe that the city never completely recovered from the blow?

The easiest answer is simply to quote Judg. 9:45: "And Abimelech fought against the city all that day; he took the city, and killed the people that were in it; and he razed the city and sowed it with salt." Verses 46–49 continue with the explicit statement that disaster also overtook "the house of El-berith."

But to what time does this narrative refer? And do the statements in it find support in the ruins of the city?

It is to find the answer to this question, among many others, that the Expedition plans to focus its attention as it completes its work. Meanwhile we have the following evidence:

(1) The series of seven Late Bronze and fourteen Iron Age floors in the rear guardroom of the East Gate breaks off abruptly during the course of the twelfth century B.C.

(2) The great fill under the Samaritan house in Field II comes from an occupational area showing the same grouping of Late Bronze and twelfth-century pottery.

(3) That Temple 2b was destroyed is indicated by the fact that the cella of the temple was disturbed by numerous pits dug through the last floor, some of them going deep into the fill below the lowest of the floors. All were filled with gray-black earth

taken from occupational debris, and all were sealed over by the thick cement floor of the Israelite warehouse. Hence it is quite certain that the pits were dug after the temple's destruction and before the erection of the Israelite building. The latter, as we shall see, could not have been built before the second half of the ninth century. In the pits there was a great deal of carbon and quantities of Iron I A (*ca.* twelfth century) pottery.

These pits were of two types. One was bottle- or flask-shaped, having a wide base (1.70 to 3 m. in diameter) and a narrow neck (*ca.* 50 cm. in diameter). Two of these were *ca.* 4.60 m. deep (15 ft.). All were unlined and unplastered. A second type was cylinder-shaped and distinguished by the regularity of its sides. Two of these began on packed earth floors 15 cm. below the lowest of the temple floors and rose through the fills and other floors with an undiminished diameter of *ca.* 1.70 m. The cylindrical pits ran in a direction precisely parallel to the orientation of the walls of Temple 2. Our first thought was that the cylinders were dug to obtain the columns and their bases after the temple had been destroyed. Yet the evenness of the sides which were still intact argued against this conjecture. One of the cylinders encountered the probably closed Temple 1a Cistern 5099A. Whoever dug the pit left the cistern open so that it was filled in with an early Iron Age debris.

The logical conclusion is that the charcoal and quantities of twelfth-century pottery found in these pits must have come from a twelfth-century destruction of the city. What the purpose of the pits was is a difficult question. Do they represent a frantic search for treasure which people in the area thought must have been contained in the temple? This might explain the flask-shaped pits. Certainly these could not have been used as cisterns or silos because their sides were not treated, that is, firmed and plastered. But this does not get us far, and the purpose of the cylinders remains an enigma to us.

7

The Courtyard Temples

Out in front, east and southeast, of the fortress-temple is a large area which Sellin called the *temenos* (sacred area). We are given little detail about the digging which he did here in an area at least 75 m. by 25 m. As shown by Fig. 10 it is certain that this was an occupied area inside both Wall D and the C Embankment. When the temple was erected over the latter, between 2 and 4 m. of fill from the mountain slopes had to be dumped in over earlier ruins to create a court, the depth of fill, of course, depending on the height of the ruins (Fig. 49)—lower, for example, under the altars than farther north.

Since this was the deepest point reached in a sizable area by the German excavations, our purpose was frankly to penetrate the earlier levels below where Sellin had stopped, without having to go to all the work and expense of removing the upper levels to get to this depth. After Lawrence Toombs had spent two weeks at the end of the 1957 season testing the nature of the problem, we began a full-scale operation in 1960, naming it Field VI. During the 1960 and 1962 campaigns James F. Ross was in charge as supervisor, with others assisting him. At the same time we opened Field VII some 50 m. to the east in a sector hitherto untouched. By working the two fields simultaneously we hoped to take VII down to where VI began, thus obtaining a complete stratification for the tell without having to go to bedrock in Field VII.

We had no hope of being able to make much sense of Sellin's work, either of what had been dug through or what was still exposed on the surface after an interval of thirty years. For the period preceding the building of the temple, much to our gratified amazement, the puzzle has fallen beautifully into place. Our regret is that we can say virtually nothing about the sector after the building of the temple until the end of the city's life. It is sad to have to report that some fifteen hundred years of the history of Shechem's most important sector was dug through and removed with almost no archaeological reporting or recording. And judging from what was over the temple and over the present surface which Steckeweh had removed immediately to the north in 1934, the stratification in the *temenos* sector was surely fairly complete.

Directly north of the surviving remnant of the courtyard fill shown in Fig. 49, a number of walls protruded from the earth as Sellin had left them (Fig. 10), whereas to the east and south the depth of excavation and surviving dump left a less likely prospect. It is in the former area that we concentrated our attention in 1960. We identified three different strata of a compound which we called the "palace" for no other reason than that it was sizable and must have had a public function. A fourth, removed by Sellin or eroded since 1927, was seen to belong to the same structure. Beneath them was occupational debris filled with pottery of the early fourth millennium B.C., and in one place there was a surface preceding the palace but close to it in date: MB II A from the period 1850–1750 B.C. The succession of four palaces dated between that period and the building of Wall A and Temple 1a of MB II C: that is, between *ca.* 1750 and 1650 B.C. or in MB II B.

Following the 1960 campaign I confess that a question mark registered an occasional impression on my mind regarding the identity of the "palace." What kind of a structure was it? Note in Figs. 63, 64 and 69 that it had a series of rooms bounded on the west by Wall D, on the east by an enclosure wall of major proportions (Wall 900), and on the north by a narrow street running along by Wall 903 and connecting with a much larger street alongside Wall 900. Obviously, one could not make much sense out of the complex until more information was obtained as to the whole: that is, what happened farther south? The difficulty in obtaining an answer was that the information was either excavated already or hidden beneath the surviving heap of Temple 1 courtyard fill.

Meanwhile, however, Prof. D. Arnulf Kuschke of Mainz, Director of the Deutsches Evangelisches Institut für Altertumswissenschaft des Heiligen Landes, had been sorting out the prewar materials of the Institut which had been stored in the basement of the Lutheran Church within the old city of Jerusalem. As already noted, he discovered some original plans of the Sellin and Welter expeditions. Among them, for example, was the original of the contour map, published in 1926 but without any elevations marked on it.[1] Our architect, G. R. H. Wright, had used the unmarked map and had supplied the elevations from his own survey (Fig. 7). It was a source of considerable satisfaction to Wright to find that the elevations given in the unpublished plans and his own figures were in agreement.

Among the Institut's papers also was an extremely precious notebook of Dr. Praschniker, Sellin's close friend and assistant of the German University in Prague. It gives the original elevations in stone-by-stone drawings of the Northwest Gate as its walls were uncovered during the 1914 digging.

Another plan of particular interest shows in some detail the discoveries of Sellin in the early phases of Field VI, particularly in the excavated areas south of the palace. By placing our 1960 discoveries in the context of those of Sellin in 1926 and 1927 (see Figs. 63–65, 69, 71), it became apparent that we were excavating a series of rooms and small courts adjacent to a large court. This latter was of far greater size in relation to the structures we had excavated than would normally be explained as part of the city's palace. In a building enclosure approximately 30 m. long (*ca.* 100 ft.) the major court took up between one-half and two-thirds of the space. The whole structure had been constructed to fit within a trapezoidal area between Wall 900 and city Wall D. This space was some 18.50 m. wide (*ca.* 60 ft.) at the structure's northern edge and, by calculation, roughly 23.50 m. (77 ft.) at its southern side. Why was this space separated so carefully from the rest of the city by the exceptionally stout Wall 900, 2.30 m. (*ca.* 7½ ft. or 5 cubits) thick? Why the especially large courtyard in a structure that already had smaller courts within it?[2]

From soundings completed in 1960 and 1962, we know that bedrock lies about 5 m. (*ca.* 16½ ft.) below the lowest floor (5010) of the temple cella at Level 13.94 m. Under the street outside Room 3 in Fig. 69, on the other hand, bedrock is at Level 9.02 m. In other words, under the fortress-temple there is a knoll of rock nearly 5 m. higher than the rock surface under the street. It is quite certain that no other temple construction was erected on that knoll. Yet one would expect a building of such major religious significance as Temple 1 to have been erected only on a spot which had had a long religious tradition. There are many illustrations of this in the ancient world. I was, therefore, a bit troubled by the blank we had drawn beneath Temple 1. After examining the original German map during the first week of the 1962 campaign, however, it occurred to me that the courtyard building may have had a religious significance. Indeed, if such were the case, then the fulcrum or focal point of the whole structure need not be below Temple 1 at all, but *below the altar* in the court.

With this in mind we decided that we must dig a deep trench across the untouched part of the temple fill below the altar of Temple 2b. This was a reluctant decision, for we had carefully reconstructed a part of that court in 1960 in order to erect *Maṣṣēbāh* 1 on it, and we had then built a wall around it to hold it in place (Fig. 39). Nevertheless, after repeated conferences, our staff decided that we had to do it; otherwise we would always feel that we should have, but did not. At the same time, what could we expect to find under there? Empty space in the middle of the court was most likely!

What we found, however, were the south and southeast walls of a smaller court which existed during the various phases of the two strata preserved of the structure within the larger court: *see* Fig. 110 and Appendix 5.

In Figs. 64 and 69 it will be noted that Walls 938 and 938a, one a rebuilding of the other, continue under the altar fill where they bond into the south wall of the inner court. And directly under them was Wall 983 of a still earlier stratum. Here, then, we have a remarkable situation. The buildings of the successive strata are all different in their internal arrangements. Yet at this spot something permanent existed, so that first Wall 983, and then Walls 984b–938a, 984a–938, 984 and once a higher 938—all these had to continue in the same place, with the floor being raised in each stage. This surely means that we do indeed have here the fulcrum of the whole courtyard structure.

Since most of the worship at ancient temples goes on in the courts, with the great altar not far away, must all temples be special buildings of the types referred to in the preceding chapter? I recalled one sacred area, not far removed from ours at Shechem in time: Stratum IX at Beth-shan, dating from the fourteenth century B.C.[3] Whatever the plan of the various rooms at Beth-shan may once have been, they certainly do not appear to have had any special architectural form when excavated. A *maṣṣēbāh* or sacred pillar, however, appears as the special cult object in an open court. During a weekend in Jerusalem, furthermore, I went through R. Naumann's convenient summary of architecture unearthed in Anatolia and Syria, *Architektur Kleinasiens* (Tübingen, 1955), and found that in the ancient kingdom of the Hittites the courtyard temple was a highly developed architectural form. Indeed, one type in the Hittite capital, Khattusas (Boğhaz-köy), had such a stylistic similarity to one of our Shechem phases that I no longer hesitated.

As a working hypothesis which best explains all factors in the situation, it would be proposed that our series of courtyard structures in the pre-fortress-temple period were courtyard temples. After consulting with our staff and with several other scholars and receiving affirmative responses to my suggestions, Lawrence Toombs and I proceeded to publish the results in the preliminary report of our Fourth Campaign.[4] A reconstruction of one of the phases is presented in Fig. 58 as an attempt to visualize the chief features of the installation.

It should be emphasized that our calling attention to the Hittite temples here and in what follows (note 10) does not *prove* that our Shechem courtyard buildings are temples. The former are very elaborate structures and they are later in date than our buildings. The reason for the allusion to them and to the structure or structures in Beth-shan IX is simply to call attention to the fact that such a thing as a courtyard temple does in fact exist. With this established, we then can look again at what we have at Shechem and see if all factors of our situation would not most easily be explained by the assumption that our MB II B enclosure was indeed a *temenos* or sacred area for purposes of worship.

As a summary of the thoughts in our minds at the conclusion of the 1962 campaign, we note the following:

(1) There is a difficulty in understanding the architectural purpose of our buildings if they are secular public buildings. Their separation from the city by a wall (our 900), almost of the strength of a city fortification, suggests that the area had a special function that needed such separation, and that the enclosed area could be viewed as a citadel of the city.

(2) The small Central Court through four strata remained in the same spot with eastern, and in three strata also the southern, walls always erected on the same lines, while the other interior walls and space arrangements could be shifted considerably in each building. Directly above the Central Court were altars and sacred pillars of the period between *ca.* 1650 and 1100 B.C. Is this likely to be accidental? Is it not more likely that the later selection of this spot for worship was determined by earlier custom?

(3) In one phase to be described below (the 901 phase) there were two small courts, in the center of each of which there were pillar bases without architectural significance. The most reasonable hypothesis concerning their use was that they held sacred pillars comparable to that in the Beth-shan IX courtyard temple.

(4) No objects whatsoever were found in our Field VI buildings, nor in the fortress-temple, to prove that they had a sacred use. This is disconcerting, and yet today there is no doubt about the purpose of the Shechem *Migdāl* or fortress. Every stratum was completely cleared of objects, a fact peculiar no matter what public function be assumed.

(5) I would not wish to press the issue of the unusual number of ovens in our courtyard buildings. But I suggest that they can be taken as an argument against the structures' being royal palaces. Kitchens would have been in too many places. On the other hand, in a courtyard temple where family feasts were frequently held, the ovens would be understandable.

(6) If our Field VI buildings are courtyard temples, they most probably are open-air precincts, with only certain rooms covered, which are independent of the royal palaces probably existing on the north side of the mound. That is, they are probably to be considered of Amorite period installation comparable in type to those of Bethel, Mamre and Beer-sheba in the Genesis traditions. This may be the reason for their difference from most other temple architecture.

(7) In Chapter 8 I shall attempt to show that there probably existed a continuity of religious tradition between Patriarchal times and the period of Abimelech, including sacred area, tree and covenant. In itself I would not call this "proof" of the purpose of the courtyard buildings, but simply one element in the total picture.

For all of these reasons, then, it does not seem unreasonable to propose that MB II B in Field VI is composed of four strata of courtyard temples, and that the preparation of the area for them in MB II A may well have been the first phase of the sacred area. As a working hypothesis we shall proceed, therefore, as though this were the case.

We shall now look more closely at each of the strata here and see what can be said about them.

The Earliest Settlement in the Fourth Millennium B.C.

Covering the bedrock throughout the west side is a fairly thick layer of occupational debris from a large encampment of people who lived here for a time in the early part of the fourth millennium. No architectural remains have been found, only many fragments of pottery. Mr. Peter Parr of the British School of Archaeology in Jerusalem was kind enough in 1960 to show me some of the "Neolithic B" pottery which the Kenyon expedition unearthed at Jericho between 1952 and 1958. It looked to me so precisely like what was coming out in the lowest levels of our Field VI that I could not tell the groups of material apart —at least from the small sorting examined from Jericho. No architecture has been left by the people who made the pottery in the places where it has been found, unless it be some insubstantial brick walls very poorly preserved. A chief surviving feature is dwelling pits over which tents, perhaps made of reed mats, must have been erected.[5] At the same time, as Robert J. Braidwood and I observed in 1941 in the H. Frankfort Prehistoric Seminar at the University of Chicago, the date of this culture must fall well within the Chalcolithic period, that is, at a time when the first metal, copper, was used for artifacts.[6]

Palestine in the early fourth millennium, then, was occupied by a seminomadic people long after northern Syria and Mesopotamia had achieved a comparatively high level of technology and artistry. Indeed, the Yarmukian people appear quite simple in interests and achievements as compared with their predecessors, who had created such a remarkable fortified village as that at Jericho during the seventh and sixth millennia B.C.

Temenos 1 (968). *Preparation of the Sacred Area* (ca. *1800* B.C.)

We have seldom found our Yarmukian levels undisturbed. In Field VI they are nearly always mixed with MB II A pottery. The activity of builders in the period 1850–1750 B.C. was so intense and serious-minded that the whole area seems to have been churned up. While there were surely people living at Shechem about 3000 B.C. and also about 2000 B.C., judging from pottery fragments, their town or city was not large enough to extend as far west as Field VI. Somewhere in the neighborhood of 1800 B.C., the area was the subject of a vast leveling and filling operation. It is possible that the valley that once crossed under the East Gate began in Field VI, east of the rock knoll under the fortress-temple. In any event, the leveling operation for MB II A use was of major proportions. In Fig. 59 an example of part of this fill is shown in a reddish-brown rocky layer deep below the footing of Wall 900. Under the earliest street (Street 9) there was a hard-packed occupation surface with a stone-lined silo or oven set in it (Fig. 60). This surface ran under Wall

900 and was cut when Wall 939 (*see below*) was erected. It lies over the rocky layer. Wherever we have dug under the walls and floors of the next phase (the 969 buildings and courts; *see below*), we have encountered walls and surfaces of this first, industrious urban activity in Field VI.

A surface with a round *tannūr* (oven) on it exists outside (west) of Wall D in Area VI.2, and runs under both that fortification and the Embankment C (Figs. 16 and 17). In Fig. 63, Wall 935 can be seen in outline running under fortification Wall D (here marked also 936). A well-made drain exists at the northwest corner of the field.

Of most importance, however, is a peculiar structure numbered 968 in Fig. 63, though only the stone edge of it is there drawn. We traced it for over 10 m. before it turned 90 degrees in an easterly direction and disappeared under the street. A probe in the street seemed to show it continuing under Wall 900. What its function was, we do not know, except that it is something extensive made by human effort. It is a kind of platform, *ca.* 1 m. high, the outer sides of which are faced with stone, while the interior is made of packed earth and stones topped by a layer of fine yellow (marly) earth. The yellowish cast to the marl surfacing seems indeed to be a characteristic of the period. In Fig. 61 the corner is shown with stones tumbled down the sides. That the earth surface of the platform here is original seems to be indicated by the fact that pottery vessels had stood upon it, but had been smashed when they fell over down the side. Jar-rims were farthest down the slope but the bases were near the top, an indication of the direction of fall.

When we first encountered the 968 platform, I thought immediately of a large earthen altar of Megiddo, its top and sides lined with stone, its size being *ca.* 26 ft. in diameter and 4½ ft. high, and its date in the same period as our structure.[7] On the other hand, we cannot rule out the possibility that it is an earthen wall, comparable perhaps to one found at Gezer.[8] As we complete our work at the site, we will make another effort to discover what 968 is, but I am not hopeful of success. The clearance of the whole area would be most difficult and expensive because of the extensive ruins above, and because the next phase destroyed so much of what was below it.

At this stage, however, it is clear that a major construction job was done in Field VI, first to level it and then to build upon it. And this was done before the earliest-known city fortification at Shechem, Wall D, was built. The structures described above were evidently outside the main confines of the city before *ca.* 1750 B.C. Yet work here was so extensive *ca.* 1800 B.C. that we must conclude that for whatever purpose the area was used, it was deemed very important. Judging from the amount of charcoal associated with the ruins of the 968 phase, we can assume that it ended in catastrophe which involved burning.

Temenos 2 (939). *Simple Courtyard Temple* (ca. 1750 B.C.)

The field numbers of this and the next two strata of the courtyard temples (939, 902, 901) derive from the eastern wall of the structures which ran parallel to Wall 900 along a street. Each was simply placed on top of the other. The correlation of the various street resurfacings with the building phases was a task given over to assistant supervisor Joseph A. Callaway during the 1960 campaign.

Between the *temenos* (sacred enclosure) Wall 900 and the outer wall of the succession of courtyard temples, nine cobblestone resurfacings of a street were found (Fig. 62). In each case (except for Streets 1–3, which we cannot check because little remains of them) the cobblestones covered one-half the space between Wall 900 and the courtyard temple, making a paved street *ca.* 1.50 m. (5 ft.) wide. The remainder of the space was a drain, usually open, but at least once a covered channel.

The earliest of the streets (No. 9) was found in an excellent state of preservation, with a slight slope to the south. Below it, the fill for the "make-up" lay upon a solid layer of ash and an occupation surface, mentioned in the preceding phase. The latter runs under enclosure Wall 900, but the make-up for the street and the street itself are laid against 900, indicating that Street 9 and the building of the enclosure are of the same period. The make-up is also laid against Wall 939, which must be contemporary with it, while the surface below it of the preceding phase is cut in order to build 939. By a similar process of analysis, Streets 8 and 7 are known to belong to the same building phase.

Most important here, however, is the knowledge that enclosure Wall 900, street, and courtyard Temple 939 all were constructed at the same time. The main architectural outlines were now established which the courtyard temple area was to retain or develop for nearly a century in MB II B.

A detailed plan of the 939 phase cannot be presented, for the reasons already suggested (*see* Fig. 63). The outer walls around the sacred courts, however, are 939 by the street, 934 crossing the center of the area and 933, which for both this and the next phase forms the outer wall, leaving a small alleyway between itself and Wall D.

The correlation of the city's first fortification, Wall D, with the 939 and Wall 900 structures is based upon the following considerations:

(1) The pottery from within Wall D cannot be dated *earlier* than this period, as explained in Chapter 5.

(2) A surface with an oven built in it from the preceding phase (MB II A) was found in Field VI, Area 2 to run under Wall D. Another wall (935) is shown in Fig. 63 also running under the fortification. Thus for both ceramic and stratigraphical reasons the first fortification was not erected until after the *Temenos* 1 phase.

(3) On the other hand, as is clear from Fig. 63, Wall 933 of the 939 or first MB II B phase presupposes the existence of Wall D as the confining element for the architecture. Thus the 939 period is the time, as far as we now can tell, when Field VI was first included within the fortifications of the city.

The walls of this phase are generally much less substantial than those of the succeeding phases. Wall 939 itself is only 60 cm. (*ca.* 2 ft.) wide. It is of interest, however, that this and nearly all surviving walls at Shechem are stone bases for brick superstructures. This is somewhat surprising, because it has often been assumed that most buildings were of stone in the hills of Palestine, where easily worked limestone is in such inexhaustible supply. The way buildings were made at Shechem, however, in all periods suggests that such a view may be fallacious.

It is probable that entrance to the compound was from the south along the cobbled street by Wall 900. The street led into what appears to have been a paved courtyard, but the precise architectural arrangements are unknown. Where the northern compound wall originally stood is also unknown, though it was probably not far from the later Wall 943. As Fig. 63 shows, the structures in the compound as a whole appear to consist of two main groups of rooms on either side of the east-west Wall 934. Quite a large building with a fine silo in it exists to the north, its main wall being 989. As previously indicated, a passageway separates Wall D from the sacred courts. The latter is a large area, its external walls showing, indeed, that they were intended to create a special enclosure. A gate into it probably existed through Wall 934 at the cobbled area between 970 and 980. From this spot an alley skirted the outside wall and turned with the western Wall 933. That is, a court must have existed here, but we can only interpret its nature from the succeeding phases, in which the successors of the strip of wall (983) in the center of the main court enclosed a smaller center court which was probably the focal spot of the worship. The floor surfaces were of packed earth, and there were generally two of them, one above the other, indicating two sub-phases to the stratum, as is also suggested by Streets 9 and 8. At least two ovens were found, as shown in Fig. 63, one of them being a rather unusual "beehive" structure. Cooking was done in them much as may still be done today: fire and coals heated flat stones on which baking plates and cooking jars could be placed. The debris or fill used to level up for the floors of the various courtyard temples contained such an unusual amount of material from the broken walls of ovens, however, that we can be certain that many more existed which have not been excavated. This is another suggestion that we have here something other than a simple palace.

Temenos 3 (902). *The Casemate-Courtyard Temple* (ca. 1725 B.C.)

In Fig. 64 it will be noted that much more has been excavated and preserved in the 902 phase. The street leads definitely into a paved open area at the northeastern corner, and the northern and southern sectors are now separated by a narrow passage which leads to the alley along Wall D at the west.

The new passage outside the southern compound thus replaces the one inside the compound in the 939 phase. In each case their apparent purpose was to provide access to a smaller Central Court within the larger complex.

The southern compound is now a far more substantial construction, the main features being a series of small rectangular rooms along the eastern and presumably the southern edge, with larger rooms at the north. The space between the two parallel walls is cut up into small rooms which surround the main court on two sides. This feature, known as casemate construction in city fortifications, is the central characteristic of the 902 phase, one not continued in the next period. The main walls are *ca.* 1 m. wide (3 ft. 3 in.) with brick superstructure once upon them. The brick, where preserved in the interior rooms, is carefully faced with a thick layer of white marl plaster. The central feature is clearly the large court, in the northwest corner of which is a smaller rectangular court (Room 12, Figs. 64 and 65). The eastern and southern dimensions of the Great Court were probably once about the same, that is just slightly over 14 m. (*ca.* 46 ft.).

The walls and rooms of the 902 compound are the best preserved in the history of the courtyard temple. At the north the main block consists of six rooms in the final phase (Rooms 9, 8, 16, 10, 13 and 15), and a small open court (11): see Figs. 64 and 65. Walls 933 and 934 are reused, the former being strengthened in Room 13 by a mud-brick addition 921. In all of these rooms a considerable portion of the floor was preserved, and in several places it was found to have been resurfaced at least once.

The rooms can be described in three groups. Along the street are the workrooms. Room 9 had two ovens in it and was thus the kitchen. In front of the ovens was a flat limestone kneading stone, and near that a stone-lined storage pit. In Room 8 were remnants of a plaster-covered bench or low table built out at right angles to the west wall, and a stone-lined pit, the bottom of which accommodated a millstone. Room 16 is divided in half by a low curb wall which encloses a plastered floor laid over a stony fill. That this was for laundry or some kind of washing operation is indicated by the drain through Wall 902 to the sewer in Street 6 (Fig. 64). The earth floor in the rest of Room 16 contained several pieces of copper slag, which led us to speculation about the city's metal industry. In the fill below the temple fragments of a blowpipe for a kiln had been found.

On each side of Wall 905a between Rooms 8 and 9 burials had been made under the floor. The one in Room 9 had a small stone vault which contained a large storage jar, the neck of which had been broken off in order to receive the body of one or more infants. Outside the jar were a dipper juglet and carinated bowl for wine or oil and bread or meat. In the jar with the skeleton were a small buff-colored juglet and some large animal bones, the remains of a food offering. Below the floor of Room 8 the intact skeleton of a small animal rested on a bed of small stones. If the decayed remains of organic matter near the head of the animal represent a food offering, one may conjecture that this was no ordinary sacrificial animal, but a special pet; for one reason or another it had been given a special burial. Since they are placed in fill or make-up for the floors, the burials belong to the beginning of the 902 phase; one cannot help but speculate as to whether they had a religious significance.

In the paved court into which the street opens in the northeast sector, another burial was encountered. A trench had been dug through the debris down to the flagstone paving of the 939 phase. A store-jar was then inserted which contained the skeleton of a four- to six-year-old child. A string of paste beads with central scaraboid was around the child's neck (Fig. 66), and four jugs, probably with food and drink, had been buried with the child (Fig. 67). This burial had been made after the fill was in place, and probably after the buildings had been erected. It thus is probably a normal burial, perhaps of the child of a priest.

The second sector with spaces marked 10 and 11, consists of a room adjacent to a small, nearly square court in the latest phase. A fragment of flagstone pavement is preserved in Room 10. Sector 14 in Fig. 15 is a part of the Great Court to the south. In Room 15 there was probably a door from the alley outside Room 903a, whence one could go through Room 15 and down into 13 by some steps. A portion of a fine flagstone floor is also preserved in a corner of the Central Court 12. The western part of Room 15, however, was destroyed by a deep pit dug here for reasons unknown by people who erected *Temenos* 5.

The evidence suggests that the whole 902 compound was violently destroyed. Street 6 is the only one that belongs to this phase, and over it was a large accumulation of debris. It is probable also that Wall 900 was destroyed at the same time. There are clearly two phases in its construction, and only a portion of its first period remains along the street. All the rest, including that by the paved court in the northeastern sector, represents a rebuilding. It is surprising, however, that in the frequent destructions of the sacred area throughout its seven-hundred-year history so few objects remain in the ruins. This fact was also noted by Sellin. It is evident that in advance of the destructions people were able to remove most everything of value.

In Fig. 58 a reconstruction of the 902 *temenos* is presented to suggest how the courtyard temple may have looked. What the superstructure was like we, of course, do not know. We have only the ground plan, of which neither the southern nor northern compound walls (corresponding to 900) has been found.

To the west of the 902 courtyard temple, it will be noted in Fig. 58, the great C Earthen Embankment was now in place. The added strength and quality of the buildings and the new security offered by this hundred-foot-wide embankment testifies to added need for protective measures, as it speaks eloquently of the added prosperity of Shechem toward the end of the seventeenth century.

It may be asked: how does one know that the C Embankment belongs to this phase of the courtyard temples? Our view is, of course, an hypothesis, but it is supported by the following considerations:

(1) The preceding 939 period saw the erection of the first fortification in Field VI, Wall D.

(2) During the next period the level of the building is already relatively high, and adjacent to the small Central Court an annex was added, the outer wall of which rested on debris above the stump of Wall D.

Hence the C Embankment is already in existence and Wall D is covered by debris before the end of the 901 phase. A process of elimination puts C, then, in the 902 period. This is, indeed, where it should be according to the discoveries of such structures elsewhere in the earliest Hyksos period when Egypt was taken over by Asiatics.

Temenos 4 (901). *The Pillar-Courtyard Temple (ca. 1700 B.C.)*

Before excavation began in Field VI, the surface complex of walls left by Sellin in 1927 belonged in part to this phase. In most places the earth had been removed below floor level, so that the actual floors of 901 were encountered only in a few places. The destruction of 902, however, had been so severe that the rebuilding could use few of the earlier walls. Wall 901 along the street is entirely new, though resting on leveling debris directly above Wall 902. It is roughly 1 m. wide by Rooms 1 and 2, but was widened to 1.50 m. along the Great Court. Fill, mostly from the destruction of *Temenos* 3, with additional marl added, was carried in and laid over the last 902 floor to a depth of nearly 1.50 m.: cf. Fig. 68.

It will be noted from the over-all plan in Fig. 69 that the casemates were abandoned in the rebuilding, the arrangement of rooms and courts was altered, and two phases are evident. During the second or last phase the western Central Court walls were rebuilt and extended westward so that Wall 912 rests on debris over the inner part of the stone base of Wall D. North of the alley, in the northern group of rooms, Walls 948 and 949 also rest over the Wall D socket. In addition, during the second phase small rooms were created in the southwest corners of the two western courts (Room 7 and the one bounded by Wall 925a in the Central Court). The level of the courtyard temple was rising rapidly with each rebuilding, so that by the second phase of 901 it was higher than the socket of Wall D and was beginning to cut into the edge of the C Embankment, especially at the north.

Street surfaces 5 and 4 belong to this phase. They lead to a small court at the north, whence the alley leads west to provide access to the sacred courts, and a narrow passage leads north around behind Wall 958. To the south a door through Wall 903 probably existed, giving access to a sizable area (4) which led into a large court to the east (Room 2) and into the Central

Court to the south. A considerable portion of the eastern court (Room 2) had its marl floor preserved, and from its surface some of the best examples of 901 period pottery were preserved. The court is rectangular, 8 by 4.50 m. (*ca.* 26¼ by 14¾ ft.), and is particularly interesting because of the presence of column bases within it. Six of them were placed in line parallel to the north wall (903) with their centers 2 m. (6½ ft.) distant from it. A heavy wall under the floor was built for them to rest on, and their tops projected above the room floor. That is, the northern part of the court was roofed, wooden columns supporting the roof, but the covered area was left open to the court between the columns. Approximately in the center of the remaining unroofed area, another column base was set on a small stone base, very solidly built. The column or post which stood on this base could have no architectural significance; it was freestanding. The suggestion can therefore be made that it was for a *maṣṣēbāh*, or sacred stone, having the same purpose as the standing stone slabs in Fortress-temples 1b and 2.

In the northwest corner of the court, at a depth of 80 cm. below the floor, a large store-jar had been buried, protected from breakage by two fragments of a large jar set around it, and by a small projection built out from the wall to form a shallow niche. Above the jar were fragments of a large carinated bowl, and leaning against the jar's base was a juglet. The bottom of the jar was filled with small bones and skull fragments of what may have been a newly-born infant. The skeleton had been placed in the jar in a sitting position and was packed in place with earth.

The Central Court in the first phase of 901 was evidently comparable to what it had been in the preceding 902 compound (Room 12). Now, however, it had a freestanding pillar within it, resting on a base exactly like that in Court 2 (Fig. 70). The rebuilding of this area in its final phase made the Central Court smaller and installed a small room in its southwest corner. At the same time a small room, No. 7, was created in Court 4.

Such in brief is Courtyard Temple 901. New ideas are present in its construction. Court 11 of the preceding 902 compound is enlarged into Court 2. Freestanding stones or posts are placed in the center of each, objects probably of sacred significance— that is, they are evidently *maṣṣēbôt*.

Temenos 5 (*909–910*). *The Enlarged Courtyard Temple* (ca. *1675* B.C.)

The last of the courtyard temples was evidently the largest of them all (Fig. 71). Two substantial east-west walls were left in place by Sellin; they were approximately 1 m. above the floors of the 901 phase (Fig. 72). A sampling of the pottery from the time of their erection was obtained from a large pit dug down through the previous courtyard temples below Walls 909 and 923. Because Sellin had dug around the walls and below their level, little of them remained when we began work, except their western end which now was on top, or at least on the upper slope of the C Embankment. With the constraint of Wall D removed, the width of the compound was extended to between 24 and 25 m. (79 to 82 ft.), and the northern wall (909) was widened to *ca.* 1.50 m., like the Great Court wall in 901.[9] What went on north and south of these walls we do not know.

Streets 3–1 do not belong with 901, and hence are assigned to this phase. We must suppose that the wall of the Great Court along the street must have followed the line of the preceding walls here, but little more can be said about the structure of this stratum.

Of special interest, however, are two small square buildings erected on top of what then existed of the C Embankment. Welter compares them to Egyptian granaries, which would appear to be a satisfactory suggestion. Granary storage would also be the simplest explanation for the heavy-walled, two-roomed structure 930–928 that was erected over part of one of the square buildings (Fig. 71). This is shown by the stratification in Field VI, Area 2 (Fig. 16), however, to be contemporary with Temple 1. So also is northern compound Wall 943.

Conclusion

In Field VI we have an unusual sequence of buildings from the early and central part of the Middle Bronze Age. Though the detailed plan of the four phases (939, 902, 901, 909–910) is different in each case, yet the eastern wall, street, and Wall 900 are on the same spot throughout. The Great Court, within which is the smaller Central Court, also holds its position. And the unshifting fulcrum under the later altar is most suggestive. Fortress-temple 1 thus did not become the first religious building to be erected on a previously neutral spot. Instead the later altar was built over a place determined by previous religious history.

As suggested at the beginning of this chapter, there exists a remarkable parallel for the courtyard temples at Shechem in the Hittite capital, Boğhazköy. Not only does that fact establish the existence of this temple-type, but Temples I and II there especially have a series of small rooms along the outer walls of the compound, the whole thus possessing a casemate character. A special entrance leads into a smaller court which is the main cult room, though unroofed.[10] These Hittite structures, though dating from the Late Bronze Age, are comparable to the Shechem Courtyard Temple 902 especially, except, of course, that the Boğhazköy buildings are larger and more elaborate, as would befit the capital of the Hittite empire at the height of its power. As for Syria-Palestine, a new temple-type is now to be added to those previously known.[11]

Though we know very little about the structures of Period 1 (968) of MB II A, what has been discovered, it is important to note, does not conform to the general outline established in the succeeding *Temenos* 2 (939). Attention is called, however, to the following:

(1) The massive filling operation to level the area suggests its preparation for an important function in the time when this sector appears to have been outside the city fortifications. From Wall 900 or the 968 structure westward our sections and those of Welter indicate that any earlier fortifications must have been farther east.

(2) The large earthen platform with stones fixed along its outer edges to prevent erosion (968) was erected for a purpose about which we dare not speculate at this time. Yet its size suggests a public function of considerable importance.

(3) The area was unoccupied previously, except for a settlement some two thousand years before. The initial preparation of the area for important public use is difficult to separate from the following period. The decision to enclose the sector within a city fortification when *Temenos* 2 was erected is probably not unrelated to its original public use.

These factors make difficult any other hypothesis than that the preparation for the first use of the area as a sacred precinct or *temenos* took place around 1800 B.C. The fact that it was outside the city at the time further suggests that it may have been a new establishment of fresh settlers in the time of the Amorite incursions.

The last two chapters and some of the main elements described in Chapter 5 can be helpfully set forth, I believe, in chart form:

Phase	Date	Expedition Stratum (by Wall No.)
Temenos 1	*ca.* 1800–1750 B.C.	968

Massive fill and leveling of the area. First structures outside known fortifications. Platform 968.

Temenos 2	*ca.* 1750–1725 B.C.	939

Simple courtyard temple and Streets 9–7 enclosed between City Wall D and *Temenos* Wall 900.

Temenos 3	*ca.* 1725–1700 B.C.	902

Casemate-courtyard temple and Street 6. Wall C and the great, 30-m.-wide, earthen embankment between C and D. Major destruction.

Temenos 4	*ca.* 1700–1675 B.C.	901

Pillar-courtyard temple and Streets 5–4. Wall 900 completely rebuilt. Wall D no longer visible when the 901 addition, Walls 912–927, was erected during the period.

Temenos 5	*ca.* 1675–1650 B.C.	909–910

Enlarged courtyard temple built over edge of C Embankment, Streets 3–1. Silos built on Embankment.

Temenos 6	*ca.* 1650–1600 B.C.	

Fortress-temple 1a, Wall A and Northwest Gate.

Temenos 7	*ca.* 1600–1550 B.C.	

Fortress-temple 1b with small *maṣṣēbôt* on either side of entrance. Altar-base with marl-brick edging. Wall B on east and north. East Gate.

Destructions (*ca.* 1550–1540 B.C.) and Gap in Occupation (*ca.* 1540–1450 B.C.)

Temenos 8	*ca.* 1450–1200 B.C.	

Fortress-temple 2a, new brick altar, first phase of podium, repair and reuse of all fortifications. *Maṣṣēbāh* 1 erected in this period or the next.

Temenos 9	*ca.* 1200–1100 B.C.	

Fortress-temple 2b, marked by raising of floor and new altar of stone. All three sacred standing stones in use. Destruction and end of sacred area.

8

The Sacred Area of Shechem in Early Biblical Tradition

Let us now examine the early stories of the Bible and see how we can put them together with the archaeological discoveries of Shechem.

The Abimelech Narrative

A good starting point, previously argued, is to maintain with Sellin that the biblical story about Abimelech in Chapter 9 of the Book of Judges is to be placed alongside the archaeological data. This narrative provides us with two firm pieces of evidence for a reconstruction: (1) A literary account matching the archaeological fact of the destruction of Bronze Age Shechem during the twelfth century B.C., together with the identity of the man responsible. This man was Abimelech, son of the famed leader Gideon and a Shechemite woman, who found the city in rebellion against him. The people of Shechem had returned to their Bronze Age, city-state pattern of government, and only three years previously had in solemn ceremony made Abimelech their king—the first and only action of this kind as far as we know during the period of Israel's tribal league.

That Shechem was an entirely foreign and pagan Canaanite enclave within the tribal league, as often previously assumed, now seems invalid. On the contrary, old tradition spoke of it as the site where the tribal league was constituted in the Promised Land (Joshua 24). Some kind of old tie existed between the new Israel and the Shechemites, so that the latter were not conquered. The city was not destroyed; it joined the covenant of the tribal league. Now with their new king the people of the city suddenly found themselves persuaded to revolt in his absence by one Gaal ben-Ebed (Judg. 9:26 ff.). Zebul, Abimelech's representative left in charge of the city, sent word to his master. Abimelech responded by destroying the city and sowing it to salt, a symbolic act denoting the "infertility" which was visited upon the city for its breach of solemn covenant.[1]

(2) A second piece of information from the Abimelech story is the statement that within the city there was a temple, "the House of El-berith," which was also destroyed.[2] The reference here without serious question is to the structure which we have designated Temple 2b. In Judges 9, therefore, we have a most important correlation between the archaeological discoveries and biblical tradition. And if Temple 2b is named in Judges 9, then there can be little doubt but that Temple 2a bore the same name.

There is still more information of interest and importance in the Abimelech narrative. After the account of Abimelech's destruction of the city is seemingly concluded in Judg. 9:45,[3] another paragraph has apparently been added (9:46–49). Verse 46 reads, as we look closely at the Hebrew: "And all the leading citizens[4] of the Migdal-Shechem (fortress) heard,[5] and they entered the *sĕrîaḥ* (stronghold?) of the house of El-berith."

As the text now stands, the implication is that when the chief people of the fortress of Shechem "heard" of Shechem's destruction, they took refuge in the *sĕrîaḥ* of the temple. Hence it has frequently been argued that Migdal-Shechem was a different locality, not in the city itself. The *sĕrîaḥ* of the temple, then, would have been in the vicinity of the *Migdāl*, and not in the temple itself. On the surface this seems obvious. Yet there are difficulties to such an interpretation:

(1) If 9:45 is the natural conclusion to the narrative of the city's destruction, then 9:46–49 is in the nature of an appendix,

probably a separate fragment of the once oral tradition. If so, then there is no certainty at all that verses 45 and 46 are to read as continuous narrative, the first being the antecedent of the second. Instead, verses 46–49 could just as well be an additional detail about what went on *during* the city's destruction. If so, then the Migdal-Shechem was a part of the city itself and the ṣĕrîaḥ a part of the temple. How does one say which interpretation of verses 46–49 is correct? With no other evidence I do not see how one can be dogmatic one way or another; verses 45–46 can be read either way. Welter certainly read the narrative as a continuous story, and a recent discussion of the ṣĕrîaḥ by Milik concludes that it was a cave on the slopes of Mt. Ebal.[6] But let us look further.

(2) Who were the people of the *Migdāl* who took refuge in the ṣĕrîaḥ? The Hebrew term almost certainly refers to the responsible male citizens whose corporate will established policy. In verse 46 they are called the ba'ălê of the Migdal-Shechem. But in verse 2 there is a reference to the ba'ălê of the city itself. These are the men who decide whether they want Abimelech, and indeed it is they who make him king (v. 6).[7] Furthermore, they have the control over the temple and are able to give money to Abimelech from the temple's treasury (v. 4). Consequently, within the city itself there cannot be two independent sources of responsibility, one over the so-called "lower city" and the other over the temple or acropolis, as has been suggested. The responsible citizens of Shechem have charge over both city and temple. Are they a different group from those mentioned in the *Migdāl*?

(3) The answer again depends upon whether the Migdal-Shechem is a separate locality. If it is separate, then it must have been large enough to accommodate the one thousand people whom Abimelech destroyed (v. 49). Yet when one studies the topography of the Shechem area, and reads Judges 9 in that context, he must ask where such a place would be. *Migdāl* is a fortress to protect something, or is a part of a city's defense system. From the standpoint of defense where would one put this particular *Migdāl*? Of course, there could be outposts to the east, west in the pass, and north and south. But this *Migdāl* is something special, supported by a large body of responsible citizenry. There simply is no logical place for such a fortress, and no evi-

dence for one anywhere else in the area, except where the city actually stood. Shechem itself was created as a great *Migdāl* to control the area. Consequently, if one were to insist on separating the Migdal-Shechem of verse 46 from the city, then the only way one could make sense out of the actual topography is to adopt Welter's view: namely, that Tell Balâṭah is Migdal-Shechem, while the city lies where the center of Nablus now is. Yet, as explained in the first chapter, that view is not possible.

In view, then, of the obvious difficulties encountered by assuming that verse 46 is to be read as a straightforward continuation of verse 45, let us start again, assuming the other possibility: namely, that verses 46–49 constitute one important detail of Abimelech's destruction of Shechem which was transmitted as a separate item in the tradition, perhaps because it was so important.[8] In this case, the Migdal-Shechem is part of the city itself. If so, then we can recall Professor Mazar's contention about the meaning of *Migdāl* in such a connection. If the town name Migdal-el, listed as a fortified city of Naphtali in Josh. 19:38, derives its name from the *Migdāl* temple of El which it contained, then Migdal-Shechem means the *Migdāl* Temple of Shechem, also known as "the Temple of El of the Covenant." Migdal-Shechem is thus identical with Beth-Millo in verse 6. Millo means a fortification set upon a "filling." One existed in Jerusalem (2 Sam. 5:9). Other examples may have been found in tenth-century district headquarters of the central government at Beth-shemesh and Lachish, where the governor's palace was erected on a filling, perhaps to raise the building above the others in the city.[9] The temple at Shechem is, of course, on deep fill. The contexts of both the references to Migdal-Shechem and Beth-Millo, however, suggest that the whole *temenos* or sacred area is referred to, not simply its most important building.

The citizenry of the Migdal-Shechem in verse 46, furthermore, must be part of the larger group referred to in verse 2 as the citizens of Shechem. The Shechem temple, as was to be the case with the Jerusalem temple later on, was also the citadel, the final point of defense. To this point people had retired for protection; one thousand were burned to death in the burning of the temple. Precisely what the *sĕrîaḥ* was cannot be known without more information about the meaning of the word. It cannot be "crypt," because the temple had none. It is interesting that the Alexandrian family of manuscripts of the Greek translation of the Old Testament renders the word by a Greek term, *oxúrōma*, which meant "fortress."[10] An Arabic word with the same consonants, *ṣarḥ*, means "tower," and Dr. Albright has pointed out that the South Arabic has a word, *ṣrḥt*, which was used in building inscriptions in the sense of "upper story, upper room."[11] With this support one can suggest that the people may have taken refuge in the tower rooms of the Shechem temple. While Temple 2 had cella walls only 2 m. thick, it was still a large and strong building, and the towers were undoubtedly capacious, since they were probably filled with storage rooms and apartments for the priestly families in charge of the building and its worship.

It is worth while in this connection to recall that the last verses of Judges 9 (50–55) preserve a good illustration of what happened in the siege of Shechem with regard to the use of the *Migdāl*. Thebez, modern *Tūbâṣ*, a dependency of Shechem about ten miles to the northeast, had apparently revolted with Shechem. Abimelech laid siege to the town and captured it.

> But the Migdal-ʿŌz[12] was in the midst of the town. Thither all the men and women, and all the leading citizens of the town, fled, and shut themselves in, and ascended to the roof of the Migdal. And Abimelech came to the Migdal and fought against it. As he drew near to the door of the Migdal to set it on fire, a certain woman threw an upper millstone upon Abimelech's head, and crushed his skull. Then he called hastily to the steward, his armor-bearer, and said to him: "Draw your sword and put me to death, lest they say of me, 'A woman killed him.'" And his steward thrust him through and he died.

If Temple 2 at Shechem still preserved its tradition of being a *Migdāl* temple, it is not at all unlikely that the name "House of the El of the Covenant" is an old one, considering the conservatism with which religious traditions are transmitted. Hence it is not at all preposterous to suppose that the temple's name in Judg. 9:46 was also the name of Temple 1 in MB II C (*ca.* 1650–1550 B.C.).

It seems to me, then, that fewer difficulties arise if Judg. 9:46–49 is interpreted as a special incident which happened *during* Abimelech's destruction of Shechem, rather than as an additional incident which happened *after* the destruction of the city. If from the standpoint of Hebrew composition and the transmission of what once was oral tradition, the pericope could be interpreted in either sense, the arguments presented seem to me to tip the scales in favor of the first.

With regard to Abimelech's tactics in capturing the city, Lawrence E. Toombs has written cogently as follows in a personal letter:

> The initial attack on the city came by way of a surprise assault on workers in the fields. Such an attack could only be delivered against the east side of the city where the fields lie and under cover of the convenient shoulder of Mt. Gerizim. Moreover the fact that the attacking troops can be brought into position without observation clearly indicates that the rebels controlled only the city and had no outposts beyond its walls, at least to the east. A detachment of Abimelech's troops blocked the gate and the workers were caught between two detachments. The East Gate geographically is the only feasible locale for this engagement and it seems logical that the assault would be driven home against that gate and adjacent fortifications. This would bring the assault forces into the city on low ground and lead to a protracted (v. 45) period of uphill house-to-house fighting. Assuming that the breaching of the gate and the entrance into the southeastern quarter of the city was what the leaders directing the defense from the acropolis area "heard," a determined rearguard action in the lower city would have given them time to organize a last-ditch defense on the higher ground around the temple. Not all of the thousand defenders would have to have been inside the actual temple. Its large forecourt would be defensible if under the cover of arrows from the tower.

Shechem in the Patriarchal Stories

With the suggestion that the name of Temple 2 preserved in Judges 9 could also have been the name of Temple 1, because the former preserved the *Migdāl* temple type, even though its broad cultic room was now more like a Canaanite sacred building, we have pushed our inquiry back into the Middle Bronze Age toward the period of the Hebrew Patriarchs. Having examined the story of the temple's destruction in the twelfth century, let us turn back to the stories in the Book of Genesis and see if they preserve any information of importance for the historian of Shechem. As we do so, certain things must here be assumed: first, that these stories were passed from generation to generation orally for centuries before the first edition of them in writing appeared in the days of David or Solomon in the tenth century B.C. It is also assumed here that archaeologists, under the lead especially of W. F. Albright, have proved that the stories derive from an actual historical epoch between *ca.* 2000 and 1700 B.C. and that with the proper use of literary and historical tools, historical information of considerable importance can be gained from them.[13]

It was over a half-century ago that Hermann Gunkel in the introduction to his significant commentary, *Genesis*,[14] stressed the importance of towns in the Book of Genesis which in later times had sanctuaries in them. The manner in which some of the stories are told suggests that they relate what later Israelites believed to be the origin of these sanctuaries. He goes on to suggest, then, that the Patriarchal "sagas," as he calls them, were preserved because each sanctuary transmitted the material of importance to itself.

While we need not enter here into a discussion of the problems relating to the transmission of tradition, the importance of particular towns where worship continued in later eras is certainly clear. Abra(ha)m is related to at least five such localities: Shechem, Bethel, Mamre, Beer-sheba and Moriah. Except for Mamre[15] each is called a *māqôm*, a common Hebrew word meaning "place," but in this case it is used with the specialized meaning, "sacred place, sacred precinct" (Gen. 12:6, 8; 13:3; 21:31–33—cf. 28:11; 26:23 ff.; 22:9, 14). A sacred tree, whether oak, terebinth or tamarisk, is mentioned at Shechem, Mamre and Beer-sheba. All are places where God revealed himself to the Patriarch, or where a solemn covenant or treaty was undertaken with the local inhabitants (cf. Gen. 14:13; 21:31–33; 26:23 ff.). Furthermore, a careful reading makes clear that the later conservators of the traditions understood them to involve the founding or the appropriation of sacred areas which were still revered in Israel. While the location of Moriah, where Abraham's faith was tested in the command to sacrifice his son

(Genesis 22), is unknown, there is no doubt that later Israel interpreted it as Jerusalem (2 Chron. 3:1). Jacob, furthermore, is credited with the establishment of the *māqôm,* or sacred area, at Penuel, a town identified by Nelson Glueck with *Tulûl edh-Dhahab* across the Jordan on the northern side of the Jabbok stream in Gilead. This is of interest because it, like Shechem, later had a *Migdāl* in it which Gideon, the father of Abimelech, destroyed (Judg. 8:8, 9, 17).

Southern, or Jerusalemite, tradition appears to have ascribed the appropriation or founding of the sacred areas at Shechem and Bethel to Abraham. Gen. 12:6–8 reads:

> And Abram passed through the land to the sacred area (*māqôm*) of Shechem, to the oak of Moreh. . . . And the Lord appeared to Abram and said: "To thy seed I will give this land." And he erected an altar there to the Lord, who had appeared to him. Then he moved on from there to the hill east of Bethel. And he pitched his tent with Bethel to the west and Ai to the east. And he built an altar there to the Lord and called on the name of the Lord.

Northern tradition, on the other hand, connected both Shechem and Bethel especially with the Patriarch Jacob. In Genesis 28 Jacob had his dream "at a certain place" where God appeared to him and repeated the promises he had made to Abraham and Isaac. In the morning the Patriarch took the stone on which he had rested his head, set it up as a *maṣṣēbāh* or sacred pillar, "and named that *māqôm* Beth-el, though Luz had formerly been the name of the town" (v. 18). On his return from Haran many years later we are told in Gen. 33:18–20 that

> Jacob came peaceably to the city of Shechem which was in the land of Canaan when he came from Paddan-Aram. And he encamped before the city, and he purchased the portion of field on which he had pitched his tent from the hands of the sons of Hamor, father of Shechem, for a hundred qesitas.[16] And he set up an altar there and named it "El, God of Israel."

In this passage the city of Shechem is spoken of as a person whose father was Hamor. That is, the city, its origin and the name of its present inhabitants are personalized after a manner typical of Patriarchal "corporate personality." A question arises, however, with regard to the name Hamor. If Shechem is a corporate entity, if its father is Hamor and the present inhabitants in the Jacob tradition are known as the Běnê-Ḥamôr ("sons of Hamor"), what does Hamor signify? The word is the common Hebrew term for "ass, donkey," and it was no more of a compliment then, than it is today. In letters written by the Amorite inhabitants of Mari on the Upper Euphrates toward the end of the eighteenth century B.C., however, there are frequent references to "killing an ass" as part of the ritual when a covenant or peace treaty was made by two parties.[17] The "Sons of the Ass" at Shechem, then, are probably to be understood as members of a confederation which had been sealed by the rite of "killing an ass." Hamor as the "father" of Shechem suggests that either the founding of the city, or else something constituent of its very being, had to do with a covenant or treaty.

This personalizing of Shechem and Hamor continues in the Dinah story of Genesis 34. It is difficult, therefore, to know for sure what historical incidents lie behind the story, though it clearly arose in clan relations. Dinah may or may not have been one of the clans of the Jacob family. In any event, the story says that Dinah on a visit to local women was seized and raped by Shechem, who promptly fell in love with her and desired her for his wife. His father then went to Jacob and asked for the girl and, indeed, for an agreement for intermarriage generally between the two families. Jacob and his sons agreed, on condition that the Shechemites be circumcised. The condition was accepted, but while the men were still incapacitated, two of Jacob's sons, Simeon and Levi, fell upon the city and slew all the males. Jacob's family then plundered the city, but Jacob remonstrated with Simeon and Levi, saying to them: "You have brought trouble on me by making me shameful among the inhabitants of the land" (Gen. 34:30). These words suggest that a solemn covenant has been violated.

The story indicates surely that even in Patriarchal tradition Shechem plays a special role not given to any other Palestinian city. A covenant involving intermarriage is made, the only exception to the general rule of no intermarriage which the tradition records (cf. Gen. 24:2–4). There is also implied the capture of the city. To the latter Jacob alludes on his deathbed in a passage, the text of which appears to have suffered somewhat at the hands of later interpreters: "And indeed I have given to you (Joseph), rather than to your brothers, one Shechem which I took from the hand of the Amorites with my sword and with my bow" (Gen. 48:22).

Whatever we are to make of this tradition, it is a very old one, because Levi is still a secular tribe, not yet set apart for priestly and religious duties as was the case at least as early as the tribal league of the twelfth to eleventh centuries. Furthermore, it is the only record of a conquest of Shechem which the Old Testament preserves. In any case, the tradition remained a strong factor in the time of Joshua. The city is not conquered; instead, it is deemed the proper place for the great covenant of the tribal league on the soil of the Promised Land (Joshua 24). In short, wherever one touches the Shechem tradition in early Israel, he encounters covenant as peculiarly associated with the city.

Is the sacred area of the Abraham and Jacob stories the same as that which we have been excavating at Shechem? Heretofore, the general view of scholars has been that the *māqôm* of Genesis is not the same as the precincts of "the Temple of El of the Covenant" in Judges 9. For one thing, the plot of ground that Jacob purchased was clearly outside the city. Yet, as we have already noted, our excavations have clearly shown that the 968 phase of ± 1800 B.C. was indeed outside any city fortifications there may have been. The sacred area was included within the city only with the erection of city Wall D not earlier than ± 1750 B.C. Hence the "outside-inside" argument can no longer be used.

Another argument that can be cited in favor of different sacred areas is the matter of the tree. Genesis 12:6 mentions the "Oak of Moreh," presumably the same as the oak under which Jacob hid the "foreign gods" in a family purification before moving on to Bethel (Gen. 35:4). This oak, like the sacred area, was not in the city in Patriarchal times; it is said to be "with Shechem" according to the Hebrew text of Gen. 35:4. That phrase is generally interpreted to mean "near, in the vicinity of"—though the Septuagint, or Greek translation, interprets it as "*in* Shechem." In any case, the Oak of Moreh has been thought by some to be the same as "the Diviners' Oak" from the direction which one company of Abimelech's forces was seen approaching the city, according to Judg. 9:37. The basis for this identification has been the supposition that Moreh, which means "teacher," could be identified with occult "teaching." This supposition has little to commend it, however, because the Hebrew word "to teach," from which Moreh derives, is not used of the occult.[18] Consequently, this argument for the separation of the Patriarchal and Abimelech sacred areas is not a good one. As we shall note below, it is much more feasible to identify the Oak of Moreh as being in the same place as "the oak of the pillar" under which Abimelech was made king, according to the same chapter of the Book of Judges (9:6).

If the chief direct arguments for the separation of the two sacred areas are no longer to be considered cogent, we still need further evidence before we identify the two without hesitation. Most important would be a continuity of religious tradition in one locality. Certain factors and inferences now to be considered point strongly to such a continuity.

The Continuity of Tradition in the Sacred Area

From the stories preserved about Abraham and Jacob we learn certain teachings and affirmations about the sacred area of Shechem in the lives of the fathers of Israel.

(1) The sacred area was either appropriated (Gen. 12:6) or first established (Gen. 33:18–20) by Abraham or Jacob, and it was outside the city. This accords remarkably with the first or 968 phase of the Shechem *temenos*, which shows evidence of elaborate preparation and building in MB II A (*ca.* 1850–1750 B.C.) and which was on the outskirts of the city of that era. That this city was of some size and importance is to be assumed by the references to it by the official of Pharaoh Sesostris III and by its inclusion among the enemies in Asia on the Brussels magical figurines.

(2) Besides having a place of worship, Shechem's role in tradition is centrally related to covenant. We infer this from the name of the "father" of the city, Hamor—which surely derives from a tradition concerning a treaty or confederation that was

a constituent aspect of the city's life. In addition, the least we can say about the historical meaning of Genesis 34 and 48:22 is that those who traced their origins back to the Jacob clan remembered both a covenant between itself and Shechem and a conquest of the city. Hence in the sense in which Jacob could be called Israel, Shechem can be said to have become "Israelite" either by confederation or conquest or both.

(3) A special tree, an oak, existed in the sacred precincts.

These Genesis stories are part of the old epic account of the origin and meaning of Israel's life in the Promised Land, an account which scholars usually designate by the combined symbols "JE," the basis of which goes back to the time of the tribal league in the twelfth to eleventh centuries. Let us now turn to a different type of literature, Joshua 24. This chapter has generally been felt to derive from very old tradition, though in its transmission it has been touched up here and there by a "Deuteronomic" editor, who included it as an appendix to the Book of Joshua. That book in turn is a part of the great Deuteronomic History of Israel in the Promised Land, extending from Deuteronomy through 2 Kings.

Joshua 24 is a story about the great covenant which brought the tribal league into being on the soil of Palestine: "And Joshua gathered all the tribes of Israel to Shechem, and he called to the elders of Israel, its (tribal) leaders, its judges and its officers, and they presented themselves before God." I find it difficult to dissociate the fact that Shechem was deemed the appropriate place for this solemn ceremony from the Patriarchal traditions, especially those about the affiliation with, and conquest of, the city preserved in north Israel.[19] In any case, what follows in verses 2–13 is the first part of the ceremony: the covenant leader quotes the Divine Suzerain, who speaks in the first person and recites the epic story of his benevolent acts to Israel.[20] What follows in verses 14–24 is the colloquy between leader and people and the leader's admonitions as the people prepare to take their vows of obedience and adherence to the covenant. Finally, the conclusion in verses 25–27 is as follows: "And Joshua made a covenant with the people in that day. . . . And he took a great stone and set it up there under the terebinth which was in the sanctuary of the Lord. And Joshua said to all the people: "Behold, this stone shall be a witness against us. . . ."

Joshua 24 preserves the record of a solemn religious cere-mony, and it is preserved in the Deuteronomic corpus of ma-terial within the Old Testament. It thus is a somewhat different type of literature from the Genesis epic sources. Nevertheless, it preserves comparable traditions:

(1) The covenant tradition at Shechem was so strong that it was deemed the appropriate place to hold the covenant cere-mony which brought the tribal league into being in Palestine. The Shechem enclave, which at the end of the thirteenth cen-tury evidently controlled a major part of the north central hill country, entered the tribal league by means of this covenant, probably accepting with the newcomers the Exodus-Sinai tradi-tions as normative. Hence whatever covenant once meant at Shechem, there was now a new covenant, which modern scholar-ship suggests was celebrated periodically for years thereafter at the site or in the vicinity.

(2) A sanctuary (Hebrew *miqdash*) is mentioned as being at Shechem.

(3) There is mention of "the terebinth,"[21] a type of tree which is a close relative of the oak, within the sacred precincts.

(4) A new element is Joshua's erection of "a great stone" under the tree in the sanctuary as the sign or commemoration of the covenant, a perpetual witness to the vows there taken.

Turning again to Judges 9 we find the temple definitely named, the name of God there employed in worship included the term "covenant," and (v. 6) we read that the responsible citizens "made Abimelech king with the oak of the pillar[22] in Shechem." Here again we have the use of the word "with" in the sense of "by," "in the vicinity of."

We have summarized, then, three different types of litera-ture: the Genesis stories (JE), an old covenant record (Joshua 24) and an old narrative about Abimelech (Judges 9). All possess differing backgrounds and to some extent a different history of transmission, and all witness to Shechem's role. Within them there are certain "constants" that strongly suggest a continuity in cultic tradition: (1) covenant as central to the self-under-standing and worship of this religious center; (2) a sacred precinct; and (3) a tree within the precinct, whether oak or terebinth. We need not suppose that it was the same tree (!), but only that a special tree within the sacred precincts was a char-

acteristic of Shechem's place of worship, so that it is mentioned
in all three sources quoted above (cf. also Deut. 11:30). We can
push back further into the mists of the past and add two poten-
tially additional "constants":

(1) It is highly probable that the special name used of God
in the Shechem sanctuary was El-berith, "the covenant El" or
"El of the covenant." In Judg. 9:4 the term "Baal-berith" is used,
meaning originally "Lord of the covenant." Professor Mazar has
suggested to me that this reading derives from a later time when
the deity worshiped in the Shechem temple was a pagan deity.
That the Deuteronomic editor so considered the deity is explicitly
stated in Judg. 8:33. Yet an earlier tradition in Josh. 24:26 refers
to the Shechem temple as *miqdash Yahweh*, "temple" or "sanctuary of Yahweh," the proper name of the God of Israel. In Gen.
33:20 the divine name at the Shechem altar is given as "El-Elohe-
Israel" ("El, God of Israel"). In all probability, therefore, the
deity of the Shechem sanctuary was of the Patriarchal El tradition, one manifestation of the God of the Fathers who was identified with Yahweh of Israel in the days of Moses and Joshua.
The relation of El-berith to other El manifestations, such as
El-bethel of Bethel (Gen. 35:7, 15; cf. 28:17, 19), El-Olam at
Beer-sheba (Gen. 21:33), and El-Shaddai (Gen. 17:1; Exod.
6:3), would appear to be clear. His special relation to covenant,
which was so important at the Shechem sanctuary, is also made
clear by the name.[23]

(2) At Bethel we know that a prominent religious symbol
was a sacred standing stone or *maṣṣēbāh* which tradition recalled
Jacob's having erected there to commemorate a theophany
wherein God repeated his promises (Gen. 28:18; 35:14). It is
not improbable that a similar object was always present in the
Shechem sacred precincts. In this case it would have been a
"witness" to the covenant which was celebrated in the various
phases of the sanctuary's history. We noted above that Josh.
24:26 says that Joshua erected a great stone under the oak in
the sanctuary as a "witness" to his covenant ceremony there.
This same *maṣṣēbāh* is probably referred to in Judg. 9:6. Let us
also recall the description of the actual objects in the excavation. In courtyard temple 901 (*Temenos* 4), dating from the first
half of the seventeenth century, there were in the first phase two

small courts, and in each one of these there was a firmly fixed column base which once held an upright stone or post (Figs. 69 and 70). Yet the areas are too large for them to have structural significance; they must have been freestanding. Such objects in a temple were surely of the category of *maṣṣēbāh*. In Fortress-temple 1b two stone slabs were erected on pedestals which flanked the doorway (Figs. 36, 37, 48). Finally, the great, white *Maṣṣēbāh* 1 was erected *on* fill placed in the courtyard of Fortress-temple 2 in the Late Bronze Age. All we can say about its date from the excavations is that it was installed some time during the life of Temple 2. Since this stone was in position when the temple was destroyed by Abimelech during the course of the twelfth century B.C., it is surely the one mentioned in Judg. 9:6. If so, then it would not appear to be overly rash to suppose that the tradition about Joshua's "great stone" is probably related to *Maṣṣēbāh* 1. Yet the idea of a *maṣṣēbāh* at Shechem did not originate with the stone; there were evidently one or more always in existence there.

The continuity of cultic tradition—needed to support the hypothesis that the *māqôm* of the Patriarchal period, and the temples of Joshua 24 and Judges 9, all point to the same sacred area which has been excavated—seems to have been present when we examine the "constants" in the various traditions: sanctuary, covenant, the special name of God as he was worshiped there, oak or terebinth and sacred pillar.

The seven-hundred-year history of the Shechem *temenos* thus permits us to join elements in the biblical tradition which hitherto could not be clearly associated. And it also gives us an additional concrete piece of evidence for the identification of the Patriarchal "God of the Fathers" with the God of the Mosaic covenant and the tribal league.

One more group of biblical verses, however, needs to be mentioned. The Deuteronomic historian who compiled from old sources the history of the conquest of Canaan by Joshua understood that as soon as Israel got a foothold in the hills north of Jerusalem, they were to go to Shechem for a covenant ceremony, there to hear the blessings of obedience and the curses of disobedience. The historian's tradition prescribed this in Deut. 11:29, and tells of its fulfillment in Josh. 8:30–35. Furthermore,

Deuteronomy 27 must derive from the same cycle of tradition. It is incomplete, for only a group of curses are listed.

This material was surely preserved, it is understood today, because these passages with Joshua 24 showed the origin of the covenant renewal ceremony that was later held annually, or at least periodically, at Shechem. Yet in these passages nothing is said about Shechem or its sanctuary. The emphasis is solely on the blessings and the curses, the former to be from Gerizim and the latter from Ebal. That is, a prominent part of the covenant renewal ceremony called for one group on the Gerizim side to repeat the blessings and another on the Ebal side to recite the curses. I suggest that the reason there is no mention of the city or its sanctuary in these three passages is precisely because they allude to a well-known ceremony which continued yearly at the site *after* the twelfth-century destruction of the sacred area. That area was never again rebuilt. Yet the ceremonies continued, with perhaps antiphonal recitation of blessings and curses, one group standing with backs toward Ebal and the other toward Gerizim. Such an hypothesis cannot be proved, but it would explain the blessings and curses passages wherein the place of the ceremony remains unmentioned.

9

Israelite Shechem

When did Shechem become an Israelite city?

Dr. Sellin addressed himself to this question in a mono-graph published in 1922, before he found the temple (in 1926).[1] He believed that it began to play an important role in Israelite life only after the time of Abimelech. The responsible citizens of Shechem mentioned in Judges 9 (the *ba'ălê Shĕkém*) were to him the common Canaanite population of the city. This was the chief support which Abimelech had there. After his conquest "the old sanctuary east of the city" became the central Israelite sanctuary, and its "old Semitic cultus" became Israelite and Yahwistic. The city itself was not completely destroyed, but the Canaanite power in it was broken and the Canaanite population destroyed.[2] What Sellin's final views were after his excavations will never be known, as they were probably contained in the manuscript destroyed with his home in Berlin in 1943.

In 1926 and 1927 Dr. F. M. Th. Böhl of Leiden, who was assisting Sellin in the excavations, addressed himself to the same question, and gave a more complex answer.[3] The Hebrew tribes, he believed, moved into Palestine in successive waves. The first main wave probably consisted of those tribes that traced their ancestry back to Jacob and the first of his wives, Leah. Genesis 34 records how two of them, Simeon and Levi, captured Shechem. This would have been at a time when Egypt was not in firm control of the country; the most reasonable hypothesis, Böhl believed, was a date in the early fourteenth century, the Amarna period.[4] Shechem at this time, then, first came under the control of groups who were to be part of the later nation of Israel. "This explains why the Books of Joshua and Judges presuppose the occupation of the city of Shechem by Israelite tribes under Joshua, although this fact is nowhere clearly stated."

In 1930 Martin Noth, one of the leading Old Testament scholars of present-day Germany, in an important study of Israel's twelve-tribe league,[5] showed how significant the system of twelve was; the names of the tribes are secondary to the number. Noth maintained that the tribes as we now know them came into being on the soil of Palestine. Various clans gradually came together in a particular region over a considerable period of time and became a tribe. Joshua 24 is a basic source for our knowledge of the history of the league or "amphictyony." Here is described, he affirms, an event which took place at the sanctuary *outside* Shechem of lasting import to the history of Israel because in a real sense it marks the birth of "Israel," a name applied to the tribal league which was constituted by a covenant ceremony. Thus Shechem can be said to be the place where Israel was created about 1200 B.C., and where the name of God used at the sanctuary was precisely "Yahweh (or 'El'), the god of Israel" (cf. Gen. 33:20).

The implications of the earlier chapters of this book make it difficult to answer the question as to when Shechem became Israelite. In a technical sense Professor Noth is correct. The "all Israel" which we meet in the Old Testament derives from the league. The name "Israel" is certainly older, but its use on the soil of Palestine after the thirteenth century refers in a special way to the Israel first organized as a league of twelve tribes. I am inclined to think that such a league was originally created under Moses at Sinai, but would agree with Noth on the importance of Shechem as the place where the Palestinian form was created, or reconstituted, as I would prefer to put it. There groups who had not emerged from Egypt with Moses, including the people of Shechem itself, became members of the league. In this sense, then, Shechem became Israelite when Yahweh, who had delivered Israel from Egyptian slavery under Moses, was identified as the same God who had been known at Shechem under his Patriarchal name, El-berith.

Professor Noth and others before him have held that the ark was at Shechem initially; that is, that Shechem was the central sanctuary of the tribal league before the site was shifted, first to Bethel and then to Shiloh in the period of the Judges. Others, especially W. F. Albright, have long opposed this view, seeing Shiloh as the special—and neutral, as regards past tradition—center of the league. The importance of Joshua 24, of Shechem's entry into the league, and of the periodic covenant ceremony rehearsed there, need not be minimized by such a view.[6]

At the same time one must agree with Dr. Böhl over against Sellin that the common people at Shechem in Abimelech's day are not adequately described by the term "Canaanites." Perhaps it would be better to suggest that they were a special Amorite enclave with old religious traditions which reached back into the first part of the second millennium and which are not identical with the religion of Canaan in the Late Bronze and Early Iron Age. Neither the population of Palestine before Israel's tribal league was established, nor the members of Israel themselves, were a homogeneous group with common background and tradition.[7] The testimony of the biblical records themselves and the archaeological exploration of the country, both testify to the regional variety which existed. The greatest single forces which worked for the unification of Israel were the covenant of the tribal league with its common religious tradition, and its understanding of God in political terms so that the covenant contained the structure of government, law and even the rules for holy war. The danger to members of the league from surviving city-states like Megiddo, Gezer and Jerusalem and from invaders like the Ammonites, Midianites and Philistines—this, too, was a powerful factor working for unity, even as it has been in modern Israel.

To what tribal area did Shechem belong in the organization of the league?

In the lists of the old clans of Manasseh, attributed to the time of Israel's conquest of Canaan and certainly reflecting the early period of the tribal league (Num. 26:31–33; Josh. 17:2; and cf. 1 Chron. 7:19), Shechem is listed along with Abiezer, Helek, Asriel, Hepher, Shemida and the five daughters of Zelophahad (Mahlah, Noah, Hoglah, Milcah and Tirzah). Furthermore, in the premonarchic boundary description given for the tribe of Manasseh, Shechem appears within the bounds of that tribe (Josh. 17:7). A study of the geography of the area makes it clear that the boundary between Ephraim and Manasseh ascended from the Jordan valley and continued west along the southern hills bounding the great plain which was the breadbasket of Shechem and the source of its economic power. Directly east of Shechem the boundary turned southward, again along the hills bordering the plain, until the latter suddenly stopped. There it crossed a ridge, then dropped down into the valleys of Ephraim. The border turned westward at the foot of or on that ridge and crossed to the valley at the foot of Tel Sheikh Abū Zarad (Tappuah) which was in Ephraim, though its land is specifically said to have been in Manasseh (Josh. 17:8). There can be no doubt, therefore, that during the period of the tribal league Shechem was included in the territory of Manasseh. That is, Shechem with the other localities listed above was absorbed into the tribal system, each becoming a clan within the tribe and personalized in the Patriarchal manner in genealogical lists.

On the other hand, in the list of Levitical cities preserved in Joshua 21, a list which with excellent arguments Albright dates to the latter part of the reign of David or to the reign of Solomon in its present form,[8] we read that the Kohathite clan of the tribe of Levi was granted cities out of the tribal area of Ephraim. Among them are Shechem and its common lands "in the hill country of Ephraim" (that is "Mt. Ephraim," if we translate literally), Beth-horon and Gezer. In this case, then, Shechem is listed in Ephraim but with a special appellative, "in Mt. Ephraim." Among the cities of refuge in Josh. 20:7 western Palestine is divided into three areas: Mt. Naphtali (central and eastern Galilee), Mt. Ephraim and Mt. Judah. Shechem is the city of refuge in Mt. Ephraim. In the genealogical tables of 1 Chronicles 7, Shechem appears with Bethel, Naaran in the Jor-

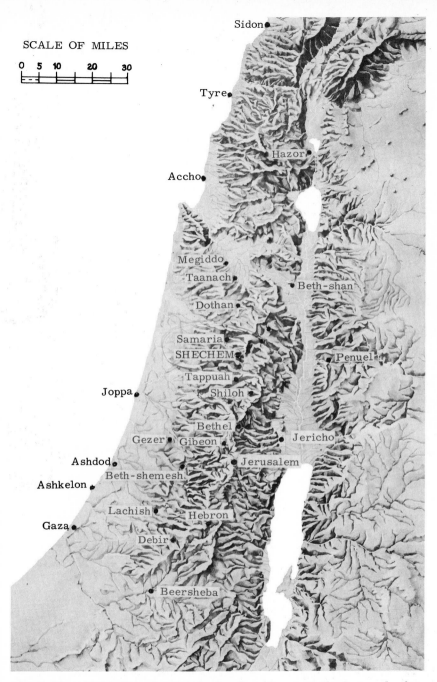

Fig. 1. Map of Palestine, showing the location of ancient Shechem and other localities mentioned in the pages which follow.

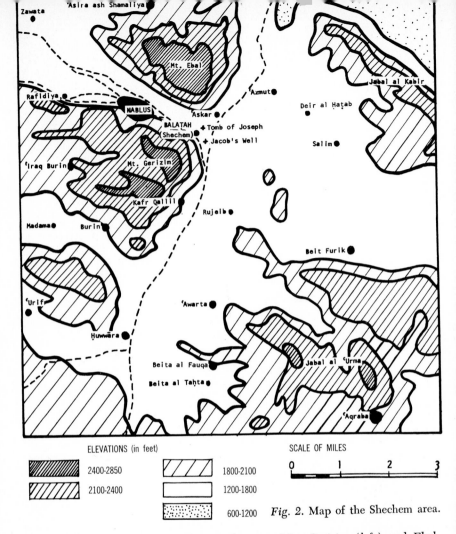

ELEVATIONS (in feet)

2400-2850

2100-2400

1800-2100

1200-1800

600-1200

SCALE OF MILES

0   1   2   3

Fig. 2. Map of the Shechem area.

Fig. 3. Looking west through the pass between Mts. Gerizim (left) and Ebal (right). Filling the pass is the low mound in which are the ruins of ancient Shechem, with the village of Balâṭah on its southern slopes. At the bottom, center, the building with the dome is the traditional site of the tomb of Joseph.

Fig. 4. Looking northeast from the summit of Mt. Gerizim. In the left, lower center, may be seen the ruins of the ancient site with the village, Balâṭah, on its slope. The road from the village leads through 'Askar on the slope of Mt. Ebal into the pass which leads northeastward to the Jordan Valley. At the lower right are the walls of an unfinished Coptic church which enclose Jacob's Well.

Fig. 5. Looking south from the slopes of Mt. Ebal over the tell (left, center) and the refugee village into the Shechem plain. Among the trees in the center before the refugee village is Jacob's Well. In the shadow of Mt. Gerizim the road from Nabdus to Jerusalem may be seen. In the lower center is the Balâṭah school, by which the Drew-McCormick's tent-camp is erected.

Fig. 6. The western fortification wall (Wall A) and the great bank of earth and marl which originally covered the mound's northwestern and western sides. Only the top layers are from excavation dump. *Fig. 7.* Contour map of the tell.

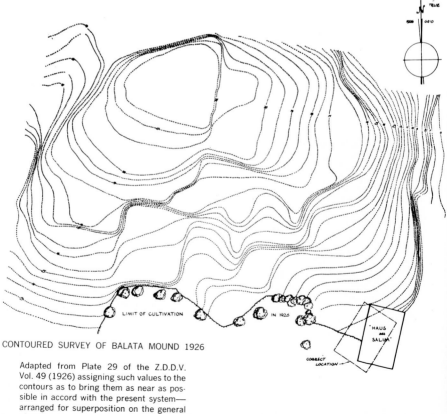

CONTOURED SURVEY OF BALATA MOUND 1926

Adapted from Plate 29 of the Z.D.D.V. Vol. 49 (1926) assigning such values to the contours as to bring them as near as possible in accord with the present system— arranged for superposition on the general plan

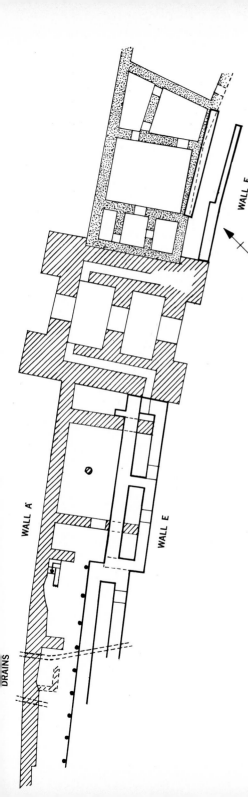

WALL E

WALL A'

WALL E

DRAINS

Fig. 8. Bishop H. M. Du Bose of North Carolina (left) and Dr. Sellin (right) at Shechem in the spring of 1926. This picture is from the possessions of Bishop Du Bose preserved by his family.

Fig. 9. Wall A (the cyclopean fortification) and the Northwest Gate as published by Sellin in 1926 (*ZDPV* 49, Taf. 33, following p. 372) with a few additions from the 1927 plan (*ibid.* 50, Taf. 22, following p. 338). The names of the fortification walls are those of the Drew-McCormick Expedition. South of the gate are the rooms designated "the Palace" by Sellin.

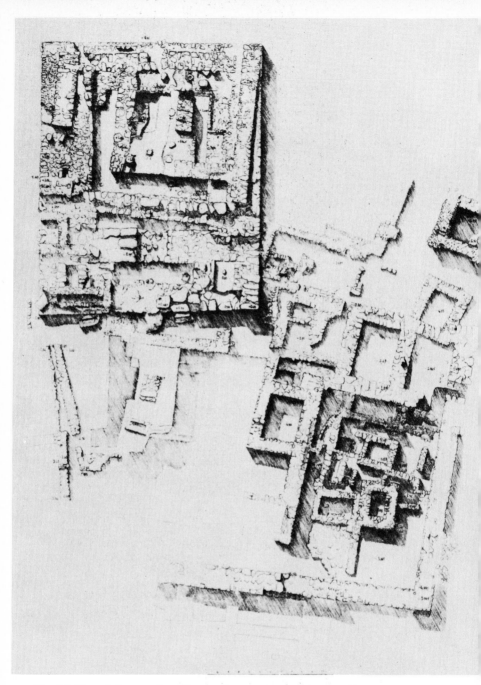

Fig. 10. Plan of the temple and ruins above it and in front of it, prepared by G. Welter from the excavations of Sellin in 1926-1927.

Fig. 11. Dumping debris from a hand-operated railroad car. Fig. 12. A pickman (left) loosening the debris. He is followed by a hoeman (center) who scrapes the earth into a rubber basket. The reed basket is for pottery fragments.

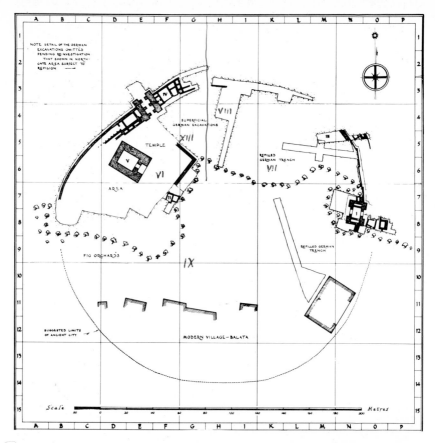

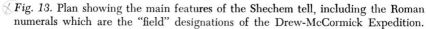

Fig. 13. Plan showing the main features of the Shechem tell, including the Roman numerals which are the "field" designations of the Drew-McCormick Expedition.

Fig. 14. The expedition camp in 1960 by the village schoolhouse. The rooms of the school were used as technical workrooms by the expedition.

Fig. 15. The staff of the fourth campaign in 1962. *Fig. 16.* A stratigraphic section, Field VI, Area 2, made in order to check the stratigraphy which Dr. Sellin had cut through and to date certain ruins still in existence. From the top down is Iron I at the point where the Steckeweh excavation stopped in 1934. Below that down to the wide chocolate-brown band that crosses the whole face of the cut are three phases of Late Bronze (*ca.* 1450-1200 B.C.). Behind the meter stick may be seen the white fill on which the temple rests. Above that to the chocolate layer are phases of Middle Bronze II C. At the bottom, right, city fortification D of early Middle Bronze II B is shown appearing (see Fig. 17).

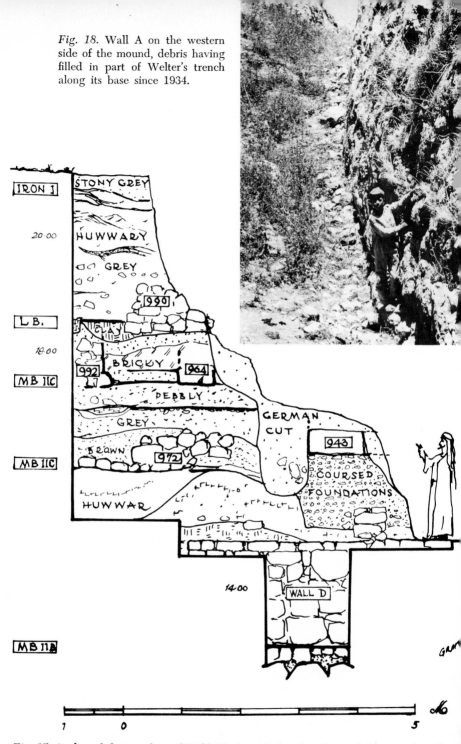

Fig. 18. Wall A on the western side of the mound, debris having filled in part of Welter's trench along its base since 1934.

IRON I

STONY GREY

20.00

HUWWADY

GREY

990

L.B.

CLAY

18.00

BRICKY

992   964

MB IIC

PEBBLY

GREY

GERMAN

CUT

943

MB IIC

BROWN

972

COURSED

FOUNDATIONS

HUWWAR

14.00

WALL D

MB IIA

GRM

1   0   5

Fig. 17. A plan of the east face of Field VI, Area 2, showing the earth layers and walls which were encountered in their relation to one another.

Fig. 19. Sketch of drain as it emerges on the face of Wall A (see also Fig. 9).

Fig. 20. Map showing the main features and digging areas on the tell.

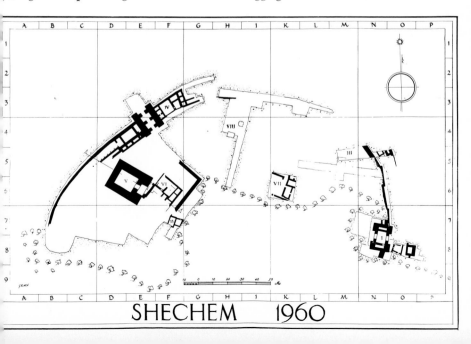

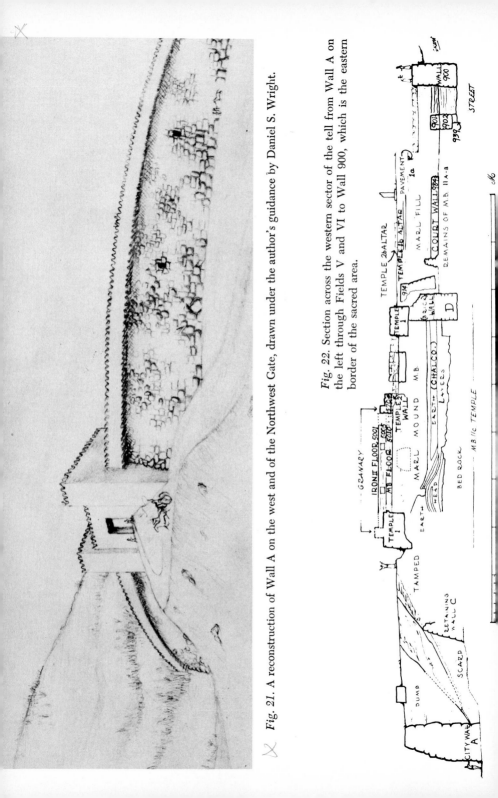

Fig. 21. A reconstruction of Wall A on the west and of the Northwest Gate, drawn under the author's guidance by Daniel S. Wright.

Fig. 22. Section across the western sector of the tell from Wall A on the left through Fields V and VI to Wall 900, which is the eastern border of the sacred area.

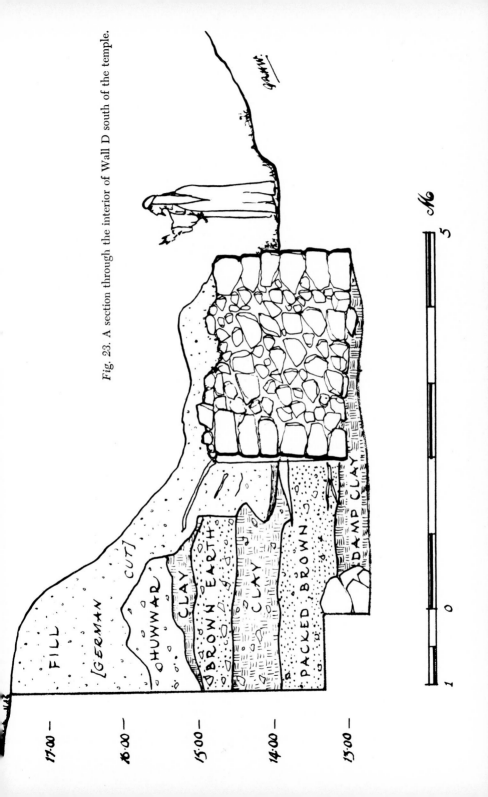

Fig. 23. A section through the interior of Wall D south of the temple.

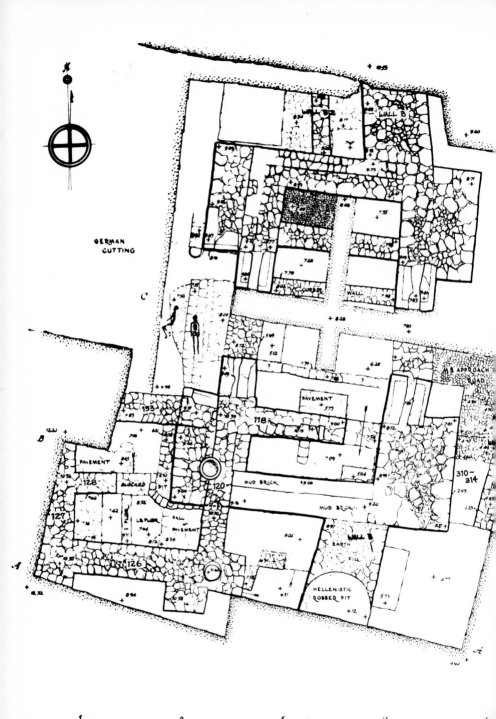

GERMAN
CUTTING

WALL B12 · WALL B

CURB OR WALL

PAVEMENT

M B APPROACH ROAD

118

PAVEMENT

133

120

MUD BRICK

310~
314

128

BLOCKED

PAVEMENT

127

LB FLOOR

MUD BRICK

310~
314

WALL OR
PAVEMENT

126

WALL B

EARTH
FILL

HELLENISTIC
ROBBER PIT

Scale

Fig. 24. Plan of the East Gate (Field I). The first phase of building here was Wall A and House 110 behind it. Then the East Gate was built, the door into the house was gradually blocked as the space outside it (310-314) was used for the street leading to the gate. The second phase of the gate saw the raising of the street level, the covering of Building 110 with a *glacis,* and the installation in the gate of the pairs of stone orthostats. In the Late Bronze Age the new guardroom is represented by Walls 120, 126-128. Another is added for Iron I A (No. 133, 12th cent. B.C.).

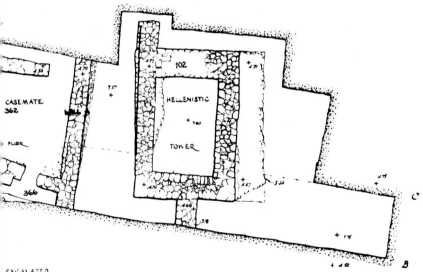

Fig. 25. Cobbled street resurfacing belonging to the first phase of the East Gate.

Fig. 26. Isometric sketch of the first phase of the East Gate.

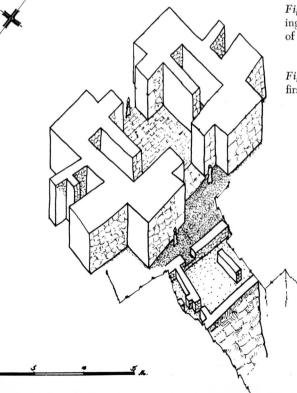

Fig. 27. View of the surviving stonework of the East Gate, with stairs leading *down into* the city.

Fig. 28. The arrangement of the orthostats of the East Gate and a chart showing their dimensions.

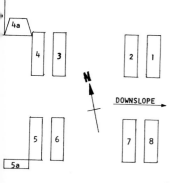

| ORTHOSTAT | APPROX. MEAN DIMENSIONS, CM. | | | ANGLE OF |
NUMBER	LENGTH	WIDTH	HEIGHT	INCLINATION
1	230	60	135	21° DOWNSLOPE
2	212	60	146	11° ''
3	187	68	125	2° UPSLOPE
4	191	65	147	1° ''
4a	108	82	140	
4b	200	52	130	
5	185	60	134	3° ''
5a	130	65	132	
6	200	48	156	29° ''
7	234	76	147	5° DOWNSLOPE
8	237	72	165	10° ''

Fig. 29. Looking southward across the inner orthostats of the East Gate. On the far side the evidence of the work of an Egyptian battering ram can be seen.

Fig. 30. The wall between court and stairwell in the south tower of the East Gate (Wall 118 in Fig. 24), showing three phases of rebuilding. At the level of the door sill in the left center is the line of flat stones for brick in the first period of the East Gate; it is nearly 2 m. above the flagstone court floor at this point. Above it is the stone repair and rebuilding erected with the second or orthostat phase of the gate's history. Debris of the Egyptian destruction of this phase filled the doorway (left) and was found piled against the wall as far as the leaning orthostat to the right (Fig. 29). Above this is the very poor earth-filled rubble wall of Stratum VI (see Chap. 9). It was slightly wider than the Middle Bronze wall beneath it and ran over the debris-filled doorway. Its northern face fell away in the winter rains of 1956-57.

Fig. 31. Reconstruction of Wall A, Wall B and the East Gate about 1575 B.C. Drawing by Daniel S. Wright.

Fig. 33. Skeleton of a colt on the floor of the last of five Late Bronze Age resurfacings of an East Gate guardroom. Directly above it were fourteen resurfacings of the 12th cent. B.C.

ig. 32. The Middle Bronze Age "casemate" Wall B 2 in Field III, surmounted by ate Bronze Wall B 3. The latter and the brick wall connecting it to Wall B suggests the latter's reuse in the Late Bronze Age. Note the door in Wall B 2 which is lled with brick and charcoal from the destroyed Middle Bronze Wall B. The urning superstructure of the latter fell through the door into the area beyond it. t the bottom is the stone socket in which the wooden doorpost for the Middle ronze door turned. It was not *in situ.* At the bottom is a floor of the earlier phase f the Wall B period.

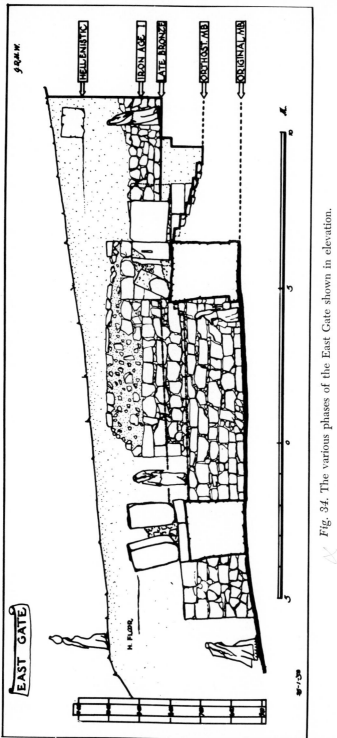

Fig. 34. The various phases of the East Gate shown in elevation.

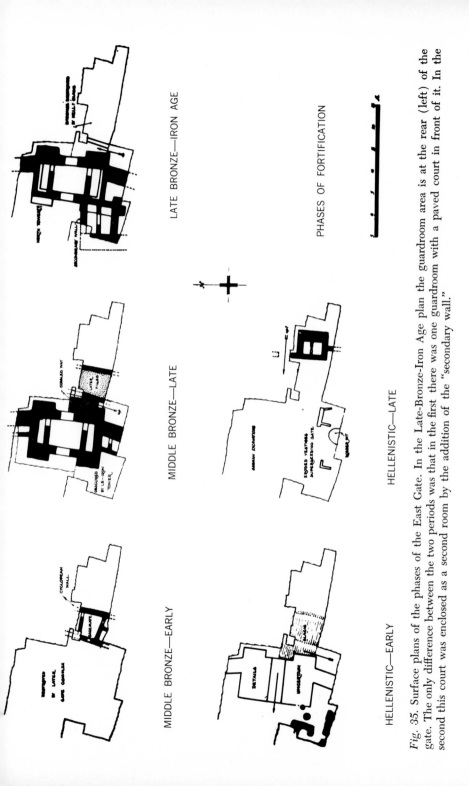

MIDDLE BRONZE—EARLY

MIDDLE BRONZE—LATE

LATE BRONZE—IRON AGE

PHASES OF FORTIFICATION

HELLENISTIC—EARLY

HELLENISTIC—LATE

Fig. 35. Surface plans of the phases of the East Gate. In the Late-Bronze-Iron Age plan the guardroom area is at the rear (left) of the gate. The only difference between the two periods was that in the first there was one guardroom with a paved court in front of it. In the second this court was enclosed as a second room by the addition of the "secondary wall."

Fig. 36. Sacred pillar 2 installed in MB II C on the left side of the temple's entrance. Fig. 37. Socket for sacred pillar 3 of MB II C on the right side of the temple's entrance.

Fig. 38. Sacred pillar 1 cemented in place in a portion of the temple's courtyard which is reconstructed. The upper edges of the stone socket are left visible in the center of each side. Fig. 39. Looking west toward the temple at the conclusion of the campaign in 1962. The stone wall around the reconstructed courtyard was erected by the Drew-McCormick Expedition in 1960 and 1962 to hold the debris in place.

Fig. 40. Looking southeast over the stone substructure for the temple. In the foreground are Walls A and E.

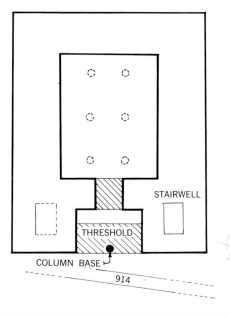

Fig. 41. The plan of fortress-temple 1a. The column bases within are hatched in from the Sellin plans. We found none of them in place ourselves for this phase.

Fig. 42. Single column base which originally stood in the portico of Temple 1a, and a fragment of a column which must originally have stood upon it.

Fig. 43. Column base used in the interior of Temple 2b.

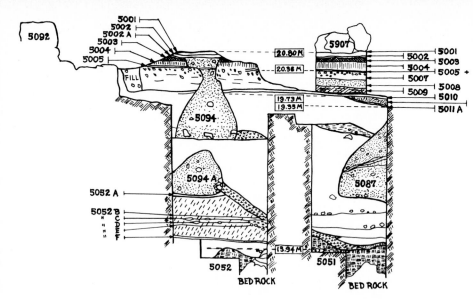

Fig. 44. Cross-section through the debris within and under the temple. Layer 5001 is the thick plaster floor of the 9th-8th cent. government tax warehouse (see Chap. 9). Layer 5002A is the imperfectly preserved floor of Temple 2b supported on Layer 5003 with 5004 as its foundation. Layer 5005 is the floor of Temple 1b and Layer 5010 that of Temple 1a. Fig. 45. Supervisor Bull holding a measuring rule between floors 5010 and 5005 of Temple 1a and 1b.

Fig. 46. The top of the stone wall of Temple I was levelled with small and often roughly cut stones and then cemented to form a flat platform for the brick super-structure. Under the Israelite granary walls in the background is brick dust with an occasional whole brick from the temple. Fig. 47. Reconstruction of Temple 1a by Daniel S. Wright. It is intended only to give a general impression of the building's vast size, with the suggestion that the heavy towers were very likely used not only for storage but also as living quarters for temple personnel.

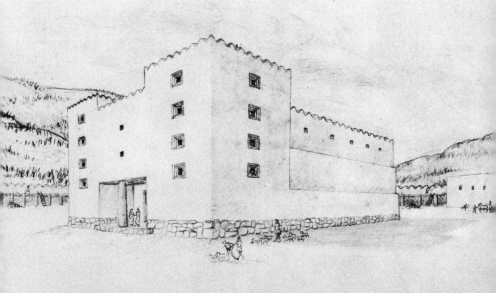

L. S. WRIGHT

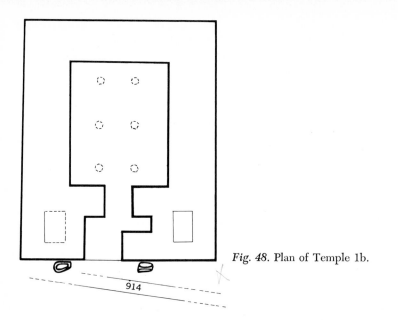

Fig. 48. Plan of Temple 1b.

914

Fig. 49. Fill thrown in over earlier temple ruins to create a courtyard for Temples and 2. The white layer at the 4th tag from the top is the cemented surface of th court of Temple 1a, which may be seen to rise slowly as a ramp to the temple's platfor (cf. Fig. 47). The white layer at the second tag is a line of marl bricks (cf. Fig. 50 which formed part of the base of the altar of Temple 1b. The fine earth below i marked by the third tag, is the brick substructure of the altar. The fill designated b the first tag was put in place for the court of Temple 2.

Fig. 50. Marl bricks used in the base of the altar of Temple 1b. Directly below them is the line of mud-bricks which formed the platform of the altar. Below that may be seen the white surfacing for the court of Temple 1a.

Fig. 51. The Megiddo fortress-temple, a building of the same type as that at Megiddo. The first phase, to the left, was probably erected as early as the 17th cent. B.C. Evidence of two subsequent rebuildings (center and right) was preserved. The last was destroyed during the latter part of the 12th cent. B.C. The podium against the rear wall in the middle and late phases is comparable to those in Shechem Temples 2a and b. Note also the thin walls of the last phase. After Gordon Loud, *Megiddo* II, p. 103, Fig. 247.

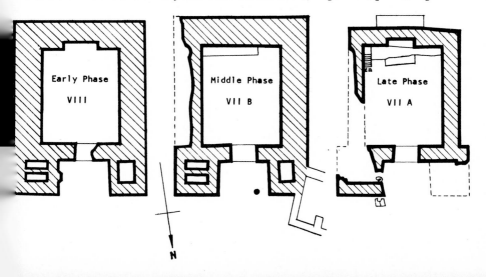

Fig. 52. A few of the scarabs found in the excavations of Shechem. No. 1 is a royal seal of King *Hpr-nb-[R]ʿ*, whose date is debated but is probably Dynasty XVII (*ca.* 1600-1570 B.C.). No. 2 also bears a royal name (*Rʿ-hpr*) of Sesostris I or II of the 20th and 19 cents. B.C., though the scarab, found in Hyksos glacis, is not that old. Nos. 3, 4, and 5 are Hyksos scarabs, Nos. 3 and 5 having been found in collapsed brick of the final Egyptian destruction of the city, *ca.* 1540 B.C., in Field III. Nos. 6-9 all probably come from the New Kingdom or Late Bronze Age. No. 8 is of special interest, though found on the surface in the East Gate, because it bears the inscription of the wife of Pharaoh Amenophis III (*ca.* 1402-1364), "The king's wife Tiy" (*hmt.t nśw.t Tiy*).

Fig. 53. A silver togglepin for pinning a cloak together, from the ruins of the city of Temple 2a (B60, Reg. 615. Length 52 mm or 2 3/32 inches).

Fig. 54. A Syro-Palestinian cylinder seal from the city of Temple 2a (B57, Reg. 71).

Fig. 55. Wall 5703 of Temple 2 on top of the stone socket of Temple 1.

Fig. 56. Reconstructed plan of Temple 2. The entry probably had towers flanking it, but no evidence remains of the plan.

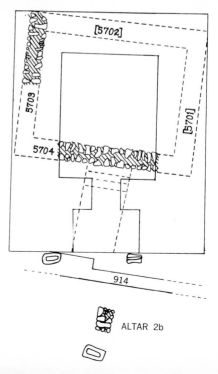

Fig. 57. Steps which led up from the floor of Temple 2a to a podium on the unused portion of the Temple 1 rear wall. The floor to which these steps belong was completely destroyed by later building. *Fig. 58.* A suggested reconstruction of a courtyard temple at Shechem, dating from the end of the 18th cent. B.C. (the 902 Phase). For plan see Fig. 64.

Fig. 59. Wall 900, the enclosure wall which separated the courtyard temples from the city, and the small stone footing on which it was erected. Deep below it the red rocky fill appears which seems to have been used to level Field VI during the course of the 19th cent. B.C.

Fig. 60. Nancy R. (Mrs. Paul W.) Lapp by a small silo set in a surface of Middle Bronze II A (*ca.* 1850-1750 B.C.) below Street 9 of *ca.* 1750 B.C.

Fig. 61. Stone-lined slope of the mysterious structure 968. The pottery was broken jars which had fallen from the top surface so that the necks and rims were farthest down the slope.

Fig. 62. Cobblestone street in the sacred area between enclosure Wall 900 (right) and Walls 901, 902 and 939 (on top of one another) to the left. In the center is Street 6 with drain. The removal of a portion of the street beside Wall 900 was done by Sellin's workmen.

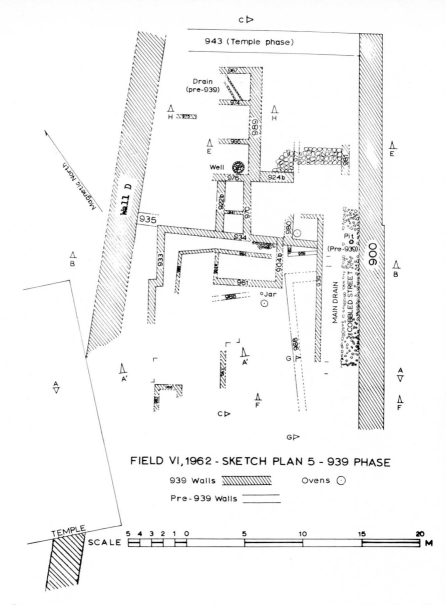

FIELD VI, 1962 - SKETCH PLAN 5 - 939 PHASE

939 Walls ▨▨▨▨▨   Ovens ⊙

Pre-939 Walls ━━━━━

SCALE 5 4 3 2 1 0   5   10   15   20
                                        M

Fig. 63. Remains of the second phase of the temenos area, designated by the wall along the street as the 939 phase.

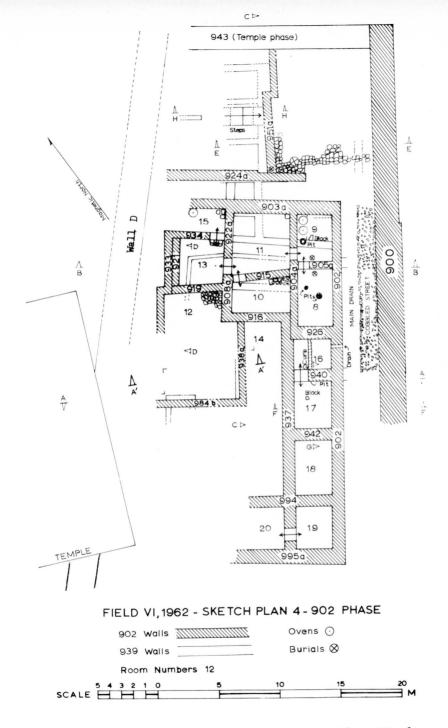

FIELD VI, 1962 - SKETCH PLAN 4 - 902 PHASE

902 Walls	▨▨▨	Ovens	☉
939 Walls	———	Burials	⊗
Room Numbers 12			

SCALE 5 4 3 2 1 0 ____ 5 ____ 10 ____ 15 ____ 20 M

Fig. 64. Plan of Temenos 3, the "Casemate" Courtyard Temple (Phase 902; cf. also Fig. 58).

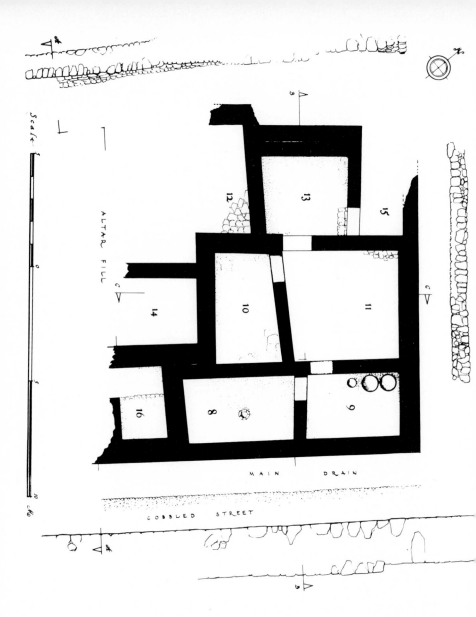

Fig. 65. Plan of rooms of the 902 phase (Temenos 3) of the Courtyard Temple as excavated in 1960. At the lower left is Wall 914, retaining the fill put in place to support the fortress-temple's towers and portico. At the upper left is the edge of city Wall D.

Fig. 66. String of beads which were around the neck of a child buried in a storage jar beneath a pavement of Temenos 3. *Fig. 67*. Vessels of the 902 and 901 phases of the Courtyard Temple. The two jugs, left and right, are from 902 phase burials. The bowl above is from mixed fill not later than the 901 phase.

Fig. 68. The excavation of the Courtyard Temples 901 and 902 in 1960. Rarely were 901 floors preserved because previous excavation had dug through them. Their level is indicated by the column bases on top of the balk at the lower left center. The excavation is at the 902 floors just before the removal of the 901 walls.

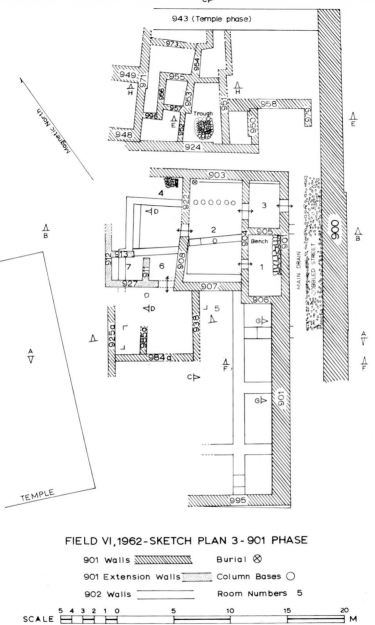

FIELD VI, 1962-SKETCH PLAN 3-901 PHASE

901 Walls ▨▨▨	Burial ⊗
901 Extension Walls ▦▦	Column Bases ○
902 Walls ────	Room Numbers 5

SCALE 5 4 3 2 1 0 ⊟⊟⊟⊟ 5 10 15 20 M

Fig. 69. Plan of Temenos 4 and the Pillar Courtyard Temple (901 phase).

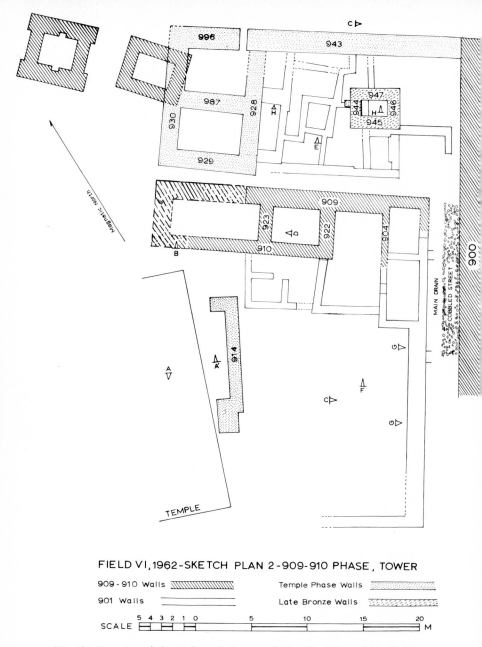

FIELD VI, 1962 - SKETCH PLAN 2 - 909 - 910 PHASE, TOWER

909 - 910 Walls		Temple Phase Walls	
901 Walls		Late Bronze Walls	

SCALE 5 4 3 2 1 0   5   10   15   20   M

Fig. 70. Remains of the Enlarged Courtyard Temple (Phase 909-910).

Fig. 71. Base for a free-standing pillar, evidently a sacred stone, in the first phase of the central court in Courtyard Temple. 901. Fig. 72. Photo taken by Kurt Galling in the summer of 1926, showing in the center left the great sacred stone of Fortress-temple 2 and altar, as they were found. Center right the high level of Walls 910 and 922 of the Enlarged Courtyard Temple is indicated (see Fig. 71).

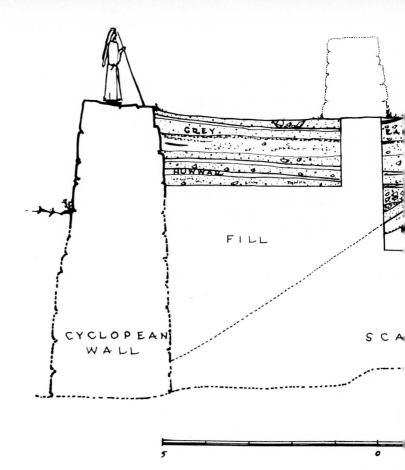

GREY

HUWWAR

FILL

CYCLOPEAN
WALL

SCA

5

0

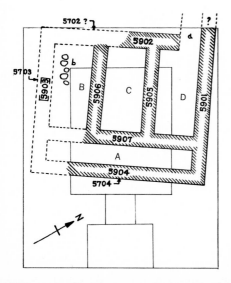

5702 ?

5902

d

b

5703

5903

B

5906

C

5905

D

5901

5907

A

5904

5704

N

Fig. 73. Plan of the Israelite government
warehouse erected over the ruins of the
fortress-temple.

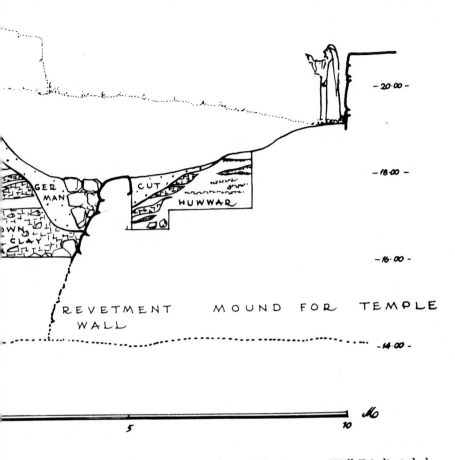

Fig. 74. Walls A and C with the position of the Casemate Wall E indicated above them (cf. Fig. 9).

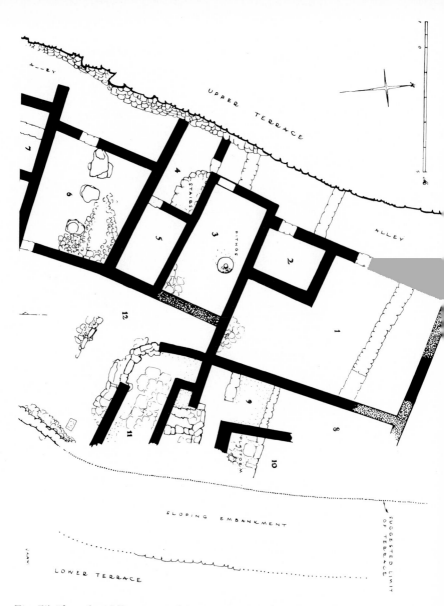

Fig. 75. Plan of middle terrace of Stratum IX B and A in Field VII.

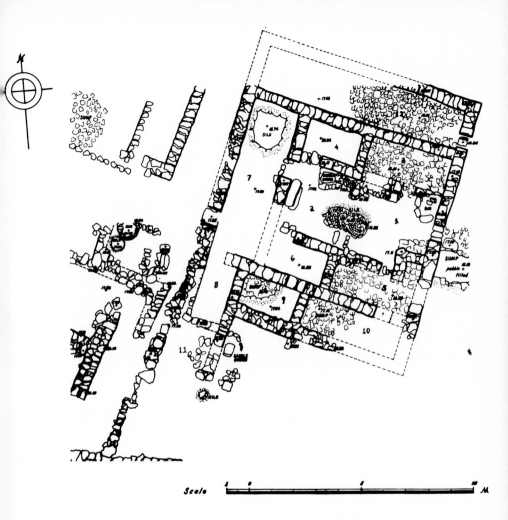

Fig. 76. Plan of House 1727 of Stratum VII.

Fig. 77. Photograph of the ruins of House 1727. Fig. 78. Pink quartzite grinding stone found in House 1727.

Fig. 79. Reconstruction of House 1728. Sketch by Daniel S. Wright.

Fig. 80. Slab of the roofing clay from House 1727, showing successive resurfacings.

Fig. 81. Middle Assyrian cylinder seal of serpentine, dating *ca.* 1200 B.C., found in debris between Strata VII and IV. *Fig. 82.* Stamp seals, of which Nos. 1, 2, 5, and 6 date from the 9th-8th cents. B.C. No. 1 was found in a sealed deposit of Stratum IX and No. 6 in destruction debris of Stratum VII. The latter is imported from Mesopotamia.

Fig. 83. An eight-sided ivory die from the 9th-8th cent., found in the government granary, Building 5900 (Fig. 73). *Fig. 84.* Ceramic ram's head, probably of the Israelite period.

Fig. 85. "Cypro-Phoenician" imported juglet, found in the debris of destruction on the floor of Room 4 of House 1727 (Fig. 76). Fig. 86. Stone installation of Stratum V (*ca.* 500 B.C.), once probably circular but destroyed by the Samaritans of Stratum IV. It was set into and its rear wall retained destruction debris of Stratum VI (7th cent.).

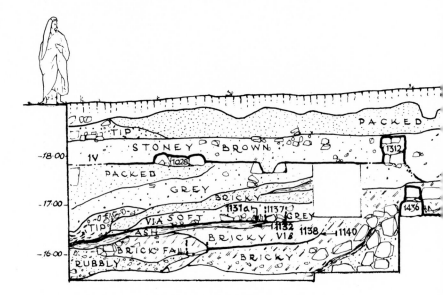

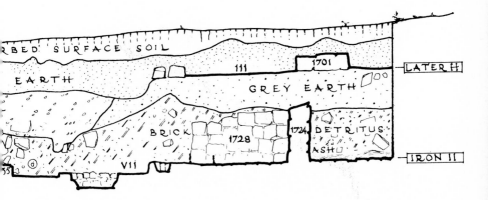

Fig. 87. North-south section through Field VII in 1962. To the right is House 1728, which was destroyed by the Assyrians in 724-23 B.C. To the left, dropping rapidly down the slope southward may be seen burned surfaces 1131a and 1140 which are evidence of two phases of Stratum VI from the late 8th and 7th cent. B.C., both of which were burned. The square hole in the middle represents one of those mistakes which leave excavators red-faced with embarrassment. In 1962 the supervisory staff of Field VII was plagued with sickness. After spending a Saturday drawing this section, Edward F. Campbell, Jr., was taken seriously ill and was kept from the "dig" for several days. During his absence the balk was pulled down to a point at the bottom of the square hole under the impression that the drawing of the section had been completed.

Fig. 88. Small black juglets for perfumed oil, dating from the 7th cent., found on a floor of a newly built guardroom at the East Gate (Field I, Area 3, Locus 1).

Fig. 89. An installation once used for extracting juice from grapes, found in 1956 in Field 1, Area 4.

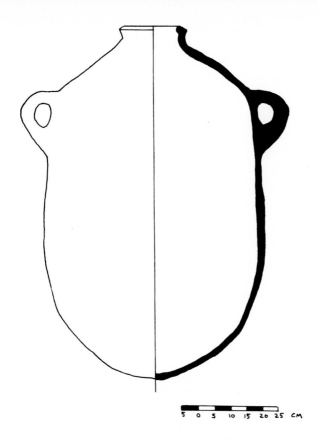

Fig. 90. A drawing of the jar which had been sunk into the earth to catch the grape juice from the press shown in Fig. 89. *Fig. 91.* A seal of beautiful blue chalcedony bearing in Hebrew letters (from left to right, *lmbn*) the inscription "(Belonging) to Mibneh" or "Miben." It is dated by Frank M. Cross, Jr., to the late 7th or early 6th cent.

Fig. 92. Seal impressions on jar handles of Stratum V, probably indicating that the wine contained in the jars came from a vineyard of which this was the seal.

Fig. 93. Seal impression on a wine jar of Stratum V bearing the impression of a roaring lion (cf. also Fig. 82:7). *Fig. 94.* Persian seal impression once affixed to a papyrus document, as the striations on the reverse side indicate. The design is dominated by the figure of the Persian king shown as a hunter.

Fig. 95. One of the two oldest coins found in Palestinian excavations. It is electrum and is imported from the Greek sland of Thasos in the late 6th cent. B.C. The design shows the deity Selinus carrying off a nymph. *Fig. 96.* A hoard of silver tetradrachmas found buried in a small pot deep below the surface levels of Stratum III in Field VII. All were coinage of the kings of Egypt following Alexander the Great who bore the throne name, Ptolemy. Each of the Ptolemies of the 3d and early 2nd century is represented (Ptolemy I-V), the latest mint date being 193 B.C. in the reign of Ptolemy V.

Fig. 97. Samaritan repair of the southeast tower of the East Gate, indicating the reuse of the structure, and probably also of Wall B, as a fortification.

Fig. 98. The sloping layers of debris at the East Gate between the tower wall of the gate (right, just outside the picture) and Wall A (left, just outside the picture; see Fig. 99). At the right center is the white surface of the Middle Bronze Age glacis, erected with the second or orthostat phase of the East Gate. This and the earth fill beneath it are cut into by an early Samaritan glacis built directly on the old one. In the upper right street levels of the Samaritan period are shown. Above the white top of the Samaritan glacis is a red brick debris spread down the slope, cut into at the left center by modern debris filling the place where a young fig tree had been. At the bottom of the picture is Building 110, erected before the East Gate at the same time as Wall A (cf. Fig. 107).

Fig. 99. Wall A as it crosses a valley in front of the East Gate. To the right is Building 110, erected at the same time as Wall A. To the right of the two-meter stick the Samaritan glacis of the first phase of Stratum IV may be seen connecting with the top of Wall A. Above it a layer of red brick debris has spilled down the slope, covering over Wall A. In the brightly lighted foreground a thick slab of the brick debris is shown as it fell over Wall A. Thus during the period of Stratum IV, Wall A was covered over. At the left of Wall A a dark earth layer with marl plaster above and below it further levels the slope over Wall A. At lower left is the tower, Building 102, evidently erected during the course of **Stratum III** (late 3rd cent. B.C.); see Figs. 24 and 107.

Fig. 100. A silo from the end of the Stratum IV period on the slope of the East Gate, dating after the slope had been leveled over Wall A (cf. Fig. 99).

Fig. 101. Cement floor of a Samaritan house or court of Stratum III B outside the city fortifications on the slope, over the silo of the latter part of Stratum IV shown in Fig. 100.

Fig. 102. Column base for an important building of Stratum IV. Fig. 103. To the left the marl and red earth resurfacing of the slope up against Wall B in the period of Stratum III (probably III B). After that was put in place, the stones of Wall B were robbed for another purpose, either at the end of Stratum III or beginning of Stratum II, and the hole was filled in, giving an excellent group of Strata IV-III Samaritan pottery. To the right in I, Area 6, the red brick debris is from the Egyptian destruction of the East Gate and Wall B in the 16th cent. (see Figs. 24 and 107).

Fig. 104. Samaritan house of Stratum III unearthed in Field II. It was used throughout the latter part of the third century and throughout the second century (Strata II-I). The walls of the building were plastered, and each room had been painted a different color. Note the excellent masonry for door (left) and window casing (center). Below the foundations are thick layers of fill which leveled a slope for the house. *Fig. 105.* An iron key used to unlock a door in the Field II Samaritan house.

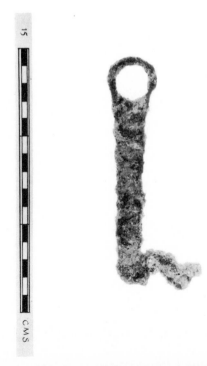

Fig. 106. Samaritan tower built on the slope in front of the East Gate late in the period of City III or early in City II. *Fig. 107.* A Samaritan by the name of Simeon has here incised his name on a jar before it was baked, using Greek letters and the Greek form of the name, "Simionide(s)."

Fig. 108. Sections through the East Gate. For their location, see the plan in Fig. 24. In sections B-B and C-C Wall A with its associated "M.B. Casemate" House and Floors 362 and 364 may be seen left of center. These date from the mid-17th cent. B.C. With the erection of the East Gate, a series of street levels, each above the other, appeared between Wall A 2 and the "Gate Tower Wall." From the second phase of the gate's first period (early 16th cent.) the "Casemate House" is filled over by a glacis, the fill for which is marked "compact grey" on the plan. The plastered surface of this slope was destroyed by subsequent erosion or Samaritan activity so that only a small piece of it remains against the gate tower (designated "white lime"). All other activity on the slope is that of the Samaritan or H(ellenistic) period. The "H striated make-up" and the 'brick dust" above it are both from the period of Stratum IV, and indicate that during that period Wall A was covered, the slope leveled, and perhaps a dry fosse created to the left by a thick plastered slope under the layers at the edge marked "grey earth and brick dust." At the left of Section A-A (top) fresh layers of fill were put in against Wall B in the period of Stratum III, after which Wall B was robbed out *ca.* 200 B.C. At approximately the same time the "Hellenistic Tower" (Section C-C, left) was erected.

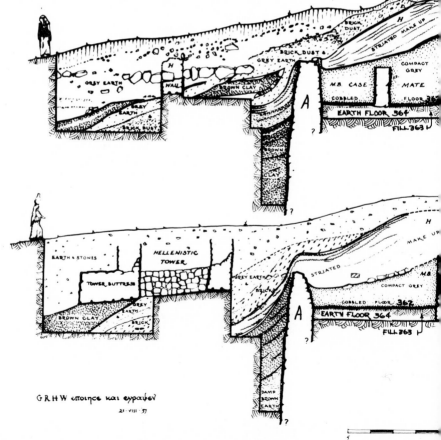

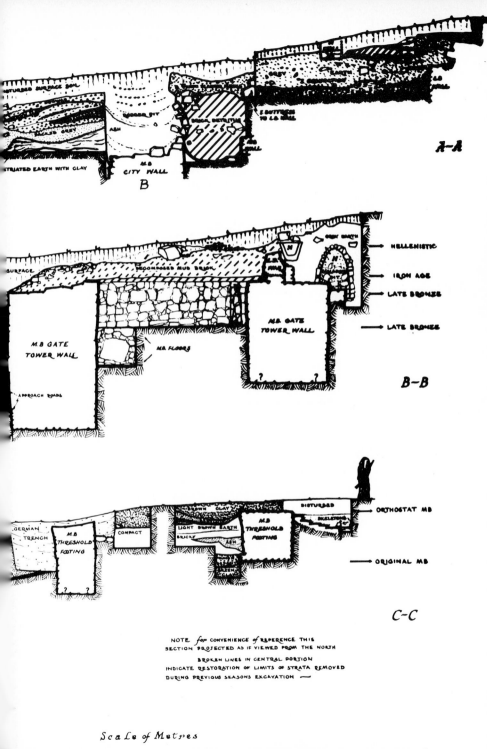

A-A

DISTURBED SURFACE SOIL

ROBBER PIT

ASH

SUGAR DISTRIBUTE

E BUTTRESS TO L.B WALL

L.B WALL

STRIATED EARTH WITH CLAY

M.B CITY WALL

B WALL

B

SURFACE

DECOMPOSED MUD BRICK

M.B FLOORS

M.B GATE TOWER WALL

APPROACH ROADS

M.B GATE TOWER WALL

HELLENISTIC

IRON AGE

LATE BRONZE

LATE BRONZE

?   ?

B-B

GERMAN TRENCH

M.B THRESHOLD FOOTING

COMPACT

LIGHT BROWN EARTH

BRICKY

ASH

CLAY

M.B THRESHOLD FOOTING

DISTURBED

BUILDINGS

ORTHOSTAT M.B

ORIGINAL M.B

?   ?

C-C

NOTE *for* CONVENIENCE *of* REFERENCE THIS
SECTION PROJECTED AS IF VIEWED FROM THE NORTH

BROKEN LINES IN CENTRAL PORTION
INDICATE RESTORATION OR LIMITS OF STRATA REMOVED
DURING PREVIOUS SEASONS EXCAVATION

Scale of Metres

5   10   15   20

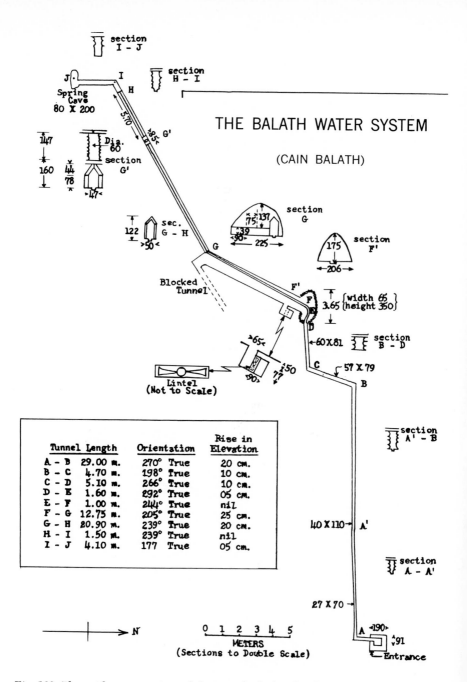

THE BALATH WATER SYSTEM

(CAIN BALATH)

Tunnel	Length	Orientation	Rise in Elevation
A – B	29.00 m.	270° True	20 cm.
B – C	4.70 m.	198° True	10 cm.
C – D	5.10 m.	266° True	10 cm.
D – E	1.60 m.	292° True	05 cm.
E – F	1.00 m.	244° True	nil
F – G	12.75 m.	205° True	25 cm.
G – H	80.90 m.	239° True	20 cm.
H – I	1.50 m.	239° True	nil
I – J	4.10 m.	177 True	05 cm.

N

0 1 2 3 4 5
METERS
(Sections to Double Scale)

Fig. 109. Plan with cross sections of the tunnel which today brings water from a spring at the foot of Mt. Gerizim into the village of Balâtah.

FIELD V AREA 13 (Temple Forecourt)

Section A-A'

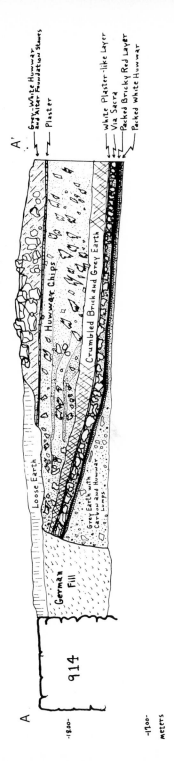
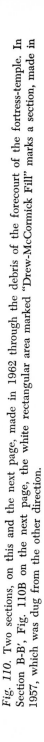

Fig. 110. Two sections, on this and the next page, made in 1962 through the debris of the forecourt of the fortress-temple. In Section B-B', Fig. 110B on the next page, the white rectangular area marked "Drew-McCormick Fill" marks a section, made in 1957, which was dug from the other direction.

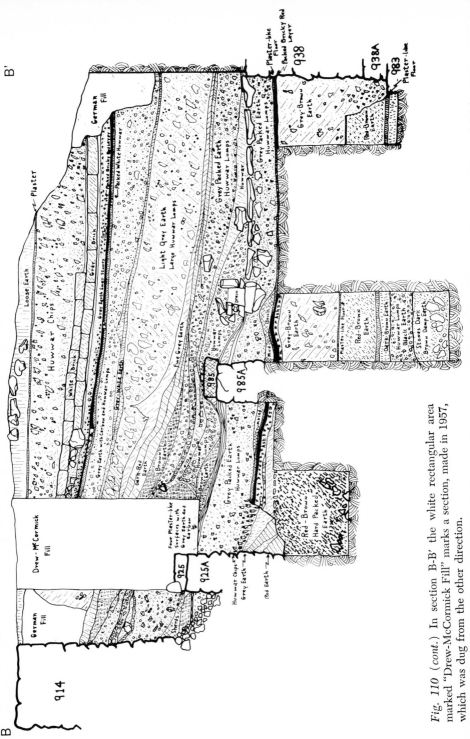

Fig. 110 (cont.) In section B-B' the white rectangular area marked "Drew-McCormick Fill" marks a section, made in 1957, which was dug from the other direction.

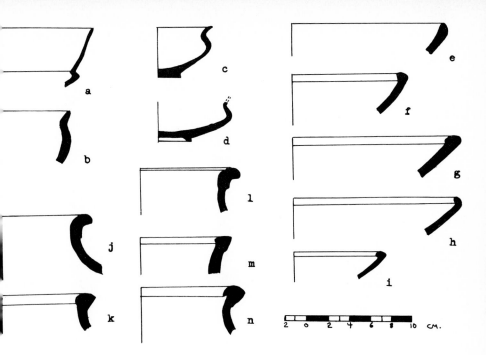

Fig. 111. Pottery from Temenos 4 (Courtyard Temple 901), dating from the early 17th cent. B.C.

a.	B57 I.8a.22	1343	Carinated Bowl	Red ware, finely levig. fast fired, cream buff slip.
b.	B62 V.13.26	208	Carinated Bowl	Buff ware, s-m lime grits, slow fired, orange-brown slip.
c.	B57 I.8a.12	877	Carinated Bowl	Red ware, s-l lime grits, slow fired.
d.	B57 I.8a.24	1354	Carinated Bowl Base	Pink buff, m-l lime grits, slow fired.
e.	B57 I.8a.24	1367	Carinated Bowl Base (trumpet foot)	Red ware, s lime grits, medium fired, burnished.
f.	B62 V.13.37	249	Platter Bowl Base	Orange buff, s lime grits, medium fired.
g.	B62 V.13.31	226	Platter Bowl	Buff ware, s lime and flint grits, slow fired, orange-brown slip burnished inside and on rim.
h.	B62 V.13.39	254	Platter Bowl	Buff ware, s lime grits, slow fired, orange-brown slip.
i.	B60 V.3.16	1436	Platter Bowl	Buff ware, s lime grits, slow fired.
j.	B62 V.13.39	253	Platter Bowl	Buff ware, s lime and silicon grits, fast fired.
k.	B57 I.11a.9	507	Platter Bowl	Red ware, s lime grits, medium fired.
l.	B57 I.8a.24	1360	Water Jar	Buff ware, l lime grits, slow fired.
m.	B57 I.8a.24	1358	Water Jar	Red ware, l lime grits, slow fired.
n.	B57 I.8a.17	1030	Water Jar	Cream buff, s lime grits, slow fired.

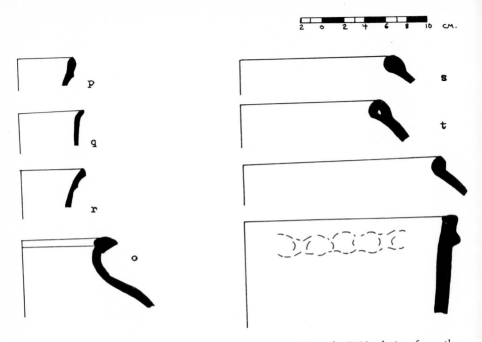

Fig. 111 (*cont.*) Pottery from Temenos 4 (Courtyard Temple 901), dating from the early 17th century B.C.

o.	B62 V.13.27	216	Store-Jar	Red ware, s-l flint and lime grits, slow fired.
p.	B60 VI.9.13	1340	Water Jar	Light gray, m lime grits, medium fired.
q.	B60 VI.50.17	6504	Water Jar	Red ware, m lime grits, fast fired.
r.	B60 VI.9.12	1330	Water Jar	Red ware, s lime grits, fast fired.
s.	B60 VI.50.3–13	5769	Cooking Pot	Buff ware, m flint and lime grits, slow fired.
t.	B60 VI.15.26	4264	Cooking Pot	Brown ochre, s flint and lime grits, slow fired.
u.	B60 VI.3d.138	482	Cooking Pot	Brown ochre, m silicon and lime grits, medium fired.
v.	B60 VI.8.21	4509	Cooking Pot	Brown ochre, l silicon and lime grits, slow fired, hand made.

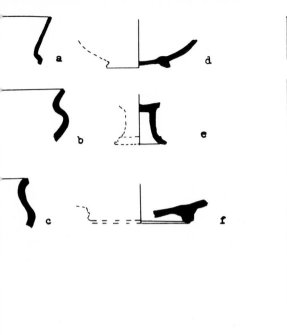
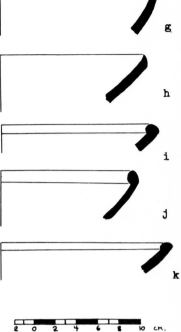

Fig. 112. Pottery from Building 110 in the East Gate (Figs. 24 and 104). It is contemporary with the earliest period of Wall A (*ca.* middle to second half of the 17th cent. B.C.), before the erection of Wall B and the East Gate.

a.	B60 VI.7.11	1236	Carinated Bowl	Red ware, finely levig, slow fired, gray slip.
b.	B60 VI.3b.50	390	Carinated Bowl	Buff ware, m lime grits, slow fired.
c.	B60 VI.18.13	4828a	Carinated Bowl	Pink buff, s silicon grits, slow fired, orange-brown burnished slip.
d.	B60 VI.4.9	1305	Carinated Bowl	Pink buff, m lime grits, slow fired, buff slip.
e.	B60 VI.3e.183	1493	Platter Bowl	Pink buff, m lime grits, medium fired.
f.	B62 VI.24.53	420	Platter Bowl	Pink buff, m-l lime grits, slow fired.
g.	B60 VI.3b.50	388	Platter Bowl	Pink buff, l lime grits, medium fired.
h.	B60 VI.15.26	4258	Platter Bowl	Buff ware, s lime grits, slow fired.
i.	B60 VI.3c.89	587	Platter Bowl	Pink buff, s lime grits, slow fired, red burnished slip inside and out.
j.	B60 VI.3d.136	447	Store-Jar	Buff ware, l lime grits, slow fired.
k.	B60 VI.3d.136	446	Store-Jar	Orange buff, l lime grits, fast fired.

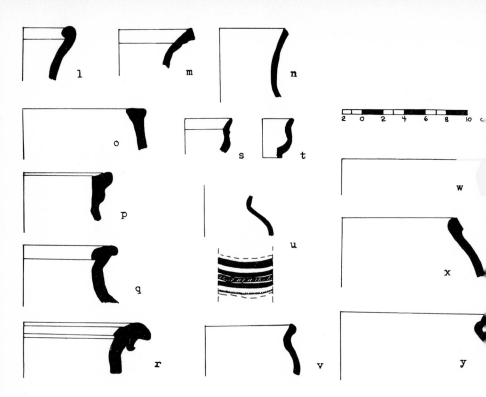

Fig. 112 (cont.) Pottery from Building 110 in the East Gate (Figs. 24 and 107). It is contemporary with the earliest period of Wall A (*ca.* middle to second half of the 17th cent. B.C.) before the erection of Wall B and the East Gate.

l.	B60 VI.14.20	4215	Store-Jar	Light gray, l lime grits, slow fired.
m.	B60 VI.3e.180	2540	Store-Jar	Pink buff, l lime grits, medium fired cream wash.
n.	B60 VI.3e.173	6129	Store-Jar	Cream buff, l lime grits, slow fired.
o.	B60 VI.3ef.228	4929	Store-Jar	Light gray, l lime grits, slow fired, cream wash.
p.	B62 V.13.40	270	Store-Jar	Buff ware, small to large lime grits, slow fired.
q.	B56 II.4	13	Store-Jar	Brown ochre, m lime grits, slow fired.
r.	B57 I.8a.25	1374	Store-Jar	Gray ware, l lime grits, slow fired, brown ochre slip.
s.	B62 V.13.21	107	Small Bowl	Buff ware, m lime grits, slow fired.
t.	B60 V.2.15	1401	Small Bowl	Pink buff, m-l lime grits, slow fired.
u.	B62 V.13.40	271	Jar	Buff ware, s lime grits, slow fired, horizontal bands of paint, black with one line of brown.
v.	B62 V.13.27	217	Cooking Pot	Brown ochre, s lime and silicon grits, slow fired.
w.	B57 I.8a.24	1359	Cooking Pot	Brown ochre, m lime and silicon grits, medium-fast fired.
x.	B62 V.13.64	290	Cooking Pot	Brown ochre, s lime and silicon grits, slow fired.
y.	B56 III.3–IV.4	12	Cooking Pot	Brown ochre, l lime grits, fast fired.

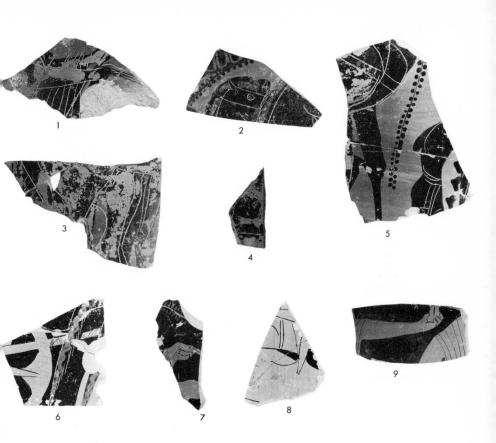

Fig. 113. Fragments of imported Greek black-figured and red-figured vessels, dating between *ca.* 525 and 475 B.C. (Stratum V).

POTTERY REGISTRY NUMBERS AND CONTEXT OF THE GREEK SHERDS.

1.	B62 1267	(VII.1.95)	Found below IV B Surface 1229–1232–1234
2.	B62 86 and 87	(VII.1.17)	Found above IV B Occupational Layer 1236, below Floor 1216
3.	B60 5330A and 928A	(VII.1.62)	Found beneath III B structures toward IV plastered Floor 1216
4.	B62 800	(VII.1.62)	Found in Stratum IV B (?) stones and pit
5.	B60 5310A	(VII.1.62)	Same context as No. 3
6.	B62	(VII——)	?
7.	B62 1266	(VII.1.93)	Same context as No. 1
8.	B62 807	(VII.1.65)	Found on IV B Surface 1229–1232–1234
9.	B62 83	(IX.3.49)	Found in Stratum V context

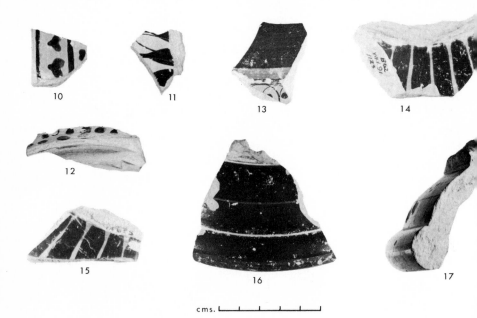

cms. └───┴───┴───┴───┘

Fig. 113 (*cont.*) Fragments of imported Greek black-figured and red-figured **vessels,** dating between *ca.* 525 and 475 B.C. (Stratum V).

POTTERY REGISTRY NUMBERS AND CONTEXT OF THE GREEK SHERDS.

10.	B60 5285	(VII.1.60)	Same context as No. 3
11.	B60 3848	(VII.4.72)	Unstratified III B context
12.	B62 159	(VII.2.3)	Found in balk cleaning
13.	B60 6249	(VII.2.126)	Found in removal IV B Wall 1123
14.	B62 1123	(VII.1.91)	From III B Pit 1522
15.	B60 5291A	(VII.1.60)	Same context as No. 3
16.	B60 5309	(VII.1.61)	Same context as No. 3
17.	B62 1536	(VII.4.141)	Found in stone heap of III B Pit 1522

dan valley north of Jericho, and Gezer (v. 28) as among the
"descendants" of Ephraim. Finally, 1 Kings 12:25 reads: "And
Jeroboam built Shechem in Mount Ephraim and dwelt there . . ."
before moving his capital, first to Penuel across the Jordan and
then to Tirzah.

These passages make it virtually certain that in the early
days of the period of the Judges the tribal areas of Ephraim
and Manasseh were distinct, and Shechem was within the latter.
During the tenth century, however, the governments of David
and Solomon were faced with the problem of the central government's establishing judicial, fiscal and military control over the
whole country. This involved dividing the land into provinces
with provincial administrators responsible to the king placed
in each. For this purpose the old tribal system would not do.
The local autonomy of tribal leaders had now to be balanced
by the fiscal and military control of the central government. In
addition, the old tribal areas by the tenth century did not always
correspond to actual boundaries or to efficient fiscal administration. The country was thus reorganized along provincial lines.
It seems probable to me that this was begun by David, who
probably succeeded in arranging Judah provincially.[9] It was
Solomon, however, who carried through the districting of the
rest of the country, undoubtedly against strong opposition, which
his father had also encountered.

In 1 Kings 4:7–19 we have a list of the twelve provincial
governors whom Solomon had placed over the northern part of
the country. Certain former tribal areas, such as Naphtali, Asher,
Issachar and Benjamin, remain more or less intact, but the rest
of the country is regrouped. The territory of north central Palestine, formerly divided into Ephraim and Manasseh, is split differently. One part is given a new name, namely "Mt. Ephraim"
(1 Kings 4:8), while northern and western Manasseh (v. 10,
Arubboth, Socoh and "all the land of Hepher") is split off as a
separate province; new districts are also created in the Plain of
Sharon (v. 11) and in the great Esdraelon plain (v. 12). The
district of Mt. Ephraim would thus include not only the former
area of Ephraim, but also Shechem with its plains to the east and
south, and southeastern Manasseh which includes especially the
Tirzah area, directly northeast of Shechem. Tirzah is readily

accessible from the Shechem plain, but it has no easy route of communication to western Manasseh, even to this day.[10]

In 1938 Père F.-M. Abel, in the second volume of his important *Géographie de la Palestine*, suggests that the chief city and residence of the provincial governor of the new district of Mt. Ephraim was probably Shechem.[11] As the main city of the province it elsewhere is listed as "Shechem in Mt. Ephraim" (Josh. 20:7; 21:21). And shortly thereafter, Jeroboam, the first king of Israel in the divided country after the death of Solomon, "built (refortified) *Shechem in Mount Ephraim,* and dwelt there" (1 Kings 12:25).

Considering the old associations and history of the city, it is not surprising that Shechem was the place where "all Israel" came to make Rehoboam, Solomon's son, their king. It was there that they revolted and decided to set up a separate state because Rehoboam would not alter any of his father's policies (1 Kings 12:1 ff.). And it was there that Jeroboam began his reign. Shechem was the natural rival to Jerusalem. Why Jeroboam did not remain there is unknown. The Omri Dynasty (*ca.* 876–842 B.C.) purchased a small village[12] on a magnificent hill and built on it their powerful capital, Samaria. Like Jerusalem, it was the personal possession of the king; and like the Jerusalem which David captured from the Jebusites, it was a city free of previous religious or political associations in the traditions of Israel. Shechem remained as a district center, and probably also as the site of a special covenant renewal ceremony, though precisely where it was then held is unknown. At any rate, the age of Shechem's greatest power was now passed, and no attempt was ever made to revive it, except in the final two centuries of the city's life.[13]

What is the archaeological evidence for Israelite Shechem?

As this is written, our work is incomplete in the investigation of the detailed history of private homes and domestic structures for the period before the ninth century B.C. Thus far we have encountered little evidence of a town of the eleventh century B.C. Following the severe destruction by Abimelech in the twelfth century, there was a very slow recovery. We know that the site was energetically "alive" in the tenth century, but thus far the evidence is solely from pottery. In Field VII at one point in

Area 9 during the last week of the 1962 campaign, digging started down through the debris of a massive burned layer into Stratum X. We presume that this layer represents the destruction of the city by Pharaoh Shishak about 918 B.C. (1 Kings 14:25–28). That would mean that Stratum X belongs to the tenth century, but we know nothing more about it than that.

As a guide to what follows, the stratification we have worked out for Israelite Shechem is again listed, together with some approximate and some specific dates which represent present hypotheses concerning the city's history during the ninth and eighth centuries.*

> Stratum IX B—*ca.* 900–860 B.C.
> Stratum IX A— *ca.* 860–810 B.C.
> Stratum VIII—*ca.* 810 B.C.–748 B.C.
> Stratum VII—*ca.* 748–724 B.C.

Most of our information comes from Fields VII and IX, the upper and lower residential quarters. In the East Gate there was considerable evidence of its reuse from pottery, but no architectural elements survive there which can be traced to this period.[14] Both Sellin and Steckeweh write of finding Israelite remains wherever they dug. The two discoveries of Sellin which we can speak about specifically from our own investigations bear upon a question discussed above: namely, the suggestion that Shechem was the administrative center of the province of Mount Ephraim.

Shechem as an Israelite Provincial Center

After Abimelech's destruction of the temple, there is no evidence that the sacred area was ever again used for sacred purposes. Indeed, what we have found suggests the secularization of the area.[15] The remains of a large building were excavated by Sellin in 1926 on top of the temple foundations. We have identified it as a government granary or warehouse: that is, a building for the storage of grain, wine and oil, received by the

[* By the end of July, 1964 three additional strata were known in addition to those here given. Strata XII and XI were those of David and Solomon in the tenth century B.C., the latter being the city destroyed by Pharaoh Shishak about 918 B.C. Stratum X is a hasty rebuilding of the city which was soon replaced by the more substantial IX B.]

government in payment of taxes. Lachish, Beth-shemesh and Debir in Judah appear to have had such structures, and Hazor and Jericho in Israel probably had them also, judging from the excavated remains. A large group of ostraca found at Samaria were evidently tax receipts for wine and oil paid to the government by wealthy landholders during the ninth and tenth years of the reign of Menahem (*ca.* 748–738 B.C.): that is, in the years 739 and 738, presumably representing a special assessment to pay a huge tribute to the King of Assyria.[16] From this we infer that Samaria, too, must have had a comparable tax warehouse.

With regard to the excavation of the temple Sellin wrote:

> The complete excavation and clearance of this building was connected with extraordinary difficulties, because we found several layers, one above the other. Already at a depth of 1 m. ran the foundations of Hellenistic houses with courtyards, in part paved. Between them lay large, undressed blocks of stone which formed the foundation walls of a large building of the Early Iron Age. They had to be uncovered, which required the removal of the Hellenistic building remains. It showed that the main direction of the walls of this building ran at a somewhat different angle than the massive structure [the temple] underneath. . . . We left them standing and dug between them. . . .[17]

In Fig. 73 there is a reconstruction of the building's plan. It must be said, however, that some things on the plan are not certain:

(1) Sellin and his architect Johannes in their drawing show Walls 5901 and 5903 running off the northwest wall of the temple (5602) as though more of the building lay in that direction. In Sellin's words, "these foundation walls, running in the direction of the palace, had apparently once been connected with the later Iron Age superstructure of the palace." As we shall see, however, and as Sellin later was to observe, a casemate city fortification ran directly behind the granary so that no "palace" existed there.

(2) In addition, the wall that was being used for the southwest wall of the granary (our hypothetical 5903) is actually Wall 5703 belonging to Temple 2 of the Late Bronze Age (see Figs. 10, 55). There is, of course, no evidence today that 5703

ran off the Temple 1 stone socket, and, since the builders of
Temple 2 were perfectly aware of the walls of the building
below, it is most improbable that they placed a corner of Temple
2 on earth or rubble off the edge of the northwestern temple
wall (5602). Johannes, on the other hand, appears quite positive
about 5901 and shows stones in place as a northwest extension
off the temple platform. As shown in the reconstruction in Fig.
73, it appeared to us that Wall 5901 continued at least to the
edge of the temple wall, while an earth-filled space appeared
at Point *a*. Consequently, we suggest an entry or back door to
the building at this point (cf. also Fig. 46).

(3) The rear Wall 5902 is reconstructed, because there are
two strips of wall here which do not line up. They must represent successive phases of building, and are not contemporary.[18]
Thus 5902 is used here in the plan, but 5702 is considered to
belong to a different phase, probably Temple 2.

The 5900 granary has the same orientation as Temple 2.
That is, its builders did not follow the plan of Temple 1, but
they were very conscious of the plan of Temple 2 and used it
for their own building both as to orientation and size. The cella
of Temple 2 thus determined the size of the interior of the
granary, provided that we are correct in reconstructing Wall
5903 on top of Temple 2's Wall 5703. Wall 5904 is not as wide
as Wall 5704 below it, but it follows the latter's inner edge. No
remnant of Temple 2 survived beneath Wall 5901, but we can
be confident that a 5701 wall once existed there, and that its
surviving stones were reused in the granary.

The builders of the granary carefully leveled the area under
their proposed building down to plaster Floor 5002A of Temple
2b, and often through it to its supporting fill 5003. Then a 10-cm.
layer of gray earth (5002) was spread where needed, and over
this a thick floor of white marl cement (5001) was laid, 20 to 25
cm. in thickness. Before this cement was completely dry the
stones for the first course of the walls were put in place, so that
they sank into the cement. The thickness of this floor and the
manner in which it formed a seal around the base of the walls
suggest that the builders attempted to create an edifice imper-
vious to vermin and to moisture.

The walls of the granary are quite different from those of any other building noted by us at the site. They are made of two rows of large unhewn stones, the spaces between which were filled with smaller stones and earth. A typical stone was of boulder size, in the range of 1 m. long, 50 cm. wide and 60 cm. high. Walls 5901 and 5902 were raised on earth and smaller leveling stones, 60 to 70 cm. above the Temple 1 walls. The boulders are precisely the same type as were used in Wall A; it is highly probable that they were robbed from that wall. Because of their size, the width of the walls varies considerably; one can get measurements from as low as 1.30 m. to as high as 1.85 m. Thick layers of cement-plaster were probably used to even out such irregularities. If one presumes that the builders were attempting an average width of *ca.* 1.65 m., then they were attempting to build walls 3½ cubits wide (*ca.* 5 ft.).

The interior of the granary provided three rooms of approximately equal size (B, C and D in Fig. 73), and a long narrow corridor (A). The latter ran the width of the granary, *ca.* 16 m. (52½ ft.), and was 2 m. (*ca.* 6½ ft.) wide. While no doorway was preserved, it seems probable that the main entrance to the building was into this corridor; from it also a wooden ladder or stairs probably rose to the roof. Incidentally, the dimensions of the corridor indicate that the builders meant it to be 4½ common cubits wide. But the length, which is 30 long or "sacred" cubits, gives an odd fraction in common cubits. This is another indication that the over-all inner dimensions of the granary are those of Temple 2 and are in long cubits (*ca.* 30 by 24). The storage rooms B, C and D are each *ca.* 4.50 by 9 m. (*ca.* 14¾ by 29 ½ ft.).[19]

This type of building with its corridor and three long rooms at right angles to it was identified many years ago by Dr. Albright as a granary (in Hebrew, *miskenet*).[20] The construction of the floor and the way the stones are set in the cement gives further support to Dr. Albright's views. The size and location of our Building 5900, furthermore, are the basis of our suggestion that it is a public or district government structure. Such granaries would account for the references to store cities (in Hebrew "cities of granaries;" cf. 1 Kings 9:19). A variation in the granary plan is also used between the tenth and ninth centuries in Israel for a common house plan. The corridor and Rooms B and D in the house plan were made into approximately the same width, while C was left open as a court (*see below* and Fig. 76).

In 1957 a sufficient number of small fragments of pottery were collected from the earth sealed *under* Walls 5901 and 5902 to enable a date in the eighth century to be established for them. Père Roland de Vaux, on a visit to the site at the time, independently gave the same date. The chief criterion among the tiny fragments was the presence of what I have called "Samaria Ware B," about which more later. Since that time we have learned that, while this ware was present in the eighth century Strata VIII and VII, it is also present in smaller quantity as early as IX B. If our chronology is correct, then the history of this ware is about 150 years (*ca.* 875–725 B.C.), though it is rare in the early period. This leads to the conclusion that the granary was probably erected either in the second half of the ninth century (Stratum IX A) or in the first part of the eighth century (Stratum VIII). A good deal of pottery from the time when the building was erected, or just before, was found sealed in the cement Floor 5001 or in its gray-earth make-up below (Layer 5002). As the typology of the pottery from Strata IX and VIII is increasingly clarified from study of the discoveries in 1962, we shall probably be able to assign the building more definitely to one of the two strata.

Wall A as it proceeds southward on the west side slowly gave way until it disappeared entirely and Dr. Sellin could find no further trace of it. That is, it was robbed of its stones which were reused by builders who cared more for houses than for fortification. Most of it appears to have been taken from the northeast and eastern sectors north of the East Gate. This gradual dismantling of a great fortification would probably have begun in a period of weakness when survival was more important than city walls, and it would have been halted in periods of strength when any part of the old fortification was deemed important for present protection. The eleventh century B.C. would have been one such period of weakness in the life of Shechem; the sixth, fifth and fourth centuries would have been another. One hint that Wall A was no longer vital on the west side is the possibility that the granary was made of stones from that fortification. Another indication is the fact that the period of Stratum IX saw the erection of a new fortification, Wall E.

In excavating what he considered to be the palace along Wall A, south of the Northwest Gate, Sellin in 1926 uncovered two long parallel stone walls which were attached to the inner corner of the tower of the Northwest Gate. He traced them from the gate to the area behind the temple for over 40 m. By 1927 he had correctly concluded that these walls were much later than the Wall A system. Parallel walls like this with occasional connecting walls form narrow long rooms or casemates into which doorways opened from within the city. Two long sections remain, one set out from the other so that the fortification was made to take a jog in order that it not come too close to the foundation of Temple 1 (Figs. 9 and 74). They had evidently been set in trenches which had been dug for them down to the stumps of the Middle Bronze Age walls which survived. In the first section next to the gate the outer of the two walls is *ca.* 1.55 m. wide, the inner *ca.* 1.10 m. and the space between *ca.* 1.55 m.[21] Three narrow casemate rooms were created in this section, the first *ca.* 4.80 m., the second *ca.* 3.95 m. and the third 3 m. The other section which begins after the jog away from the temple has both walls *ca.* 1.55 m. wide.

Sellin also reports that he found the double casemate walls in the area of Squares H–I 3, where their remains today are above the socle of Wall B at this point (Fig. 20). There is a strong suggestion in the ruins still remaining that these were a rebuilding of the fortifications which followed the course of Wall B on the north side around to the inner northeast corner of the Northwest Gate. That is, fortification E was a casemate repair of the Wall B system, probably using the East Gate and clearly using the Northwest Gate. South of the latter, where no city wall except Wall A had been needed before, it was continued, undoubtedly around the whole western and southern sides, though only the one section of it now remains.

During the last week of the 1962 campaign, Robert Bull dismantled a small section of fortification E in order to find some pottery fragments, if possible, sealed in earth *under* the stones of the wall. He succeeded in collecting a few which appeared to belong to Stratum IX, but nothing more precise than that can be said. Whether this casemate refortification of Shechem is to be credited to Jeroboam I (1 Kings 12:25), as at first glance would appear probable, cannot be made certain by the small pottery group so far discovered. This type of fortification was introduced into Palestine during the tenth century by the united monarchy, and continued in use for royal building at Samaria, where its most beautiful workmanship is displayed. The Shechem casemate thus has good analogues, and it represents royal fortification of a district center during the early part of the divided monarchy.

Stratum IX B (ca. 900–860 B.C.)

Our evidence for this stratum comes solely from Field VII, and the dating, while approximate, is tentative. In this sector the city of the ninth to eighth centuries sloped southeastward in the direction of the East Gate. Terraces were constructed to give the houses solid foundations, and one of them happened to cross in the center of Field VII (Fig. 75). It was between 13 and 14 m. wide, and it appears to have held that width throughout Strata IX through VII. This was because the terrace walls established in IX were rebuilt and reused three times before the destruction visited upon the city by the Assyrian army. Preceding IX and at the end of VII, the destructions visited upon the city are so massive as to cause major rebuilding and a change in city plans.

The reconstructed ground plan of IX B divides itself into three sectors (Fig. 75). The terrace wall to the left, 70 cm. wide, held the earth of the upper terrace in place. To the right of it on the middle terrace there was a narrow street which gave access to the complex, Rooms 1–5. Room 1 is over 5 m. wide, and it must thus have been an unroofed court with a small enclosure, Room 2, set into its southeast corner. Rooms 3–5 were presumably living quarters. Room 4 had a nicely built stone structure in one corner which may have been part of a stairway to a second story. Room 3 had the top part of a large jar sunk in its floor, neck and rim down. We assumed, of course, that it was a drain, except that there did not appear to be any outlet for the water (Fig. 75). Assistant supervisor Albert Glock, how-

ever, noted clear traces of burning around the periphery of the
vessel, and called our attention to a similar installation in Stratum V A at Hazor (dated *ca.* 745–732 B.C.) and another from
the latter part of the seventh century at Meṣad Ḥashavyahu on
the coastal plain. In these cases, it is quite clear that the vessels
were ovens.[22] It was a quick way to make an oven: simply to
cut a large storage jar in two parts, and use the upper part,
presumably because of the wide shoulders. The more typical
house oven of any period is more complex; it is made of a special
clay mixed with coarse binding material, and outside and inside
layers of large sherds may be stuck into the mixture. A round pit
in the ground was prepared; the material was formed in place
around it and permitted to extend a few inches above ground.
A fire built in it would then have hardened the walls.

Between Rooms 4–5 and 6 there is a wall, 7 m. long,
which blocks passage southward. Rooms 6 and 7, accordingly,
must be entered from another alley, access to which was somewhere south of our excavated area. Room 6 is a court, half roofed
over on the northern side. Two wooden pillars on stone bases
once supported the shelter. These bases are large boulders,
crudely cut to cubic forms, *ca.* 50 cm. in diameter, two forming
each base. The upper stones on the plan are quite crude and
belong to Stratum IX A, as does also the large flat stone on an
uneven base next to the door.

The third sector is along the eastern edge of the terrace,
including Rooms 8–12. They rest on a kind of platform created
to hold them up, but the edges are unclear because they have
crumbled away down the slope. Later building has left the rest
fragmentary, though more detail may make matters clearer when
excavation here is completed.

The walls are only one stone in thickness, and they appear
very insubstantial, though they remain standing to a height of
1 m., and in some places to 1.50 m. As we shall note subsequently,
however, this type of wall is typical in houses of the ninth and
eighth centuries at Shechem. While occasionally walls may be
two stones in thickness, the single-stone wall, only some 40 cm.
thick, is the more common. However, by the time a covering of
12 to 25 cm. of mud-plaster was put on each side, the wall width
was more substantial, between 64 and 90 cm., probably representing 1½ or 2 cubits.

All of the walls shown in Fig. 75 were peculiar in that the east-west walls tilted to the north, and the north-south walls tilted to the west. To field supervisor Horn this suggested that an earthquake may have been the cause; otherwise why was the tilting so consistent? Ashy destruction layers were present, though not found consistently throughout the stratum. If earthquake was the sufficient natural cause for the end of IX B, then we cannot date it other than to say that it probably occurred during the period approximately 880 to 830 B.C. It is of interest to note, however, that another Israelite provincial city, Hazor, has in its Stratum IX a city contemporary with ours. If a political interruption in the life of Israel is to be sought as the explanation for the end of Shechem IX B and Hazor IX, then it was probably the war between Ben-hadad of Damascus and Ahab of Israel (1 Kings 20). Ben-hadad had succeeded in taking his army into the heart of Israel and had invested Samaria itself. Ahab had gathered all of his provincial officers and troops, thus presumably leaving the provincial capitals virtually defenseless, before a severe defeat was visited upon Ben-hadad. We are not informed of the date of this event, but since it occurred before Damascus and Israel were allied against Assyria in the battle of Qarqar in 853 B.C., we will not be far wrong if we assume it to have been in the period between 860 and 855 B.C.[23]

Stratum IX A (ca. 860–810 B.C.)

Following some sort of violent disaster which befell IX B, radical measures were needed to shore up foundations and to rebuild house superstructures. In so doing, rearrangements of space were occasionally undertaken. A heavy accumulation of debris was leveled over the earlier floors. New ones were installed 20 in. above the lower floors on top of the debris, some of very fine flagstones. Others of tamped earth show on occasion several resurfacings. Doors were blocked. Court 1 was subdivided into rooms. The alley to the east of it had supporting walls running across it to the terrace wall. Room 6 was reused, but large flat slabs were placed on top of the earlier pillar bases, and another was installed next to the door, so that there were now three new flat bases for pillars to support the roof over the half-open court. To the east the platform at the edge of the terrace was kept in good repair, but the surviving architecture thus far is too fragmentary and complex to give a clear picture as to the nature of the rooms here. At the southeastern corner of the middle terrace the people of Stratum VI (seventh century) had dug through eighth-century levels down as far as IX B in some places.

The disentangling of Strata IX and VIII was so intricate a task that again we are left without clear evidence as to what brought the city of IX A to an end. Whatever it was, destruction was so bad that the people of City VIII had to rebuild completely, and they did so on an entirely new plan, disregarding the IX house walls entirely. In this case we surely can look to the wars between the Aramaean state of Damascus and Israel for the cause. Before an Assyrian army of Adad-nirari III destroyed Damascus in 805 B.C., Hazael, the Aramaean king whom the Assyrians called a "son of nobody" (i.e., a commoner), dealt blow after blow upon both Israel and Judah, until by about 810 B.C. Judah even had to pay tribute to him while Israel was completely at his mercy (2 Kings 12:17–13:23). Megiddo, Hazor and Tirzah all had a severe disrupting of city life at this time, and the end of Shechem IX A is probably to be attributed to the same disasters.

Stratum VIII (ca. 810–748 B.C.)

We can say very little about the houses of Shechem during this period. The builders of Stratum VII had destroyed virtually everything down to Stratum IX A walls, and the only pieces of VIII that survived were those set within IX rooms and whose surviving tops were at about the same level as those of IX. We know that the upper terrace wall continued in use, and the walls of a large building erected against it extended eastward across nearly the whole terrace.

Field IX, south of Field VI and directly behind the first walls of the modern village, is a 121-sq.-m. plot which was opened to serve as an additional check on stratigraphy. In 1962 we found it to be a residential quarter of a much poorer quality than that in Field VII. In both the Samaritan and Israelite periods, building remains and objects in the lower quarter suggest poverty. Almost every building phase was badly, if not completely, robbed of building material by the people of the next phase, as though nothing that could be used was overlooked. This meant that the digging had to be carefully done by debris phases, each one of which contained a great mixture of pottery from earlier periods. Dating could de done only by assessing the latest material in each phase. In 1962, excavation had gone from the surface where, under debris of previous excavation washed down from Sellin's dump between Fields IX and VI, a medieval cemetery was encountered. By the end of the 1962 campaign, however, digging had reached Stratum IX A where both flag-stone- and cement-floored structures were encountered which appear to have been rebuilt twice in Stratum VIII. That is, the extensive building and rebuilding in these phases suggest an era of relative peace, with the evidence pointing toward a consider-able period of political security. This situation clearly agrees with the dating suggested by the stratified ceramic evidence in Field VII that the era in question is that of the Israelite kings Joash and Jeroboam II (ca. 798–748 B.C.) before the beginning of Israel's impoverishment and civil turmoil in the reign of Mena-hem (ca. 748–738 B.C.).

This long stable period saw the production in Israel of the most beautiful pottery which Iron Age Palestine produced. It has been called "Samaria Ware" because it was first found in quantity by the Harvard excavators at Samaria between 1908 and 1910. At Shechem this pottery first appears in Stratum IX A, with a few pieces sealed in the leveling fill for IX A floors. Potters began to make it during the Omri Dynasty (ca. 876–842 B.C.). It reached its height in quantity and excellence during the pros-perous period of Stratum VIII (ca. 810–748 B.C.), and continued in use during Stratum VII (ca. 748-724 B.C.) The destruction of Israel by the Assyrian army marked the virtual end of its manu-facture. The final decades of Israel's life, when the country suffered severely from Assyrian pressure and political instability, saw the quality of the pottery decline. Indeed, it is amazing how quickly social and economic factors are reflected in the architecture and artifacts which survive in a country.

This is the first time that the chronology of Samaria Ware has been pin-pointed. Its history of nearly one hundred fifty years is much more extensive than I had previously supposed. As for its places of manufacture, these seem to have been confined to the central hill country of Palestine as far south as Bethel: that is, to the areas contiguous to Samaria, Israel's remarkable capital city. The ware seems not to have been made in Judah nor at Hazor of Galilee. Its ancestry can be traced back to fine red polished bowls and jugs which appear at least as early as the time of Solomon.

In Stratum VIII at Hazor, dating to the period of the Omri Dynasty in the ninth century, beautiful red bowls appear which in 1959 I labeled "Samaria Ware A."[24] It is a fairly thick ware, containing a considerable amount of gritty binding material; after firing, it becomes quite hard and often retains a dark-colored core. Over this a thick red or brownish-red slip (colored surface covering) was placed before the vessel was fired. This was allowed to dry. Then the vessel was put back on the wheel and turned while the potter gave it a spiral burnish: that is, while the vessel was turning he held a narrow wooden or bone tool against the interior walls. Starting at the bottom in parallel bands, he pressed the tool against the paste and gradually brought it up over the rim, occasionally continuing down the outside. In Judah he would have stopped at this point and put the bowl in a kiln. If in firing the temperature is not allowed to rise over about 900 degrees Fahrenheit, the parallel or spiral lines made by the tool will shine after baking. The vessel can then be said to have been "ring-burnished" or "spirally burnished." Only on rare occasions were ninth-century bowls hand-burnished without the potter's wheel. Pitchers, on the other hand, when burnished, were generally done by hand in vertical strokes. In Israel, after burnishing but before baking, an additional step was taken for a few of the finest vessels: the potter would rub the ware lightly over the burnished area with a cloth or piece of leather, so that the bowl would emerge from the kiln with a shiny or lustrous finish.

Samaria Ware A of this type appears not only at Hazor, but also at Megiddo, Samaria and Shechem. It seems to go back into the tenth century, when more hand- than wheel-burnishing was common. At Shechem the treatment continued on common bowls as late as Stratum VII, though by then they were not polished.

While individual pieces of Ware A can be attractive, the most beautiful pottery is what I have called "Samaria Ware B," the kind generally referred to in the past as Samaria Ware before the term was extended to the A type by the excavators at Hazor. This is quite a different type of pottery. The clay for it was extremely well mixed; the binding material introduced into it was very fine grits; the color after firing was predominately buff, often with a slight tan tint; and the pottery was exceptionally light in weight. Over the clay before baking a thick red covering or slip, brighter in color than on A ware, was applied, usually over the whole vessel except perhaps under the base. It was then burnished, but the polishing after burnish on the best vessels was so carefully done that it not infrequently obscured the burnishing lines.

Certain special shapes occur in this ware. One is a bowl on a high ring foot. By Stratum VIII times, both at Samaria and at Shechem, potters often made this vessel so fast and carelessly that the red slip, applied like paint, would trickle down the sides on to the ring foot, giving a messy appearance to the vessel. The shape and paste may still be good, but the finish is careless. Another fine piece of "tableware" is a plate on which the red slip has been applied while the vessel was turning on the wheel; bands or rings, especially on the bottom, were left uncolored by the slip, the only color being provided by the clay itself. At Shechem, however, almost any small vessel, including the lamp, can appear in Samaria Ware. The light, chalky paste and the red burnished and polished slip make the ware easily distinguishable. The only difference between the ninth- and eighth-century ware, as far as we now see, seems to be that the earlier Samaria Ware B tends to have deeper red tints than the later. Yet in both Strata IX A and VIII the best plates in this pottery remind one of the beautiful Roman dinner plates called *terra sigillata*.

Stratum VII (ca. 748–724 B.C.)

The buildings of Stratum VIII were evidently so badly ruined in Field VII that they were not reused. Instead, the structures of City VII are entirely new. This shift in strata is comparable to that between Strata VI and V at Hazor in Galilee.

Both Shechem VII and Hazor V represent the final years of an independent Israel, the time of the increasing Assyrian pressure with the resulting political instability and increasing impoverishment of Israel. The decline in quality of Samaria Ware B in Stratum VII is a clear reflection of the situation. If we look at the history to find a political reason for the shift in strata at both Hazor and Shechem, we are led to the brief period of civil war *ca.* 748–747 B.C. before Menahem (*ca.* 748–738 B.C.) succeeded in establishing himself firmly on the throne. And once there, we are informed that he "smote" the Shechem area, specifically Tappuah[25] to the south, "and every one in it and its borders as far as Tirzah" to the northeast "because they did not open to him"[26] (2 Kings 15:16). The area from Tappuah to Tirzah is precisely the Shechem area, though the city for some reason is unmentioned.

On the middle terrace in Stratum VII was a fine building, House 1727 (Figs. 76 and 77). "Room" 12 on the north side was a paved alley leading to another building; it does not appear to be an integral part of the house, and there were no doorways leading from it into the house. With that left out of consideration, 1727 is almost exactly square, slightly more than 10 m. on a side (*ca.* 33 ft. or 23 cubits). Along the eastern side was a street, supported by a kind of platform to prevent it from eroding down the steep slope to the next terrace. Beside the door leading into the building there was a large sump so that rain water would drain into it instead of into the house. It was roughly circular with a diameter of *ca.* 2.25 m. (*ca.* 8½ ft.) and nearly a meter of depth. In addition to stones the sump had purposely been filled with a great quantity of pottery of the Stratum VIII period: that is, from the time just preceding the erection of the building.

A gate by the sump opened into an open court (Fig. 76, Areas 1–2), flanked to the north by two rooms (Nos. 3–4) and to the south by two more (5–6). The length of the court and its parallel side rooms is *ca.* 6.70 m. (*ca.* 22 ft.), which is precisely 15 cubits. Room 7 across the back is the same length. Thus, omitting the widths of the interior walls, the depth of the court and the width of the rear room show that the building was carefully planned after a known architectural model. Indeed, we now know that this type of house was a common Israelite architectural style between the tenth and eighth centuries, excellent examples having been found at Tirzah, Hazor and Mizpah.[27] The long narrow spaces on each side of the central court and across the back can be used in different ways, but the basic plan remains the same. That plan seems also to have been adapted for use in country forts and may be related to the casement principle in fortification as well as to the plan of state granaries (cf. Fig. 73).[28]

Thus the parallels to House 1727, especially at Tirzah and Mizpah where even the dimensions are closely similar, make it clear that the architectural form consists of Rooms 1–7. This means that Rooms 8–11 to the south are additions to the primary plan. The reason for these additions may well be that the building housed a family which was engaged in industrial pursuits. Let us note briefly the installations within the building:

As one entered the court from the street, a small storage bin was immediately to the right. Rooms 3 and 5 were paved with cobblestone floors. The roof of Room 3 was supported in the center by wooden posts which stood on two stone pillars. The south side was open to the court except for a small screening wall. Directly in the center of the court was a large hearth, roughly oval in shape and nearly 2 m. (6½ ft.) in length. It is filled with stones level with the dirt floor of the court, and under them, 26 cm. (10½ inches) below the surface, is a large wine press with vat of Stratum VII B. Plaster or slaked lime coated the rim stones, and manifold evidence of fire lay on the loosely placed stones of the interior. A small bin appears to have existed at the southern edge. One possibility is that the installation may have been for slaking lime. Some of our native workers suggested that it could have been used as an open kiln for pottery, since comparable hearths are occasionally still used today for this purpose.

A large and heavy saddle quern was in place along the court, and the bottom portion of a jar set within a small circle of stones stood nearby to receive the flour or feed ground by hand on the stone. Two hand crushers or grinders lay beside the quern. One was of the ordinary type, made of volcanic lava (basalt), flat on one side and rounded above. The other was larger, 46 cm. long, 16 cm. wide at the center, and 11 cm. high (ca. 18 by 6¼ by 4¼ inches). It is made of pink quartzite, so hard and yet so smooth on its bottom surface that one concludes that it could be, and probably was, used for other purposes than grinding flour. Its weight, 39 lb., 9 oz., further suggests its use for something other than flour. One suggestion is that it was used to grind stones smooth and square which were now in use at points where specially strong masonry was needed. One large stone of this type was in the wall of Room 4 (*see* Figs. 76 and 77). Another was placed by the doorway leading into Room 7, apparently as a means of strengthening the wall at that point.

If the quartzite grinding stone was indeed used to grind such stones smooth, then its Hebrew name may have been *megērāh*.[29] Ashlar, that is, finely cut masonry, was introduced into Israel in all probability by the Phoenician artisans hired by David and Solomon. I Kings 7:9, for example, says that in the royal buildings erected by Solomon in Jerusalem were "costly stones, hewn according to measure, . . . (?) by means of the *megērāh*." The process by which limestone was prepared for building would have been as follows: after the blocks were split off the bedrock at the quarry, they would have been "hewn according to measure" by an adze (*garzen*), and then ground smooth by a hard rubbing stone. Hence the last phrase of the above verse must surely mean just this. A very difficult passage in 2 Sam. 12:31 says that David put the conquered Amorites "on the *megērāh* [probably grinding stone], and on iron *hārîs*(es) and on iron *magzērāh*(s)." While not generally understood in this manner, the verse surely means that the people were put to work in the quarries, the last two terms probably referring to the newly-introduced iron handpicks and adzes used to hew the stones.

The main living room on the ground floor of the house was Room 7 with its silo. A small door in the rear opened on the upper terrace. A short corridor, Room 8, led to a small addition which may have been the kitchen area, for here was found a smaller and more typical saddle quern and grinding stone for flour. The quern seems to have been in place when found; with it was a small silo for grain. This area was badly ruined by subsequent building operations in Stratum VI, so that its plan is unclear. Rooms 9 and 10 each had a large stone-filled sump, connected by an underground drain. This suggests some other purpose than would have been present in an ordinary home, but what it was, was a matter of conjecture.

Of particular interest is the evidence as to the building's construction. The walls are only one stone in thickness, *ca.* 40 cm. wide (15–16 in.). These were built up at least a meter in height and then given heavy coats of mud-plaster to make a wall base at least 60 to 80 cm. wide. If a 2-cubit wall was erected, then it would have been about 89 cm. (35 in.) thick. Above this, brick was apparently used. Two nearly whole wall bricks were recovered, *ca.* 37 cm. by 32 cm. by 12 cm. (*ca.* 12 by 11⅞ by 4¾ in.), the second figure not being exact because of uncertainty as to whether a face was preserved on one side. Clear outlines of ceiling beams were discovered in Sector 2 of the court, having evidently slid off the superstructure to the north when the walls collapsed. They were halves of logs laid with the rounded surface up, and they seem to have been laid in pairs, the two logs in a pair touching one another (see Fig. 79). The pairs were separated from each other by a space between 9 and 12 cm. The diameter of the beams varied between 15 and 22 cm. At least part of the house evidently had a second story, because over the ceiling beams and beneath much of the brick detritus were chunks of flat-surfaced floorplaster, 6 to 7 cm. thick. This floor material had three layers, the top one being a smoothed and highly polished surface about one cm. thick, sprinkled with crystals of feldspar or other quartzlike material. Great chunks of smoothed mud and straw roofing material, laid in layers as many as eight in number, were recovered in 1960, especially from Room 7 (Fig. 80). That is, the roofs were of the typical clay-straw variety, which had to be rolled after a rain and frequently resurfaced.

When excavated, the debris from the collapse of the house was nearly a meter thick over Rooms 4 and 7 and over Sector 2 in the court. The debris consisted of remains of brick, mud-plaster, slabs of roofing material and clay pieces from the floor of the second story, interlaced with charcoal from burned beams. On the floor were broken pottery vessels covered with dark ash, indicating the burning-collapse sequence. When the beams had burned, the superstructure collapsed. Storage jars were evidently on the roof, because the broken remains of them were in the upper layers of the brick and clay detritus. On the eastern side stones from the building, with burned debris, had tumbled in a mass down the steep slope of the terrace.

It is clear that the building was destroyed while the house was in full occupation and before its occupants had occasion to remove its contents. It is impossible not to associate this event with the conquest of Israel by the Assyrian emperor, Shalmaneser V, in 724 or 723 B.C. The capital, Samaria, held out under siege until the winter months of 722–721, but the other cities and towns were probably overrun and destroyed quickly during the first months of the campaign in 724 B.C. (2 Kings 17:1–6).

Among the objects found in Israelite Shechem, the most interesting has been a fine collection of seals. Figure 81 is a Middle Assyrian cylinder seal, imported to Shechem *ca.* 1200 B.C., to the city destroyed by Abimelech (B60, Reg. 661). It is a pierced cylinder, 36 mm. in height and 13 mm. in diameter (*ca.* 1⅜ in. and ½ in. respectively), made of serpentine. At the center of the design is a winged disk over a highly stylized "tree of life." To the right is a winged animal with horn(s), hooves and bull's head and tail. Over the animal and to the right of the winged disk are the seven stars of the Pleiades and the moon crescent. A major clue to the date of the seal is the manner in which the animal is drawn. While clearly a bull is intended, its slim body is like that of a horse. In Middle Assyrian seals the horse first appears as a mythological creature, and the bodies of bulls on the seals are drawn like those of the horse.[30]

In Fig. 82 is a selection of various stamp seals of a variety of dates. No. 1 (B62, Reg. 529) is from Stratum IX B. It is a scarab of white steatite, the design with the human hand being unique, as far as I am aware.[30a] No. 2 is an ivory seal with a pierced oval top (B62, Reg. 491). Its design appears to be a winged beetle, and it comes from the debris of Strata IX–VII in Field IX. No. 3 is a white steatite scarab (B62, Reg. 511), found in context of the Israelite period, though its design bears in hieroglyphs the name "Rameses" derived from the Nineteenth Egyptian Dynasty (late fourteenth and thirteenth century). No. 4 is a scarab (B62, Reg. 73) of white steatite picked up on the surface of the mound near Field VII. Prof. S. H. Horn in his study of our scarabs believes it to be from the Hyksos period (seventeenth to early sixteenth century). No. 5 is a scaraboid of dark stone (B62, No. 5), with a design influenced by Assyrian motifs: a winged disk and lunar crescent over a sacred tree which seems to have the seven stars of the Pleiades at its sides. It, too, was found on the surface. No. 6 is a beautiful pierced marble scaraboid (B62, Reg. 475) found in the destruction debris of Stratum VII. It is imported from Mesopotamia, its design showing two figures with altar between, a star as a divine symbol above and the Pleiades at the left. No. 7 is another scaraboid (B62, 121), made of ivory, showing a roaring lion. It is probably to be related to the lion stamped on a jar handle of Stratum V (see Fig. 93).

An object of special interest is the eight-sided die shown in Fig. 83 (B60, Reg. 698), made of ivory. Most ancient dice are like modern ones, but this one is very different. It was found with ninth or early eighth century pottery inside the thick cement of the floor of the Government granary (Fig. 73) over the temple in Field V. The fine ram's head in Fig. 84 (B62, Reg. 28) was found in mixed fill, but probably dates from the same era. Figure 85 is a beautiful "Cypro-Phoenician" imported juglet (B60, Reg. 725), found in the debris on the floor of Room 4 in the Stratum VII house shown in Figs. 76, 77, and 79.

Reoccupation

The destruction of Israel was for breach of a vassal treaty imposed by the Assyrian monarch. The last Israelite king, Hoshea, "became his vassal and paid him tribute. But the king of Assyria found conspiracy in Hoshea because he had sent messengers to So, king of Egypt, and had not offered tribute to the King of Assyria (as he was supposed to do) year by year" (2 Kings 17:3–4). Since this was the second rebellion in a decade, retaliation was swift and terrible. The country was laid completely waste, most of its inhabitants slaughtered, and according to Assyrian report 27,290 of the leading citizens taken into exile. Thus a dark age descended upon Israel. There were undoubtedly some survivors who had escaped the slaughter, and we are told that "the king of Assyria brought people from Babylon, Cuthah, Avva, Hamath and Sepharvaim and settled them in the cities of Samaria in place of the people of Israel" (2 Kings 17:24).

It is this reoccupation that is represented by Stratum VI.

The presence of foreigners in the country is attested by a considerable quantity of "Assyrian Palace Ware," a pottery which followed Mesopotamian models, though most of it was locally made. Yet little of Stratum VI remains. Room 10 of the VII house was reused and a new cobblestone floor was laid, but the remainder of the house shows no evidence of rebuilding. For some reason the brick detritus over the house was left intact in its west central and northwestern parts. On the south the people of both Strata VI and V seem to have built against it. Directly south of the street platform appeared an odd structure (No. 1127) which field supervisors called the "fish pond" (Fig. 86). It was a rough half-circle, ca. 3.20 m. in diameter (10½ ft.), of carefully laid cobbling, surrounded by a thin curving wall erected against the debris behind it. The most reasonable suggestion is that the structure was originally a circular platform for a wood or skin shelter or tent; its eastern part was destroyed by the Samaritans of Stratum IV. Above the cobbled surface in several places were traces of hard-packed earth with grass impressions. A few Samaritan sherds of Stratum IV appeared in almost every pottery basket right down to the surface of the cobbling. Beneath it, however, there was nothing clearly later than Stratum V.

The debris behind the 1127 cobbling, into which it was set, belongs to Stratum VI. As we began to dig a section through it across to 1127, we came upon a dark layer of occupation debris and below it a layer of slaked lime, numbered 1131a, running down the slope to the south. It was about 5 cm. thick and gave off a distinct smell of oxidation. In this layer and under it there was a huge quantity of broken pottery, most of which was from jars made of a ware that had a distinctive brick-red color. Most of the sherds were lime encrusted: a hot fire had burned the limestone of the walls into powder which hardened over the pottery when soaked by the winter rain. Charcoal chunks and flecks abounded in the debris. Below this was a layer of burned debris (1132) as much as 15 cm. thick in places, its slope being more gradual than 1131a. It is probably the floor or surface of the VI occupation and was designated VI A. Below the floor of 1132 there was another layer of debris, ca. 50 cm. (19½ inches) thick, a yellow soil from decomposed brick (Layer 1138). Under that was a dark smudged layer on a second surface (Layer 1140). These two layers were an earlier phase and designated VI B.

Figure 87 is a north-south cross-section through the center of Field VII. At the center, Wall 1436 is the south wall of Room 5 in the VII house. To the left may be seen the layers of VI A and B; these were set deeply in the debris of the slope, so that below them was a burned surface of Stratum IX B.

In Field IX the city's slum area during both the Israelite and Samaritan periods, the evidence for the reoccupation in Stratum VI is even clearer. Stratum VI A contains plastered floors and yellow mud-brick walls usually set on a course of flat stones. The bricks evidently once contained straw as a binder. On the floor of one building was an ashy destruction layer. Localized masses of broken pottery, including crushed storage jars, suggest that the destruction was sudden and that the building's contents were not removed. A basalt grinding stone lay on the floor and a small mortar was upside down in the debris. Also in the debris on the floor were two slingstones and an iron arrowhead (Reg. 453). A bronze spear point (433) and an iron spearpoint (427) were found elsewhere in the same phase. Indeed, throughout the field the evidence is clear for a massive destruction of the town of VI A. Collapsed walls and accumulated debris within which Stratum V structures were built suggest that an interval of time elapsed between the destruction of VI A and the reoccupation of V. Directly below VI A were the floors of VI B, also covered by an ash layer. Spear points 452 and 471, which may suggest military action, were found in this layer. The fact that very little debris accumulation was present over this destruction layer suggests prompt rebuilding, and indeed VI A follows the same lines of building as VI B. While the people of Stratum VI were poor enough, the objects left in their buildings suggest that they were better off in this sector than their successors in Cities V and IV.

It seems clear that the people of VI reused the East Gate. A portion of a burned floor was found in 1956 in the East Gate (I.3. Loc. 1) with three small perfumed-oil juglets on it (Fig. 88). The burned marks turned on a course of very poor, earth-filled repair of the stairwell in the tower (see Fig. 30).[31] Behind it in Area 4 there was a grape press with vat, the press being a flat stone with grooves in it where the grapes were pressed. The grooves permitted the juice to run into a jar which was sunk into the earth below the stone (Figs. 89 and 90).

The pottery of VI A and B is in the tradition of that in Stratum VII, but is much later—indeed, farther distant from VII than the ceramics of VIII. Consequently, the two destructions of VI, probably not far apart in time, must have occurred during the seventh century, preferably in the latter part of the century. What caused the trouble we cannot say with certainty, though the simplest explanation would be the conquest of Samaria and Galilee by the Judean king, Josiah, *ca.* 628–627 B.C. (cf. 2 Chron. 34:3–7). This king, with the decline of effective Assyrian control, moved rapidly to unite Palestine under his rule. Yet at this point the suggestion of Josiah cannot be more than a hypothesis.

The fact that most of the pottery follows earlier Palestinian tradition, except for the bowls made on Mesopotamian models, indicates that not all the people of the reoccupation were foreigners by any means. In any event, foreigners and natives had quickly adapted to the situation. A small and very beautiful Hebrew seal was found which belonged to a man in the city of Stratum VI, or else shortly thereafter in Stratum V. It was found in debris disturbed by later building and must be dated by the manner in which the letters on it, *lmbn*, were made (Fig. 91).[32] It is made of a deep-blue piece of clear chalcedony, which Professor Clifford Frondel of the Department of Geology of Harvard University terms exceptional in depth of color and translucency— quite rare, indeed, and undoubtedly highly valued. The letters, incised in a very formal manner, mean "Belonging to Mibneh" or "Miben." This is a shortened form of a name that once may have been "Mibneyahu" or "Mibne-El," meaning "Creature of Yahweh" or "Creature of God." Below the letters is a symbol that once probably looked like a mace, stood upright, and was the symbol of a Mesopotamian deity. Now it is only a decorative device, though it is the first time it has been found on a seal in this manner.

Both in 1960 and in 1962, in the fill between the earliest Samaritan level and the latest Israelite, we found pieces of pottery that belonged in neither. In 1960 we were almost certain that there was a lost or eroded stratum belonging to the sixth century B.C. The foundation for the round house, 1127, referred to above was the first time we encountered an architectural element which we felt could be ascribed to the period we now call the town of Stratum V. In Field IX a definite level throughout could be discerned. Construction is characterized by bricks made of a fine gray earth lacking any binding material and laid either on the ground or on a single foundation course of field stones. The bricks are square, *ca.* 25 to 30 cm. (*ca.* 11¾ in.) on a side and 15 cm. (5⅞ in.) thick. Floors were made of coarse marl cement with a rather rough surface. Everywhere, both in Fields IX and VII, there is evidence of poverty. Lines of debris in Field IX suggest that the occupation was terminated by fire during Persian times.

Fortunately a number of pieces of imported black- and red-figured vases were found in the debris with local Stratum V sherds (Fig. 113). They are treated briefly in Appendix 6 below by Nancy R. Lapp, who finds that they all are to be dated between *ca.* 525 and 475 B.C. The latest cannot be much before 480 B.C., so that the end of Stratum V must have taken place about that time or a little later. That age is a dark one as far as the history of Palestine is concerned, and we simply do not know what happened. We know that Bethel, Gibeon and Gibeah have pottery similar to the local wares in Stratum V, and all four sites may have had their history interrupted in the same period. In any case, Shechem's tell was to remain unoccupied for nearly one hundred fifty years. The reason we know so little about Strata V and VI is that during that period they were eroded by weather and farming.

A number of seal impressions, one seal and a very old coin from Stratum V are objects of special interest. In Fig. 92 are seven jar handles with a peculiar stamp on them. Nos. 1 and 2, 5 and 6 all appear to have been made by the same stamp, and it is not improbable that all of them were. The egg-shaped design with cross-bar in the center, ear-like projections at the top, and seven straight marks below are somewhat enigmatic. The jars probably contained wine, and the stamp with equal probability designated the vineyard from which the wine came.[33]

Fig. 93 shows another jar handle of Stratum V with the

impression of a stamp bearing a rather crude depiction of a roaring lion. Note also the ivory scaraboid with similar motif in Fig. 82 (No. 7). The fill in which it was found contained such a mixture of things that the seal could date anywhere between the ninth and third centuries B.C. Yet the motif of the roaring lion suggests the same period.[34]

Fig. 94 is a small lump of hard clay bearing a Persian seal impression. On the back were the impressions of a papyrus document to which it was attached; the object was the actual seal affixed to a papyrus document, whether official or private we cannot say. The figure is that of the king as a hunter, a common motif on Persian seals. The symbol to the left may represent the Zoroastrian deity Ahura-Mazda.

In Fig. 95 are obverse and reverse of one of the oldest coins found thus far in Palestine. It came from the faraway Greek island of Thasos. Its presence at Shechem, together with the pieces of imported Greek pottery, show that close commercial relations with Greece had begun by the last quarter of the sixth century and continued during the fifth. Lamia Rustum Shehadeh, a Lebanese graduate student in the Department of Near Eastern Languages and Literature of Harvard University, has prepared the following description and analysis of this unique object in Palestinian archaeology:

> The coin is B56, Reg. 6, discovered in mixed debris in Field I, Area 4. It is made of an alloy of silver and white gold (electrum), is 2 cm. in diameter and weighs 145 grains.
>
> *Obverse.* Silenus in a kneeling-running position is carrying off a nymph. An ancient incision across the coin cleaves the head of Silenus in two. There is no border.
>
> *Reverse.* A quarter incuse square; no border.
>
> The type is characteristic of the coins of Thasos in the late sixth century B.C. Thasos was rich in wine and its main deity was Dionysius, the god of wine. Its main cult was the worship of Silenus, companion of Dionysius. This type is represented on the city's earliest coins, *ca.* 560–465 B.C.[35]
>
> The way the type is adapted to the field by making Silenus kneel is important in dating this coin. It was the custom in the early period of coinage among the Greeks to adapt the type to the field, as in reverting the head of

an animal, or in a "heraldic arrangement," or the so-called
kneeling (actually running) figures. This method continued to be used until the figure was represented in its natural attitude and the circular field was filled up by legends,
symbols and the like.[36]

The incision across the coin was common in the earliest
coins of Greece. It was done to test the genuineness of the metal
at a time when coinage was new and its value not trusted. Another coin of the same general period as ours is an Attic silver
tetradrachma, found at Giv'at Ram (Sheikh Bader) in western
Jerusalem. It belongs to a coin series minted by Peisistratus in
Paeonia between 555 and 459 B.C.[37]

The commercial relationship between Greece and Palestine
in this early period is not well known. One might suppose that
all of the Greek material described above should date before
or during the Persian attempts to conquer Greece in 490 and 480
B.C., but this is by no means certain.

10

The Samaritans at Shechem

At the end of the first season of excavation in 1956 it seemed clear that the Shechem tell remained unoccupied throughout most of the Persian period of the fifth and fourth centuries B.C. It was also clear, however, that a great number of people had lived there during the third and second centuries B.C. The question was then posed: Why this extensive reoccupation of a deserted mound? This would be a story of interest if we could reconstruct it. And why was the mound again deserted by the first century, so that when Jesus met the Samaritan woman at Jacob's Well, there could have been nothing more than a village around the spring—one comparable to modern Balâṭah?

Finding answers to these questions was complicated by two considerations: (1) The source material for the history of Palestine in the intertestamental period is both scanty and full of problems; and (2) no one as yet knew enough about the pottery of the country during this dark age to enable him to date any discoveries with confidence or precision. In 1956 and 1957 my own judgments about dating this period were based on very few criteria, none of which was precise. I was well acquainted with a large bowl of the Persian period which had a series of ridges or "corrugations" down the outside. In the surface pottery of the East Gate a species of this bowl seemed to be present, but with only one ridge which served as a kind of collar at the rim. Hence I guessed that we were at the end of the series and not earlier than the fourth to third centuries. There were many fragments of black-glazed Greek pottery which I knew to be post-Persian and pre-Roman. Lamps were made on Greek models, examples of the old Palestinian saucer lamps being rare. A certain jar-rim type found might be a predecessor of one found at Bethel in 1934, where I had my first experience in field work; this Bethel type was closely similar to the jars in the first cave where Dead Sea Scrolls had been found. Furthermore, Qumran, the community center of the Scroll people, had recently been excavated by Père R. de Vaux. A study of the pottery dump at that site confirmed my impression that these late Shechem common dishes, jugs and jars were earlier than those at Qumran. Consequently, the final end of Shechem as a city could not have been much later than about 100 B.C.[1]

Fortunately, we were at work in the historical period when stamped coinage was now used for money. The excavations have produced a large number of coins. Except for the early coin of the Stratum V period, mentioned in the preceding chapter, the earliest of the series is from the late fourth century. Two floor levels, for example, were discovered by Lawrence Toombs in 1957 immediately under the surface of the ground above the Laba'yu and Abimelech period guardrooms of the East Gate. On the lowest level was a saucer lamp of the Persian period type, together with a coin of Alexander the Great (ca. 333–323 B.C.). Altogether we have found a large number of coins of Ptolemy I, one of Alexander's generals, who ruled Egypt and Palestine after the death of the great conqueror. A small hoard of fifteen of his coins, dating between 305 and 285 B.C., was found together on the east slope in Field I during 1956.[2] Our most spectacular coin discovery, however, came in 1960 when a small jug was discovered in Field VII which was filled with thirty-five silver tetradrachmas, representing every Ptolemy from I to V (Fig. 96). One belonged to Ptolemy I (312–285 B.C.); sixteen and probably three more were of Ptolemy II (285–246 B.C.), six of them dated to the year of issue; one was of Ptolemy III (246–221 B.C.); two bear the name of Ptolemy IV (221–204 B.C.); four and probably eight more were of Ptolemy V (204–181 B.C.). Two of the Ptolemy V coins were dated, one in 198 B.C. and the other in 193 B.C.[3]

It was Ptolemy V who lost Palestine to Antiochus III (223–187 B.C), a monarch of the Seleucid Dynasty which ruled Syria. Most of the second-century coins found, therefore, bear the names of the Seleucid kings. The latest coin which has been found in context bears the town name Antiochia (Ptolemais, Akke; modern Acre) and is dated 112–111 B.C.[4] Thus our coins confirmed the conclusions already derived from pottery study: namely, Shechem was resettled as a city not long before Alexander the Great and ceased to exist not long after *ca.* 110 B.C.

Between the 1957 and the 1960 campaigns one young member of the staff, Paul W. Lapp, who had been working for his doctorate under Dr. Albright until the latter's retirement, returned to Harvard Divinity School to complete his work for the degree. He found it possible to arrange a critically dated corpus of Palestinian pottery from the last two centuries B.C. and the first century A.D.[5] In doing so he solved the problem of the stratigraphy of debris over, in and under the house in Field II, with the result that a sizable group of pottery from the second half of the second century B.C. was now distinguished as characterizing our Stratum I. During the 1960 and 1962 campaigns three additional building periods were discerned, to which we were able to give approximate dates. For historical reasons to be given below it was now believed possible to date the beginning of the new city in 331 B.C., and to suggest its end *ca.* 107 B.C. The stratification, then, may now be listed as follows:

Stratum IV B and A—331 B.C.–*ca.* 250 B.C.
Stratum III B and A—*ca.* 250–190 B.C.
Stratum II—*ca.* 190–150 B.C.
Stratum I—*ca.* 150–107 B.C.

1. The Samaritan Reoccupation of Shechem (Stratum IV)

During the third and second centuries B.C. the area around ¹ m was held by a people whose religion was an offshoot Judaism centered in Jerusalem. When Nehemiah was busy in Jerusalem getting the fortification walls rebuilt *ca.* 440 B.C., he was bitterly opposed by the governors of neighboring Persian provinces, who did not wish to see Jerusalem re-created as a rival. One of them was Sanballat, the governor of Samaria (Nehemiah 4 and 6), whose reactions give the impression that he was a man of considerable strength and vigor. The Jews, in their newly fortified Jerusalem with their newly rebuilt temple, wanted nothing to do with him or with his people. It stands to reason that the rebuilding of Shechem was the work of Samaritans, and they appear to have done a very thorough job of it. Within the course of time they even built a temple for themselves, a rival to the temple in Jerusalem, on the top of Mt. Gerizim above the rebuilt Shechem.

Our primary evidence of their work in the first period is at the East Gate. The Middle Bronze orthostats were known; the sunken street between them was reused; and we know that at least the south tower was rebuilt. We do not know how extensive the rebuilding was because at the edge of the tell only a fragment of a rebuilt wall behind the southeastern pair of orthostats was discovered (Fig. 97). Other evidence clearly suggests, however, that Wall B was reused. Its stone socket was evidently preserved in good shape, and the Samaritans needed only to add a new brick superstructure. The street seems to have turned southward along the ridge outside the gate, just as it had in earlier times (see Figs. 98 and 108).

It was on the bank in front of the gate, however, that the most vivid evidence of hard work in refortifying the city was present. Wall A here was still standing to a considerable height, though evidently this was not the case in Field III. The slope was leveled and cemented in place in a manner quite similar to the cemented glacis at the end of the Middle Bronze Age. In fact, the new Samaritan one cut through all debris of the intervening centuries and was placed directly on the fill of the original Middle Bronze glacis.

During the course of Stratum IV on the slope there appeared on it a layer of orange-red brick debris, with many fragments of brick and charcoal. This brick debris had been smoothed down the slope, so that it fell over and filled in behind the surviving stump of Wall A. Over the debris a new surfacing of the slope was created. From this we infer that during the course of the late fourth or early third century fighting had taken place and the brick superstructure of the East Gate had fallen down the slope. If so, then the brick is that of early Stratum IV fortification. It is very different from earlier Bronze and Iron Age brick found on the site. It is red in color, indicating a kiln-fired product, and in size is roughly square, *ca.* 15 to 20 cm. on a side. Figures 98 and 99 show sections through the debris on the bank in Strata IV and III, and the new preparation of the slope against the stone base of Wall B in Stratum III. Figure 100 shows a bin or silo, evidently belonging to Stratum IV A in Area 1 near the eastern edge of our 1956 trench. Below it the plastered slope of the bank descended so steeply as to lead one to suspect that a dry fosse had been created here after Wall A had been covered over. The filling of the fosse with black earth and covering over the silo installation represent a leveling of the area for people who evidently lived outside the fortifications. Over the silo (Fig. 100) there was a fill and then a pavement with the small stone bowl, shown in Fig. 101. This appears to have been put in place some time during the course of Stratum III.

Precisely how the mound was refortified on the west and north is not known, and previous excavation makes it now impossible to find out. There is a probability that the surviving fragments of brick superstructure left by Sellin over the outer piers of the Northwest Gate, derive from the Samaritan refortification, but we have no way of being sure.

Within the city only a few fragments of Strata I and II have survived the centuries of cultivation and erosion. The two phases of Stratum IV and the two of Stratum III, however, are still present. Yet the builders of Stratum III so thoroughly demolished the ruins of IV that in Field VII not a single coherent building can be reconstructed. Floors are to be found, but most walls have been robbed of their stone for subsequent building. Figure 102 shows a large and very well made column base still in place. It indicates that in the city of Stratum IV the Samaritans had erected a sizable building deemed sufficiently important for so large a column in the doorway. Yet in the area excavated every vestige of this building had been destroyed by subsequent builders.

From this fragmentary evidence in Fields I and VII, then, we are led to conclude that the rebuilding of Shechem at the end of the fourth century was a major work that involved a complete city, its refortification and the construction of major public buildings. The evidence of the poverty of part of the new population, however, was clear in Field IX. Here two phases were present, but there was no sign of major building activity whatever. In the earliest, IV B, there were only mud-brick huts, some of them perhaps little more than tents, judging from the insubstantial foundations. While the public works were rapidly carried out, the people who lived in Field IX did not fare well at all.

The Reason for the Samaritan Construction of Shechem[6]

The question as to the historical reason for, and meaning of, this sudden and elaborate reconstruction of the city at the end of the fourth century necessitates a study of such historical sources as we have for the period. The difficulty, however, is that the worth of these sources is difficult to ascertain, and there has been no agreement whatever on any reconstruction of the events connected with the Samaritans, the establishment of their temple on Mt. Gerizim, or their relation to the cities of Samaria and Shechem. Yet we now have one definite historical datum that must be explained: for the sudden and extensive reconstruction of a "dead" city there must have been some reason. To find and to answer the question about Shechem, we must attempt a historical analysis of part of the debated material.

The primary source of difficulty is Josephus, the historian of the Jewish people who wrote toward the end of the first century A.D. In his *Antiquities XI*, 302 ff., he presents a story of the high priest Jaddua and a brother, named Manasseh, who are supposed to be living in the time of Alexander the Great. Yet it is quite obvious that Josephus believes this Jaddua to be the successor to Johanan and the last high priest mentioned by the Chronicler (Neh. 12:11, 22). Furthermore, a leading figure in the drama is a Sanballat who is governor of Samaria, one easily confused with the contemporary and adversary of Nehemiah.[7] In any event, a paraphrastic interpretation of Josephus' story is as follows:

Darius of Persia (Darius III, 336–331 B.C.; not Darius II,

423–404 B.C.) sent to Samaria a man named Sanballat to be governor or satrap, a Cuthaean from which race, says Josephus, the Samaritans came. This Sanballat, in order to cement good will with the Jews in Jerusalem, gave his daughter Nikaso to a certain Manasseh, brother of high priest Jaddua. The elders in Jerusalem, however, resented this marriage to a foreigner; and Manasseh had to go to his father-in-law and tell him that the marriage had to be annulled. Thereupon Sanballat, confident of the good will and favor of Darius, promised Manasseh many favors, including the high priesthood of the Samaritans. So Manasseh stayed with Sanballat, thinking that Darius would finally give him the high priestly office. Many from Jerusalem deserted to Manasseh, and Sanballat gave them money, land and places to live. The difficulty, however, was that Sanballat and Manasseh were sure that Darius would defeat Alexander the Great. When the opposite happened, and when in 332 B.C. Alexander was besieging Tyre, Sanballat went to see him, offered him 8,000 Samaritans to assist the siege, and accepted his rule. In return Alexander gave his consent for the Samaritans to build a temple on Mt. Gerizim, for Sanballat pleaded that he had with him Manasseh, brother of the high priest, together with many of his countrymen. It was also an advantage to Alexander to have the Jews split into two groups instead of being united, because they had always caused trouble to their rulers. So the temple was built and Manasseh was appointed its high priest. But before matters proceeded further, Sanballat died, after Alexander had spent seven months on the siege of Tyre and two months on that of Gaza.

Ralph Marcus, in his analysis of Josephus' narrative about Alexander in Palestine,[8] accepts the opinion that Josephus uses three different sources: one treats the Samaritans and another the Jews, with neither taking much account of their neighbors. The third source is definitely hostile to the Samaritans. The first is the source just summarized regarding the origin of the Samaritan temple at the time of Alexander the Great.

Josephus' use of the second source begins in *Antiquities*, XI, 326; it tells the story of Alexander's visit to Jerusalem after the conclusion of the siege of Gaza in the fall of 332 B.C. The story is a colorful narrative about Alexander's plan to subdue

Jerusalem, but he is so overcome by the extraordinary dignity and the religious (non-military) nature of his reception that he saves the city and accords the Jews special privileges, including the privilege of living by their own laws and the non-payment of tribute in the seventh year. He is said to be especially impressed when shown the Book of Daniel containing a prophecy concerning himself! Marcus concludes after analysis that this narrative is unhistorical, that Alexander never went to Jerusalem, that the source from which the story comes was composed after Julius Caesar's expedition against Egypt, and that the details of the two generals' expeditions have been mixed.[9]

Finally in Book XI, 340 ff., we come on the third, or anti-Samaritan, source. This tells us that the Samaritans, "whose chief city at that time was Shechem (*Sikima*), which lay beside Mt. Garizein and was inhabited by apostates from the Jewish nation, seeing that Alexander had so signally honored the Jews, decided to profess themselves Jews. For such is the nature of the Samaritans, as we have already shown somewhere above.[10] When the Jews are in difficulties, they deny that they have any kinship with them, thereby indeed admitting the truth, but whenever they see some splended bit of good fortune come to them, they suddenly grasp at the connection with them, saying that they are related to them and tracing their line back to Ephraim and Manasseh, the descendants of Joseph." So now as Alexander left Jerusalem, the Samaritans met him, here called "the Shechemites," bringing along the soldiers whom Sanballat had sent earlier, invited him to come to Shechem to do honor to their temple, and to remit the seventh-year taxes. Alexander deferred decision, but took Sanballat's soldiers with him to Egypt, where he gave them allotments of land. After the death of Alexander and the division of his empire, the temple on Mt. Gerizim remained. Thus it was always a place of refuge for anyone who got into trouble in Jerusalem. Such a man "would flee to the Shechemites, saying that he had been unjustly expelled."

This third source would appear related to the second in the common concern with the remission of the taxes during the Sabbatical year. And we note that in this source Shechem is explicitly said to be the capital city of the Samaritans, who are also called "Shechemites" (*Sikimîtai*), while no mention is made of the city of Samaria, which had been the capital of the Persian province.

We now turn to Quintius Curtius' *History of Alexander,* the only work in Latin devoted exclusively to the life of that monarch that has survived, one probably written during the first half of the first century A.D., though the date is debated. Here we learn that Alexander placed one Andromachus as governor over Coelê-Syria,[11] and that the Samaritans had burned him alive, while Alexander was in Egypt.[12] "To avenge his murder, he hastened to the spot with all possible speed, and on his arrival those who had been guilty of so great a crime were delivered to him."[13]

To this bit of information Eusebius,[14] Jerome and Syncellus[15] add that Alexander took Samaria and settled Macedonians in the city. The only trouble with this information is that another passage in Eusebius,[16] dated by the Olympiad 121 (296–295 B.C.), says: "Demetrius Poliorcetes, king of Asia, captured all of the Samaritan city which had been settled by Perdiccas." Though attempts have been made to harmonize the two passages, Marcus concludes:[17]

> There is, therefore, a contradiction between the two passages in Eusebius; in one he says that Alexander settled the Macedonians in Samaria, in the other that Perdiccas did so. The historicity of the former fact must therefore be judged on the basis of the statements of Curtius and Syncellus alone. Now Syncellus is not a particularly trustworthy source for this period, while Curtius merely says that Alexander appointed Menon as prefect in place of Andromachus. We cannot be certain that Alexander was in Samaria for any length of time.

From all this it seems to me that we may accept the following as fairly certain:

(1) The substantial reliability of Josephus' first source about the Samaritans: namely, the story about the founding of the temple on Mt. Gerizim by permission of Alexander the Great, and about the 8,000 Samaritan soldiers given to aid Alexander's campaign, whom he settled in Egypt as a provincial guard.

(2) The statement of Curtius that while Alexander was in Egypt the Samaritans cremated alive Andromachus, prefect of Coelê-Syria, to which the territory of the Samaritans belonged.

Now regarding the skepticism of Marcus concerning the Eusebius-Syncellus information that Alexander retaliated by destroying Samaria and giving it over to the Macedonians, we must make the following observations:

(1) The Samaritan revolt was the first trouble recorded for Alexander after his conquest of Syria-Palestine and Egypt. One would have expected a prompt and strong reaction from him.

(2) At Samaria beautifully constructed round towers were built in this general period, and J. W. Crowfoot has argued strongly (in my opinion successfully), that they represent a completely non-Palestinian type of fortification, and that their prototypes are to be sought in the Greek world.[18] Historically, then, they would most easily be explained as having been erected as a renewal of the city's fortifications by settlers from Greece—thus by inference supporting the Eusebius-Syncellus report. (Yet the Perdiccas reference cited above could also provide a historical setting.)

(3) Herod the Great built the great temple to Augustus and a Doric stadium in Samaria, at which time it was a completely pagan city. It is doubtful whether he would have done so had not the city had a long pagan history. It was certainly non-Samaritan in any event (though Eusebius' second reference to a settlement of Macedonians by Perdiccas in 296/295 B.C. could as easily account for this as a settlement by Alexander).

(4) When Alexander conquered a region, it would appear that he settled some soldiers in it, gave them land and thus expected them to defend it and remain loyal to him. There is thus nothing intrinsically wrong with the Alexander settlement record, and for that matter nothing wrong with a later Perdiccas settlement either. In the case of Samaria Alexander did not need to leave soldiers there originally because 8,000 Samaritan soldiers were given him. But after trouble, what would be more natural than to settle a garrison in the area's former capital city and with the garrison, his own government official to be in charge?

(5) The problem of the reoccupation of Shechem demands explanation. It seems to me that the simplest view is provided by taking the Eusebius-Syncellus statement at face value about Alexander's destruction of Samaria and turning it over to Macedonians. This would mean that the Samaritans were forced to

establish a new capital, and the logical place was old Shechem, at a time when Samaritans were so anxious to maintain their claims over against the Jews and Jerusalem. This would account for the following:

(a) The archaeological evidence from Shechem which suggests its re-establishment not later than the last third of the fourth century;

(b) The Samaritans appear to have made elaborate attempts to refortify the city, surely in order both to make it defensible against Judean threats particularly, and by implication to create as strong a rival to Jerusalem as Samaria had been for the past six and one-half centuries;

(c) The third or anti-Samaritan source in Josephus would thus have solid historical tradition behind it in claiming by implication that Shechem[19] was the Samaritan capital in the Alexander period.[20]

At about the same time that this reinterpretation of the events which led to the rebuilding of Shechem as the Samaritan capital appeared in print,[21] a remarkable discovery gave strong support to my contention that we must take the late tradition about Alexander's destruction of Samaria in 331 B.C. very seriously. In April, 1962, news of a new manuscript discovery came to Père de Vaux, Mr. Yusuf Saad, Curator of the Palestine Archaeological Museum, and Dr. Paul W. Lapp of the American Schools of Oriental Research in Jerusalem. Dr. Lapp identified a papyrus sample from the find as written in an Aramaic script of the fourth century B.C. He also found that the city of Samaria was clearly mentioned on it. The discovery had been made by the indefatigable Ta'amireh Bedouin—the people who had found the Dead Sea Scrolls—in a cave in the Wadi ed-Dâliyeh. This is located about a dozen miles north of Jericho in the almost inaccessible clefts rising to the western hills from the Jordan valley.

On November 19 my colleague, Frank M. Cross, Jr., had completed negotiations for the purchase of several papyrus scrolls for the Palestine Archaeological Museum. The money for the purchase came from a fund set up by Mrs. Elizabeth Bechtel in the American Schools of Oriental Research, for which Professor Cross was the representative. Thus, while the scrolls would remain in Jordan, the purchase secured the publication rights for the American Schools of Oriental Research. Within a short time Professor Cross had identified the manuscripts as economic documents from Samaria, some of them explicitly dated. One, for example, has the date: "the twentieth day of Adar, year 2, (the same year being) the accession year of Darius the king, in Samaria . . ." Since there is only one Persian king who died in the second year of his reign, Arses, the document was written on March 18, 335 B.C., a year which was also the accession year of Darius III. A coin found with the scrolls in the cave was determined to belong to the last years of Darius III, who reigned from 335 to his displacement by Alexander the Great in 331 B.C.

From January 7 to 18, 1963, Dr. Lapp began the excavation of the cave amidst great difficulties of supply, dust and bats. The Bedouin reported that they had counted some 300 skeletons lying on mats in the cave. The excavation turned up additional papyrus fragments, skeletons of men, women and children of all ages, large quantities of cloth, some of it beautifully embroidered, wood, olive and date pits, sycamine nuts and mat fragments. There was also found a quantity of homogeneous pottery which in type immediately precedes our earliest Samaritan pottery found in Shechem IV A and B.

What were all those Samaritans doing in that cave so far from home? The most reasonable hypothesis is that they had fled Alexander the Great's punitive expedition against Samaria in 331 B.C., the story reported by the late traditions mentioned above. As Dr. Lapp explains it, Alexander's troops evidently found the hiding place of the fugitives from Samaria and suffocated them by building a large fire at the cave's mouth. In any case, the refugees had perished simultaneously.[22]

Shechem, then, was Samaria's replacement as the Samaritan capital. This explains why so large a building program, the creation literally of a new city, was carried out in a comparatively brief period.

The City's Last Years

What caused the disruption in the city's life at the end of Stratum IV A we do not know. A new surface was prepared on the slope, including a quantity of marl-filled dark earth which carried the slope up against Wall B (Figs. 103 and 108). The comparatively steep angle of the layers of the earth ascending the slope to Wall B and the complete covering of Wall A make one suspect that the street which passed through the gate now for the first time came down the bank directly east or northeast, though no sign of it now remains.

In Field VII the terraces by now had been eliminated entirely. A street ran northeast-southwest across the field. Houses, one with a flagstone court, could be entered on each side of the street. Street walls were about 1 m. thick and the inner walls 70 to 80 cm. thick. They all had nicely laid foundations consisting of two rows of stones filled with smaller stones. The walls above these stone bases were of brick, different in type from that used in the fortification, one example being flat and square like Middle Bronze brick (*ca.* 33 cm. on a side). In Field II a very fine house was erected in Stratum III, as earlier noted (Fig. 104), two rooms of it surviving in the area excavated. Its walls had been plastered, and each room was painted a different color. Where an interior door had hung in one of them, an iron key and three iron nails from it survived, though the wood was gone (Fig. 105). This house was to remain in use for over a century, until the end of the city's life.

Two phases of Stratum III, the second (III A) being a rebuilding of the first with a slight rearrangement of interior rooms, appeared in Field VII. New floors were installed in III A including a new flagstone paving in a court. The hoard of thirty-five silver tetradrachmas mentioned above (*see* Fig. 96) was buried in its small jug some two feet below the surface levels of Stratum III. It evidently belonged to someone who lived at the end of City III's life. The latest coin in the hoard was minted in 193 B.C., and on this basis we have suggested a date of about 190 B.C. for the end of the stratum. We had assumed that warfare destroyed the city in 198 B.C., or in the year immediately preceding, when the armies of Ptolemy V and Antiochus III had been struggling for the control of Palestine. This war culminated in the battle of Paneas and the defeat of Ptolemy V in 198 B.C.

Josephus tells us, however, that shortly after the defeat of Ptolemy V, Antiochus III made a treaty of friendship with him and gave his daughter Cleopatra in marriage to the Egyptian monarch in 193 B.C. (The more famous Cleopatra lived 150 years later.) To Ptolemy the young woman brought as a dowry the assignment of Coelê-Syria, Samaria (which included Shechem), Judea and Phoenicia.[23] Ralph Marcus, in a note on this Josephus story, observes that this dowry gift is mentioned in several ancient sources, one of which says that Antiochus acted so generously in order to be free to war on the Romans. Yet whether the assignment of revenues of lower Syria, Phoenicia and Palestine to Ptolemy lasted very long may be doubted. In any case, both kings died within a short time, and Palestine was firmly in control of the Seleucids.

With the end of City III all attempts at a strong fortification of the Samaritan capital ceased. Figure 103 shows a place south of the East Gate where the stones of Wall B were removed, possibly in order to build the insubstantial tower which was erected directly east of the East Gate in the latter part of City III or early in City II (Fig. 106). Little remains of Stratum II, and we have no knowledge of the nature of the city or the reasons for the shift to Stratum I. A sherd belonging either to Stratum III or II (*ca.* 250–150 B.C.) is shown in Fig. 107. On it a Samaritan, named Simeon, had inscribed his name in Greek letters before the vessel was baked reading "Simionide[s]."

The evidence for tracing the history of Shechem during its last century is meager. As is the case with all mounds which remain unoccupied for any lengthy period of time, the surface layers were destroyed by cultivation. It is probable that Shechem was unharmed by Antiochus IV Epiphanes (175–164 B.C.), the king who caused such trouble in Jerusalem in his attempt forcibly to stamp out Judaism and to hellenize the Jews. Josephus says that after the terrible events of 168 B.C. in Jerusalem, the Samaritans made a special appeal to Antiochus to spare their temple on Mt. Gerizim, asking that it be known as the temple of Zeus Hellenios and saying that they themselves were not Jews at all in origin.[24]

The end of Shechem as a city was evidently brought about by the Jews from Jerusalem. John Hyrcanus (134–104 B.C.), as the leader of an independent Jewish state with its capital at Jerusalem, achieved a position of considerable power. Deciding to put an end to the Samaritan rivalry, in 128 B.C. he destroyed the Samaritan temple on Mt. Gerizim, and in 107 B.C. he campaigned successfully against Samaria.[25] The final destruction of Shechem and the covering over of Wall A on the west and of the ruins of the Northwest Gate were probably his work at about the same time.[26]

With this destruction the biography of Shechem comes to its end. The Samaritans moved elsewhere, and, when they did so, they left behind them a curtain rung down on a fascinating past. Having ceased to pursue political goals or to create trouble for anyone, they have been permitted to live in Nablus as a special colony to this day, though they are greatly reduced in numbers. When we tell them about our excavations and show them the work of their ancestors, they can only shake their heads sadly, because their tradition has lost all memory of the site.

Appendix 1

Principles of Field Technique

The success or failure of an archaeological expedition depends on the skill of its field supervisors and their assistants. Since the act of digging destroys evidence almost as soon as it is uncovered, the expedition relies on the correctness of their technique, the keenness of their observation, and the accuracy of their reporting to preserve otherwise irreplaceable data.

When at 5 A.M. sharp the supervisor picks up the deep air-travel bag which contains the miscellaneous tools of his trade[1] and walks up the slope of the mound to join his crew of workmen, he is about to face a complex and demanding set of scientific problems. In essence he must try to do three jobs at the same time: direct the excavation, record his findings and interpret

---

[1] A notebook in which alternate pages are millimeter paper (for recording the progress of the excavation), a pottery notebook, small bags for the objects recovered, labels for the pottery baskets and for marking levels in the balk, bent nails for fastening labels in the balk, several lengths of stout cord, half a dozen nine-inch spikes, a steel tape and a cloth tape both graduated in the metric system, a plumb bob, a spirit level, a trowel, a paintbrush, a handpick and a good knife, as well as pencils, erasers and a ballpoint pen.

what he sees so that it makes architectural and historical sense. In doing this the supervisor constantly faces three difficulties: the top-to-bottom hazard, the surface obsession and myopia.

(1) In archaeology everything appears upside down, so that the supervisor sees the future before he is allowed to look at the past. He encounters the effect before the cause, the destruction of a city before its foundation. His technique must make allowance for this wrong-end-to view of events and provide him with a way of going back at any point to recheck what has already been done.

(2) Working on a nearly flat surface tends to obscure the obvious fact that the structures being excavated once stood in three dimensions, and that in what now appears as a few inches of dark soil half a dozen generations of human beings lived and died. In the face of this difficulty, the supervisor must adopt a method which allows him to think, to dig and to report three-dimensionally.

(3) The supervisor lives in a small world. The painstaking observation demanded of him tends to shrink his vision to the small area under his immediate charge. Unfortunately, however, the ancient builders lacked the foresight to erect their structures in neat five-meter squares. Their walls run through the balks into squares being dug by other supervisors, and the structures of one area have meaning only as part of the city as a whole. Alertness to what is going on around him in his own and other fields is a necessary qualification for successful field supervision.

Archaeological technique, which to the novice often seems meticulous to the point of being finicky, is in reality a common-sense method of minimizing errors which can easily arise from these three sources.

The basic strategy of the supervisor is simple enough. His aim is to uncover the whole of a contemporary level at the same time. He would like to have the walls and floors of a building, and the outside surfaces (streets, courtyards and the like), which were in use with it, all exposed simultaneously. The whole building complex can then be drawn in plan and photographed as a unit, after which the excavator is free to remove it and go down to the next level. If the ancient city had been built on a flat surface this process would be relatively easy, but in fact there are as many humps and hollows in an ancient town as in a modern farmyard. Consequently, the excavator must dig, not by depth below surface (which is usually absolutely meaningless), but by the color and texture of the soil. If, for example, he encounters a layer of fine, loose, reddish earth, produced by the weathering of baked mud-brick, he will take off that layer in its entirety, no matter how irregular or uneven it may be. When it is removed, he will examine the surface below, determine its nature and composition and remove it, proceeding, thus, step by step until he reaches the level of a floor, a street or some other significant architectural feature.

Since the supervisor has no way of knowing what levels lie beneath his feet, he will not try to excavate the whole surface of his five-meter square at once. Instead he will make a small probe trench in one end of his square. When he has determined the sequence of levels in the small exploratory trench, he can more intelligently remove them from the entire square. In this process the supervisor does not work mechanically. He is perpetually asking himself questions. "What is the composition of this layer?" "Where did it come from?" "What is its function?" "How is it related to the walls and floors in the area?"

The great enemy of careful excavation is loose dirt lying in the square and masking the nature of the surfaces being dug. The constant cry of the supervisor is, therefore, "*Nadif*" ("clean it up").

This excavation technique yields a series of detailed plans, one for each of the successive occupation levels uncovered. The local plans can be linked together to give a plan of the entire field at each stage of occupation. The field plans may then be put in their place on the general plan of the mound and a composite picture of the city, stratum by stratum, built up. Every plan is accompanied by a sequence of black-and-white photographs, showing the various features of the level as they appeared in the course of excavation. These plans and photographs form the *horizontal* component of the record.

How may the vertical relationship of these plans to one another be determined and recorded? This is where the sides of the squares (the balks) play an all-important role. A field supervisor, staring at the side of the trench and mumbling to himself, is not touched by the sun. He is trying to relate what he is doing now to what he did last week. Or, more significantly, he is reversing the upside-down nature of his work and reasoning from cause to effect. The level which appeared during excavation as an unlovely jumble of brick and plaster is seen as the fallen wall of a house. The layer of charcoal above it appears clearly in the balk as the burned reeds and beams of a roof which fell in flames on the floor. The plasterlike layer is proved to be the floor of the house, for in the balk it runs up against the stone wall. And the compact gray earth layer under the plaster is recognizable as the make-up laid down and leveled up to take the floor. The excavator may have been aware of all this in the course of the digging. The point is that the balk makes this sequence *demonstrable*.

As an aid to both excavation and reporting the supervisor gives each soil layer as he comes to it a number in his notebook, and enters a full description of the layer opposite this number.[2] To assist his memory (especially since drying out causes unexpected changes in soil color) he labels each level in the balk with a tag, bearing the notebook number of that level. Each object found in the dig and every basket of pottery sent down to the washing shed is identified by the layer from which it came. Thus, every artifact is related to its appropriate level, and can be assembled for study together with all the other objects from the same level. In a sense, what the pottery experts are doing in their long hours of sorting and deliberating over sherds is attempting to date the soil layers which the field supervisors have isolated and identified.

Having produced and read his balk, the supervisor is not yet finished with it. He must now draw it accurately to scale on millimeter paper.[3] To do this he fastens a stout cord across the balk at some convenient place with nine-inch spikes, running it horizontal with a spirit level. This is his "datum line." From the same spikes, and parallel to the cord, he stretches a cloth tape,

[2] In the Shechem excavation numbers are assigned to walls, structures and loci. Soil layers are also given numbers in the field notes, though in the sections published in this book the numbers have not always been transferred to the plans.

[3] The scale used in "master sections" is normally 1:50. Where it is desirable to show more detail, esp. in the case of small subsidiary sections, or sections in crucial areas, 1:25 is used.

to give him the horizontal distances along the datum. Working from the line he draws the significant features of his balk, taking vertical distances from datum with a plumb line. The finished drawing is called a "section," and numerous examples appear in this book. The excavator does not wait until his square has reached bedrock before drawing his sections, but produces them in convenient stages, extending them downward as excavation proceeds. When the section of a cross-balk has been drawn and photographed the balk may be removed, but it is an inflexible rule not to take down a balk until it is properly recorded. The careful removal of a balk is often an invaluable check on the accuracy of interpretations already made.

With a frequency shattering to the supervisor's peace of mind, features (for example, a pit, a silo, a bench or a burial) turn up, isolated in the center of the square, where they will not appear in any section. As soon as the top of such a structure is observed the supervisor lays out a subsidiary section connecting this structure *at right angles* with one of the main sections. This anticipates problems which are bound to arise, viz. from what level was the structure built and what is the history of its repair and reuse? The digging itself may answer the questions conclusively, but only the subsidiary section, tying in with the main drawing, can *prove* the point in the final excavation report.

A "master section" (e.g. Fig. 108), running across a whole field, will include areas under the care of several supervisors. In this case it is desirable to have the section drawn by the professional hand of the chief architect, so that the drawing will be uniform in quality and will correspond in style with other master drawings in the final report. Where this procedure is adopted, the section is produced through a long series of consultations among the director, the chief architect, and the supervisors, while the work is still in progress. The critical judgment of half a dozen persons all intimately involved in the excavation and a number of notebook sections are thus combined to produce a result which is likely to be far more accurate than the interpretation of any single individual.[4]

---

[4] The comment on the Shechem East Gate Sections E–W found in Franken and Franken-Battershill, *A Primer of Old Testament Archaeology*, p. 12—"However it is not the excavator who has drawn this section, who ought to interpret all his material from it, studying the live section meticu-

Two notebooks, a sheaf of sections, and a dozen plans may seem a small reward for seven weeks of hard labor under a relentless sun, but these plans and sections, taken together, form the necessary three-dimensional record of the excavation, and are the framework around which the final definitive publication of the expedition will be built.

---

lously day by day as it grows, but his architect at the end of the season's work"—should be read in the light of the above paragraph. The sentence with which the "Primer" continues—"Moreover, here we can figure out the stratigraphy of this particular part of the site, but during the excavation no attempt was made to separate the finds from the various levels as they occurred in the drawing"—is simply false.

Appendix 2

Shechem in the Amarna Archive

In 1887 a collection of cuneiform tablets was found in Egypt among ruins 190 miles upriver from Cairo, which were to cause quite a sensation. The tablets came from Amarna, later identified as the ruins of Egypt's capital during the reign of the extraordinary Akhenaten (*ca.* 1364–1347). The Akkadian language had even been used in Egypt, at least for diplomatic correspondence, and some of the tablets showed that scribes were trained at the court to write the cuneiform script. For of the 377 texts, 22 are scribal exercises or (in the case of 4 of the texts) copies of myths done for practice by budding scribes. The remaining 355 are letters; 43 are exchanges between either Amenophis III or Akhenaten and rulers on a par with them—kings of Babylon, Assyria, Mitanni, Arzawa in Asia Minor, Cyprus and Hatti. All the rest involve vassals of Egypt who governed city-states in Syria and Palestine.

One of these city-states was Shechem. Strategically located in a sparsely settled region, Shechem dominated an extensive territory, and its ruler, Lab'ayu, was ready to extend his holdings, given the slightest opportunity. The Amarna Letters tell us very little directly about Shechem—it is mentioned by name only once—and even leave a trace of doubt that Lab'ayu really had his headquarters there; but that its fate was in his hands is made clear. After his death, two sons of his are found ranging over much of the same territory, although we cannot be sure they made Shechem their center; the one man who refers to himself as a son of Lab'ayu is at Pella. The greater part of our information about the city-state of Shechem, about Lab'ayu, and about his sons, comes from the complaints of neighbors. Lab'ayu and his sons themselves appear not to have had much occasion to complain to the court!

The 355 letters from Amarna doubtless formed only a part of the total correspondence concerning Syro-Palestine during the "Amarna period." The earliest letters in the collection came to Egypt during the final years of Amenophis III's reign, when the capital was at Thebes; a selection of the letters from that period was taken along to the new capital to serve as background for the running of the empire. Probably the great majority of the letters from the final years of Akhenaten were taken back to Thebes when the court returned thither shortly after Akhenaten's death. The letters in the Amarna collection, then, were not a full archive from the start. Furthermore, they were found by peasants who did not know their value, and it was some months before they were secured for proper study; it is reported that many tablets were lost in the interval.

Nevertheless, the historical picture which emerges from the archive as we have it makes fairly consistent sense, and it covers the entire period from the last few years of Amenophis III to the end of Akhenaten's seventeen-year reign, or from *ca.* 1370 to *ca.* 1345. We do not seem to have any letters from the central hill country of Palestine, however, which can be securely dated to the final years of this period.[1]

Letters concerning Lab'ayu and his sons are presented here in approximate chronological order. Uncertain words are italicized, while reconstructions of breaks in the text appear in brackets. Parentheses surround both glosses by the scribes and certain explanations offered by the editor.

[1] On the historical background of the Amarna Letters, on the chronology of the period and for full bibliography, *see* the author's *The Chronology of the Amarna Letters*, Baltimore, 1964.

Letter 244[2]

To the king, my lord and my sungod, say: Thus Biridiya, a true servant of the king. At the feet of the king,
my lord and my sungod, seven times and seven times I
fall. Let the king, my lord, know that since the archers
returned[3] Lab'ayu has shown me enmity. We are not able
to harvest our fields/ (harvest),[4] and we are not able to
go out of the gate/ (gate) because of Lab'ayu. If it be
known that you have not given archers, then behold he
will certainly set his face to take Megiddo. So let the king
rescue[5] his city, so that Lab'ayu will not seize it. Truly,
the city is doomed through death due to pestilence and
disease. Pray let the king give 100 guard-troops to watch
over his city. Then Lab'ayu will not seize it. Truly,
Lab'ayu has no other intention: he seeks to destroy
Megiddo.

[2] The basic publication of the Amarna Tablets is J. A. Knudtzon, *Die
El-Amarna-Tafeln,* Leipzig, 1915. He published 358 texts, and his numbering of them remains standard. Nineteen tablets have appeared since;
they are given numbers consecutively on up to 377 by most scholars,
after C. H. Gordon, *Orientalia,* XVI, 1947, pp. 1–2. The only English publication of the full corpus (not including 370–377, which appeared first in
the Gordon article) is S. A. B. Mercer, *The Tell el-Amarna Tablets,* 2 vols.;
Toronto, 1939. Of much greater importance is the work of W. F. Albright
in a series of articles (*see* the Bibliography in *The Chronology of the
Amarna Letters*), and in his translation of twenty-six of the letters in J. B.
Pritchard, ed., *Ancient Near Eastern Texts Relating to the Old Testament,*
Princeton, 1955, pp. 483–490, including 244, 245, 250, 252, 254, 256, 280,
289, 365, 366 and 369. The translations presented in this Appendix are
heavily dependent on Albright's work.

[3] The verb used here literally means "entered." The rest of the letter
makes clear that the archers have not just arrived; the implication is just
the opposite. Often in the letters the verb "to enter" means "to enter the
presence of the Pharaoh." That must be the meaning here also; the archers
have returned to Egypt.

[4] Or: "We are not able to pluck the wool." Often in the Amarna Letters, scribes use Canaanite words as glosses to elucidate the more difficult
Akkadian expressions, placing a diagonal mark with the stylus before the
gloss. Biridiya's scribe does this particularly often. Here the meaning of
the Canaanite word is "to harvest," but the Akkadian, *kasiga baqani,* is
difficult. The verb *baqanu* usually means "to pluck the wool from sheep,"
but it is used for plucking hair from one's beard and for stripping leaves
from plants. The word *kasiga* is here translated "field" on the basis of the
demonstration by E. A. Speiser, *Journal of the American Oriental Society*
LII, 1932, pp. 363 ff., that a similar word in the Nuzi tablets means "a
corner of a field." B. Meissner, in *Archiv für Orientforschung* V, 1928–1929,
p. 184, argues from a vocabulary text in which the two Akkadian words
appear as equivalent in meaning, that the whole expression simply means
"to pluck wool."

[5] Here and in other places in the letters, the verb *naqamu* means ap-

Biridiya is one of many city-state governors who bears an Indo-Aryan name. He writes to the court of Amenophis III in Egypt to complain of Lab'ayu's threat to Megiddo, a city located twenty-five miles north of Shechem. Biridiya had had a supporting force from Egypt to aid him, but they had been withdrawn. Egypt pursued a policy of letting the vassals work out their own affairs, at least as long as tribute poured in, and, in spite of repeated requests for a show of force by Egypt, we have few indications that Egyptian troops were much in evidence. It is noteworthy that a mere token force of a hundred men would have served Biridiya's purpose; this would have indicated clearly on whose side Egypt stood.

The Amarna Letters depict deplorable conditions for the subjects of the ruthless governors. A number of the letters note that illness is a serious problem, and even a healthy subject would have to fight in the ruler's defensive (or offensive) bands in the constant petty bickering, or work in the forced labor battalion (see Letter 365, also from Biridiya), or even be sold into slavery (see Letter 369 and the letters of Rib-Adda of Byblos, who complains regularly that he must sell his serfs into slavery in order to have grain enough to stay alive).

Megiddo was not Lab'ayu's only target. His own letters (see below) describe his being at Gezer, thirty miles southeast of Shechem. Shuwardata, from the Hebron area fifty miles south of Shechem, complains that Lab'ayu has troubled his cities. In Letter 366, Shuwardata tells of defeating the " 'Apiru-chief" (or the verb may mean he killed him). We will see later that Shuwardata could easily have been using this term to designate Lab'ayu, although we know that Shuwardata was not the cause of Lab'ayu's death.

Still another ruler, Bayadu, whose location is unknown, reports news of Lab'ayu. Unfortunately, the context is broken and the lines can be read in either of two ways: "Lab'ayu has taken him and he stands against the cities of the king, my lord," or "They have taken Lab'ayu, and they stand against the cities . . ." (237:2ff.). Two other letters, 249 and 263, mention

---

proximately what it means in biblical Hebrew, namely "to vindicate," which means to rescue the deserving and punish the disloyal. This yields such meanings as "rescue" and "preserve."

Lab'ayu in broken contexts; both imply that he has allied himself to Milkilu of Gezer and to the latter's father-in-law Tagu, who holds territory along the coastal plain just south of Mt. Carmel. There is the distinct implication in both cases that Lab'ayu is up to no good.

Letter 252[6]

> To the king, my lord, say: Thus Lab'ayu, thy servant. At the feet of my lord I fall. As to what thou hast written to me—"Are the men strong who have seized the city? How can the men be resisted?"—in combat the city was taken, although I had sworn a peace-oath, and, when I took the oath, a *rabū* (an Egyptian official) was with me. The city was taken and (so was) my god. I have been slandered/(attacked)[7] before the king, my lord.
>
> Further, when ants are smitten, they do not (simply) take (it), but they bite the hand of the man who smites them. How can I hesitate these days[8] when two of my cities have been seized?
>
> Further, if thou wert to command: "Now fall down beneath them and let them smite you," my enemy would be resisted. The men who seized the city (and) my god (or: the city of my god), despoilers of my father, indeed they would be resisted!

This letter replies to a dispatch from the court. The normal tone of such replies in the Amarna Letters is one of abject humility. Not so with Lab'ayu. The king's dispatch had at least shown an interest in his problem, and Lab'ayu intended to maintain his right. His right in this instance is connected with his ancestral town, since he considers the attackers to be despoilers of his father and reports that the image of his ancestral patron deity was taken. All of this in spite of his oath to maintain peace.

Lab'ayu hammers home his determination by using a marvelous proverb about the ant (recall Prov. 6:6 and 30:25). At the point where the proverb begins, the truculence of the letter is

[6] W. F. Albright, *BASOR* 89, Feb. 1943, pp. 29–32.

[7] The scribe began an Akkadian idiom which he only partially recalled; he gets it correct in 254:16 ("They eat my pieces"). His Canaanite gloss here makes it certain what he meant.

[8] Again the scribe mixed an idiom, starting with the singular word for "day" and then switching to a plural demonstrative adjective; we have to let the second word suggest his final intention.

heightened further in that the language shifts to Lab'ayu's native tongue, Canaanite, and stays in it to the end of the letter. The proverb is not the only one in the Amarna Letters. Tagu uses one about bricks in a wall in Letter 266. Such picturesque language affords a fascinating glimpse into the by no means unsophisticated world of fourteenth-century Canaan.

Letter 253

To the king, my lord and my sungod: Thus Lab'ayu, thy servant and the dust on which thou dost tread. At the feet of the king, my lord, seven times, seven times, I fall.[9] [I] have heard the words which the king, my lord, wrote to me on a tablet. [*Behold*, I] am the servant of the king, [as was] my [father] and my father's [father]—servants of the king from [*long ago*]. And I have [not] transgressed, nor have I sinned. Behold my transgression and behold my sin: that I entered the city of Gezer. Thus I said (or: say): "May the king show favor to us." And behold now there is no other intention than serving the king. So whatever the king says, I hear. Let the king, my lord, place me under the care of (that is: appoint me into the hand of) my commissioner [so as to] protect the city [of the king].

Lab'ayu's tone in this letter is much less defiant. He comes from a line of loyal governors and himself is loyal. Perhaps his forefathers reigned in the same city as he now holds, namely Shechem; in that case it is probably his ancestral city and hence the subject of Letter 252. About Lab'ayu's visit to Gezer we hear more in Letter 254.

Letter 254

To the king, my lord and my sungod: Thus Lab'ayu, thy servant and the dust on which thou dost tread. At the feet of the king, my lord and my sungod, seven times, seven times, I fall. I have heard the words which the king wrote to me; now who am I that the king should lose his land on my account? Look, I am a true servant of the king, and I have not transgressed, nor have I sinned, nor

---

[9] Much of the introductory paragraph of this tablet is broken, but Lab'ayu's name is certain and the rest is so formulaic as to be easily reconstructed.

have I held back my tribute, nor have I held back the
requests of my commissioner. Now they slander me (that
is: they eat my pieces) wickedly, but let not the king,
my lord, hold my transgression against me. Further, my
transgression is this, that I entered the city of Gezer and
said publicly:[10] "Will the king take what is mine and not
likewise what is Milkilu's?" I know the deeds of Milkilu
against me!

Further, the king has written concerning my son. I did
not know that my son was associating with the 'Apiru.
Now have I not given him into Addaya's hand?

Further, if the king were to write for my wife, how
could I withhold her? If the king were to write to me:
"Plunge a bronze dagger into your heart and die," how
could I but do the command of the king?

Year [3]2

In this letter, Lab'ayu's eloquence concerning his loyalty
reaches new heights, as he protests his regular performance of
all that he is supposed to do, and expresses horror that the king
could think otherwise of him. His son has been turned over to
Addaya, as the king has demanded. Addaya will appear again
in the correspondence of Abdu-Heba of Jerusalem, as an official
with headquarters at the Egyptian administrative center, Gaza.
He appears to have been (287:45 ff.) the outgoing commissioner
of central Palestine at that time; perhaps he is the one referred
to as commissioner earlier in 254 and in 253. It is noteworthy
that the 'Apiru are a sufficiently clear and present danger that
the court wants its vassals to avoid them, but it is interesting
that it is Lab'ayu's son, not Lab'ayu, who is accused of associating with them.

The blameless Lab'ayu admits one transgression. A rift has
developed between Milkilu and Lab'ayu, two men who are the
closest of allies from all other indications, and Lab'ayu sees that
Milkilu has accused him before the king. What Lab'ayu says he
has done is to proclaim in Milkilu's city that he thinks they
should both be treated in the same way. Perhaps Milkilu has
obtained some concession from Egypt, such as a relief from
tribute. Given the obscure meaning of all this, it may be perilous

---

10 With this adverb, the scribe employs a good Akkadian form. Just
a few lines before, on the adverb "wickedly," he used a good Canaanite-
Hebrew form, the infinitive absolute. This mixing is the most typical feature of the language of the Amarna Letters.

to speculate about Lab'ayu's words cited in Letter 253 ("May the king show favor to us" or possibly "The king has shown favor to us"). Perhaps Lab'ayu is asking that the king settle the dispute between the two crafty governors. We can also be sure that he is taking the opportunity to express his hope that he might receive the same concession Milkilu has.

At the bottom of Letter 254 appears an Egyptian scribal docket, dating the receipt of the letter. The year number has the units figure 2 and a part of a tens figure which is not clear. It can be 10, 20 or 30. The date refers to the year in the king's reign; if it be 12, that would be well along in Akhenaten's seventeen-year reign or else quite early in Amenophis III's thirty-eight-year reign. Were the reading 22 correct, it could apply only to Amenophis III. That would be sixteen years before Amenophis III's death, and a date so early, let alone one twenty-six years before his death, seems very unlikely. All the other information from the letters suggests that only the last few years of Amenophis III are represented. In short, the choice falls between the twelfth year of Akhenaten and the thirty-second year of Amenophis III. There are many reasons to suggest that the latter is correct; the events here described belong at the beginning of the time range covered by the letters. This letter came first to Thebes, around 1370, and was taken to Amarna when Akhenaten established his new capital there in his fifth year.

Letter 245

(This letter must have come to the court on two tablets, for this tablet is whole, but the text begins in the middle of a dispatch.)

> Further, I entreated my brothers: "If the gods of the king, my lord, grant that we capture Lab'ayu, then we will send him alive/ (alive) to the king, our lord." But my mare was felled by an arrow/ (shot)[11] and I took my place

---

[11] The gloss appears to be from the verb "to shoot" (Hebrew *yarâ*), while the Akkadian verb may be *nasahu* with a Canaanite passive inflection (cf. another use of this verb in 250:45, where I have translated "smashed").

behind him/(after him)[12] and rode with Yashdata; but
before my arrival, they had killed him/(struck him
down).[13] Truly, Yashdata is thy servant, and he went
with me into the battle. Now indeed [   ] the life
of the ki[ng   (two lines are unclear)   ] of the king,
my lo[rd   ] Now Zurata took La[b'ayu] from Megiddo and he promised me: "I will send him by ship/
(ship) to the king." So Zurata took him, but he allowed
him to return to his home from Hannathon, for Zurata
took his ransom money in his hand/(in his hand).

Further, what have I done to the king, my lord, that he
should belittle me/(belittle me), and honor/(honor) my
younger brothers? For it is Zurata who let Lab'ayu return,
just as it was Zurata who let Ba'lu-mihir return, to their
homes. Now let the king, my lord, know!

Three lines of evidence point to Biridiya as the author of
this letter: the handwriting is that of the scribe in his other
letters; Yashdata, in a letter of his own (248), reports that he
is with Biridiya; and the situation recalls Biridiya's letter 244.

The best explanation of what has happened here begins by
assuming that Lab'ayu had been taken into custody on a previous
occasion, probably at the king's direction. He was to be sent to
Egypt to account for his actions; Aziru of Amurru was required
to do the same, as Letters 162 and 164–169 inform us. Zurata, of
the seaport of Accho, was to take him thither and send him off
by ship to Egypt. On the way, at Hannathon (See Josh. 19:14),
he accepted ransom from Lab'ayu and let him go. Biridiya should
have known better than to trust Zurata, even though he apparently was his younger brother. Zurata had already done the same
thing with Ba'lu-mihir, and we have evidence to suggest that
Zurata did not improve his record with the court in subsequent
years. In a letter written fairly early in Akhenaten's reign, Burna-
buriash, king of Babylon, complains that a caravan of his has

---

[12] Albright translates "and I alighted afterwards . . ." which may
prove to be better. It is certainly unusual to have the antecedent of a
pronominal suffix follow the suffix, as my translation requires. The verb
means "to stand, take a stand," and can bear either translation.

[13] The Akkadian verb is *dâku,* the same as the one used by Shuwardata in Letter 366, cited in the comment on Letter 244. The gloss also
does not have to mean "kill." However, the context demands the death of
Lab'ayu, and Letter 250 confirms that this came about in the Esdraelon
(see below).

been ambushed at Hannathon (probably Tell el-Bedeiwiyeh,
fifteen miles southeast of Accho) by a party which included
Zurata's son (8:17 ff.).

In short order, a second force was raised, still with the plan
to take Lab'ayu alive, but Biridiya was delayed in getting to the
scene of the skirmish, and his allies had dispatched Lab'ayu by
the time he got there. Lab'ayu's epitaph is provided us by Shuwardata, who shortly thereafter wrote to the court (280:30–35):
"Further, Lab'ayu is dead, who took our cities, but behold Abdu-
Heba is another Lab'ayu, and he has taken our cities." The
death of the most notorious of the city-state governors has hardly
lessened the collective chaos in Canaan at all.

Letter 289

To the king, my lord, [say]: Thus Abdu-Heba, thy
servant. At the two feet of my lord, [the king], seven times
and seven times [I fall]. Behold Milkilu: he does not cut
himself off from the sons of Lab'ayu and [from] the
sons of Arzawa,[14] in desiring the land of the king for
themselves. Concerning a governor who does such a
deed, why does the king not inquire about him? Behold
Milkilu and Tagu: the deed which they have done is this,
that they have taken the city of Rubutu. And now as for
Jerusalem—truly this land is the king's—why is it that it
is as loyal as the city of Gaza to the king? Behold, the land
of the city of Gath-carmel is Tagu's, but men of the city
of Gath are a garrison in Beth-shan! Now shall we do as
Lab'ayu, who gave the land of Shechem to the 'Apiru (or:
made the land of Shechem into 'Apiru territory)? Milkilu
has written to Tagu and the sons of <Lab'ayu>[15]: "Truly
you are of my house. Give all that they desire to the

[14] Or Arzayu (since letter 62:27 gives that as the name of a survivor
of a raid on Sumur in Syria). In Letter 32, from the kingdom of Arzawa,
the name *Kalbaya* occurs three times. When the Amarna Letters were first
published, *Kalbaya* was read *Labbaya*, for the first sign can have either
value. It appeared, then, that Shechem's Lab'ayu had had contact with a
region in Asia Minor at least 300 miles away. Now, however, it appears
that the two pairs of names have nothing to do with one another. *See*
Albright, *BASOR* 89, Feb. 1943, p. 16, n. 51a, and Campbell, *The Chronology of the Amarna Letters*, pp. 39–41.

[15] The scribe apparently left out the name by mistake. There is little
doubt what it should be. Three lines later the scribe omits the preposition
before Jerusalem.

men of Keilah and let us indeed break off <with> Jerusalem."

The guard which thou didst send with Haya, the son of Miyarē', Addaya has taken, and has placed in his house in Gaza. [And] he has sent twenty men to the land of Egypt. Let my king know for a certainty that there is no guard of the king with me. As surely as my king lives, Pawure the commissioner has taken leave of me and is in Gaza. So let the king provide for him. All of the land of the king has revolted. Send Yanhamu and let him check on the land of the king my [lord].

To the scribe of the king, [my lord]: Thus Abdu-Heba, thy servant. Present eloquent words to the king. Much life indeed to you! I am thy servant.

This letter is quite typical of the six long and detailed dispatches from the harried king of Jerusalem. From him we gain our most consistent picture of the constant turmoil in the Palestinian hill country. With Lab'ayu now dead, Milkilu, his erstwhile ally, has continued to plot mischief with Tagu, Milkilu's father-in-law, and with the sons of Lab'ayu. They have taken a town called Rubutu; from the context it is hard for us to be sure whether this is one of Abdu-Heba's towns, located close to Jerusalem[16] or a town located between Gezer and Gath-carmel in the flanks of the hill country.[17] Gath-carmel must be located at a point along the Carmel range west of the Esdraelon plain, possibly at modern Jett (but see below). In any case, Abdu-Heba does not seem to be so much worried about losing one of his own towns as he is about Tagu's ability to get away with expanding his territory while at the same time holding a trusted position in the eyes of the court, which involves supplying troops to the Egyptian outpost at Beth-shan.

Abdu-Heba's words about Lab'ayu are illuminating. Half in despair and half in threat, he asks whether he should do as Lab'ayu did with his city, turn it over to the 'Apiru. But this raises the question of the identity of the 'Apiru. In 287:30–32, Abdu-Heba accuses Milkilu and the sons of Lab'ayu of giving the land to the 'Apiru. In 290 Shuwardata is included, as victories

---

[16] With F.-M. Abel, *Géographie de la Palestine* II, Paris, 1938, p. 27 and map 1; and, most recently, W. Helck, *Die Beziehungen Ägyptens zu Vorderasien im 3. und 2. Jahrtausend v. Chr.*, Wiesbaden, 1962, p. 189.

[17] With Albright, *ANET*, p. 488, n. 18.

of Milkilu and his allies are described as victories of the 'Apiru. But in 271 Milkilu and Shuwardata appeal for help against the 'Apiru! In short, while the 'Apiru do have a separate identity in the Amarna Letters, one often uses the term simply to condemn one's current enemy. The term comes to mean little more than "rebellious against the king (in my opinion)." We are left to wonder whether Abdu-Heba's statement about Lab'ayu means that Lab'ayu has fallen in with a sinister group of aliens or has simply made his city rebellious. It is probably true that the Egyptian court had difficulty telling which was the actual situation also.

It remains true, however, that the term 'Apiru does have reference, in the Amarna Letters as in documents from other places in the Near East covering almost the entire second millennium B.C., to an element of the population which lacks societal status and legal rights. These people lived on the fringes of society, making allies where they could and sometimes offering their services as soldiers to whoever would feed them.[18] 'Apiru serve Biryawaza, loyal prince of the Damascus area, as part of his punitive force on the side of Egypt in Letter 195:24–32. It should be noted that these 'Apiru have not come from somewhere else to Palestine, but are indigenous outlaws; hence it is easy to see how the designation can become a term of opprobrium in the mouth of an Abdu-Heba.

The list of officials and governors given in Letter 289 allows us to keep abreast of the chronological question. With Lab'ayu dead and Milkilu and Tagu alive, with Yanhamu, Haya and Pawure functioning in Egyptian official capacities, and with Addaya in the picture, we are in the middle of the chronological spread of the Amarna Letters, probably during the first five to seven years of Akhenaten's reign.

Letter 250

To the king, my lord, say: Thus Ba'lu-UR.SAG,[19] thy servant. At the feet of the king, my lord, seven times and

[18] On the 'Apiru, see J. Bottéro, Le probléme des Ḥabiru, Paris, 1954; M. Greenberg, The Ḥab/piru, New Haven, 1955; Campbell, The Biblical Archaeologist XXIII, 1960, pp. 13–20; and Albright, BASOR 163, Oct. 1961, pp. 53–54.

[19] The ideogram UR.SAG stands for Akkadian words meaning "hero, warrior." It is not certain what Canaanite word would serve for this idea.

seven times I fall. Let the king, my lord, know that the
two sons of the transgressor against the king, my lord, the
two sons of Lab'ayu, have set their minds to destroy the
land of the king, my lord, after the *death* of their father
(or: after their father had wreaked havoc).[20] Now let
the king, my lord, know that the two sons of Lab'ayu daily
press upon me: "Why did you give Giti-padalla into the
hands of the king, your lord, a city which Lab'ayu, our
father, had taken?" And thus the two sons of Lab'ayu say
to me: "Make war on the people of the land of Qena,
because they killed our father; and if you will not make
war, then we will become your enemies."

Then I replied to them: "May the gods of the king, my
lord, preserve me from making war on the men of the
land of Qena, servants of the king, my lord." May it appear right to the king, my lord, that he send one of his
commissioners to Biryawaza, and say to him: ["Are you
going to mar]ch forth against the two sons of Lab'ayu, or
are you a transgressor against the king?"

(There follow twelve lines in which some signs can be read
but from which no connected sense emerges. Milkilu and the
sons of Lab'ayu are named, and the section closes with "after the
death of Milkilu and Lab'ayu" or "after Milkilu and Lab'ayu had
wreaked havoc.") Resuming:

And thus the two sons of Lab'ayu say: "Make war, as
did our father, against the king, your lord, when he at-
tacked Shunama and Burquna and Harabu and smashed

[20] The verbal root *ḫalaqu* is used twice in this sentence, once to mean
"destroy" and once where the meaning is not clear (either "to die" or "to
wreak havoc"). The point is that the forms are different; in the former
instance, the form is a D infinitive (a conjugation of the verb in which
the middle root letter is doubled), while in the latter instance the form
is *ḫuliq*, without doubling. Perhaps the scribe wrote the word "defec-
tively," standing for *ḫulliq*, which happens often enough. In that case, we
have a D permansive and can translate "wreaked havoc." The trouble is
that the same form appears again in the same letter at the end of the
broken section, and there it has a plural subject (Milkilu and Lab'ayu).
If it is a permansive, it should have a plural ending, but it does not. Perhaps the form is correctly written with only one *l* and is a Canaanite
participle of the Qal conjugation; the vowel pattern *u–i* indicates this form
on three other occasions at least in letters from Palestine (256:9, 288:11
and later in this letter at line 47). In that case, the meaning might be "to
die" as is indicated by the use of this verbal root in parallelism with the
common verb "to die" in the Ugaritic epics. The syntax remains quite
difficult; what we might most like to have is a Qal infinitive (which
thought apparently inspired the author's erroneous suggestion in *The
Chronology of the Amarna Letters*, p. 109, n. 4).

them/ (*smote them*), and seized Giti-rimuni, and *be-
trayed the helpers*[21] of the king, your lord.

But I answered them: "May the gods of the king, my
lord, preserve me from a deed of hostility against the
king, my lord. The king, my lord, I serve, I and my
brothers who heed me." However, Milkilu's messenger
does not leave the side of the sons of Lab'ayu at any
time (that is: daily). Behold, Milkilu seeks to destroy the
land of the king, my lord, but I have no other intention:
I serve the king, my lord, and the word which the king,
my lord, speaks, I heed!

While this letter bristles with minor difficulties, the thread
of the story is clear enough. Ba'lu-UR.SAG would have the king
recognize his complete loyalty, demonstrated by his resistance
to the demands and threats of the sons of Lab'ayu. Ba'lu-UR.
SAG controls Giti-padalla, a city once taken by Lab'ayu, and he
is connected with the activities of the people of Qena. Four other
towns are mentioned, all of which Lab'ayu had seized. Three are
in the Esdraelon plain, in the vicinity of Megiddo: Shunem lies
across the plain, ten miles due east of Megiddo; Gath-rimmon
lies six miles south and east of Megiddo, near Taanach; Burquna
lies eleven miles southeast of Megiddo, near modern Jenin, the
site of ancient Qena. We cannot locate Harabu, although Shuwardata cites a town with a similar name in Letter 281 as an
example of what the king's archers can do if they will only come
to his aid.

Where, then, do we place Ba'lu-UR.SAG? Albright has
argued plausibly that Giti-padalla lay along the mountain flank
south of Carmel, over the ridge from the Esdraelon, at modern
Jett, where some have located Tagu's town of Gath-carmel.[22]

---

[21] The phrase consists of a form of the verb *patû*, used as it is used
in 2 Sam. 3:25, plus the wedge which usually indicates that a gloss will
follow, plus *uziri*, which Albright takes as another Canaanite participle
(see preceding note) with a plural construct ending. The verb would be
'*zr*, "to help." Perhaps Ba'lu-UR.SAG's scribe did not use the gloss-wedge
to indicate that he was going to give a synonym, but rather simply to
mark unusual words. In that case, the curious verb form translated "*smote
them*" just above could be a form of the verb *naqamu* and mean "let me be
rescued."

[22] *BASOR* 104, Dec. 1946, pp. 25–26. Favoring Gath-carmel at Jett
are G. E. Wright and F. V. Filson, *The Westminster Historical Atlas to the
Bible*, Philadelphia, 1956, Map IV, and Helck, work cited in footnote 16,
pp. 190 and 198.

This is fifteen miles westward from both Megiddo and Qena. Ba'lu-UR.SAG's knowledge of Milkilu's movements favors a location between the Esdraelon and Gezer. Furthermore, the tone of the messages from the sons of Lab'ayu suggests that Ba'lu-UR.SAG was expected to join the rebellious allies, and hence that he occupies territory previously held by one of their number. Tagu is strangely absent from the events in Letter 250; very possibly Ba'lu-UR.SAG was Tagu's successor, and has proved to be quite different in his attitude toward Egypt.

Why, then, does Ba'lu-UR.SAG call for help from Biryawaza of the Damascene? There is strong evidence to suggest that Biryawaza was trusted by Egypt to a degree beyond most of his contemporaries. He held authority over governors throughout most of southern Syria and perhaps even Galilee. Rib-Adda of Byblos and Zatatna of Accho both are aware of his long official arm (Letters 129 and 234). The fact that Ba'lu-UR.SAG appeals for help from him simply reflects the extent of Biryawaza's official authority.

Ba'lu-UR.SAG tells us that there are two sons of Lab'ayu, and that they and Milkilu have continued in Lab'ayu's footsteps. They seek to avenge their father's death and to restore the limits of his holdings. They are threatening the same cities as had their father; even the beleaguered Biridiya, in what is presumably the last preserved letter from him to the court, reports that he now feels the pressure of the two sons of Lab'ayu "who have given their silver to the 'Apiru . . ." (246:rev. 5–7).

Letter 255

To the king, my lord and my sungod, say: Thus Mut-ba'lu, thy servant, the dust of [thy] feet, the clay of thy footsteps. At the feet of the king, my lord, seven times, seven times I fall. The king, my lord, has sent to me Haya to say: "Caravans of the land of Hanagalbat, behold they were sent. So send them on!" Who am I that the caravans of the king, my lord, should not be sent on? Look, [Lab]-'ayu, my father [*served*] the king, his lord, [*and he*] sent on every caravan [which] the king sent to the land of Hana-galbat. Let the king, my lord, send caravans to the land of Karduniash. I will bring them through. They will be carefully guarded!

There must remain a slight doubt about reading Lab'ayu in line 15 of this letter, but apparently Mut-ba'lu describes himself as one of the sons of the infamous rebel. In Letter 256 we learn that Mut-ba'lu was located at Pella[23] on the east side of the Jordan valley, just opposite the Egyptian outpost of Beth-shan. In Letter 255 he is responding to the accusation that he has been interfering with caravans passing down the Esdraelon and past Pella on their way to Mitanni (Hanagalbat); in the light of what Egypt has been hearing from Lab'ayu's neighbors, it is hard to imagine that Mut-ba'lu succeeded in exonerating himself by invoking his father's sterling record! Nevertheless, he tries to establish his trustworthiness by vouching for the safety not only of caravans to and from Mitanni but also of caravans to Babylon (Karduniash). Some idea of the richness of these caravans can be gained from looking at the lists preserved as Tablets 13 and 14 of the Amarna collection, and from noting that the transshipment of gold and other precious minerals and woods is the constant subject of many of the royal letters in the archive.

Mut-ba'lu addressed his Letter 256 to Yanhamu, and he mentions Haya in Letter 255. These two figures flourished in the middle years of the Amarna period, approximately during the first half of the reign of Akhenaten. Mut-ba'lu was at Pella, then, at about the same time as Milkilu and the two sons of Lab'ayu were active in the Plain of Esdraelon and along the coastal plain. If Mut-ba'lu is one of these "two sons of Lab'ayu," it would mean that the entire center of Palestine, even over to Transjordan, was under their control, and this under the very nose of the Egyptian outpost at Beth-shan. It would mean also that the letters of the woman governor of Zaphon (273–274), located about thirteen miles south of Pella,[24] are probably referring to the sons of Lab'ayu when they speak of the revolt of the 'Apiru, this at a time when the sons of Milkilu have entered the picture.

Finally, then, we can put together a picture which sees Lab'ayu in control of the entire central part of Palestine's hill country; his sons may already during his lifetime have been posted in cities on the east of the Jordan. After his death, for about a decade, his sons and their allies may have controlled the land

23 Albright, *BASOR* 89, Feb. 1943, pp. 7–15.
24 N. Glueck, *ibid.*, 90, April 1943, pp. 2–23.

from the Mediterranean coast to Gilead, and even farther north in Transjordan to the region opposite the Sea of Galilee.[25] Whether Egypt moved to break this stranglehold remains a question. Letters in the Amarna collection which can clearly be dated late in Akhenaten's reign are confined to Syria, or else are colorless and uninformative.[26] As we have noted, most of the letters from these later years were taken back to Thebes when the court abandoned Amarna. What few letters there are barely suggest a general quieting down of the countryside, and a return of firmer Egyptian control, perhaps achieved by the arrival of an expeditionary force. It may be that Shechem and its rulers did not retain for long the impressive control which for a short time had made them the most notorious brigands of their day.

[25] The territory of his ally Ayyab extended in that direction; *see* Albright, *ibid.*, 89, Feb. 1943, pp. 7–15, esp. p. 9.

[26] Included are four from Yapahu, governor of Gezer, who still fears 'Apiru trouble and seems little better off than his predecessors (297–300).

Appendix 3

Two Cuneiform Tables From Shechem

Professor Albright,[1] in an article on the two Shechem cuneiform tablets here discussed, pointed to the meager yield of such materials thus far coming from Palestine. It is clear that the fifteenth, fourteenth and thirteenth centuries B.C. saw the regular use of this writing medium for all sorts of things; the two items from Shechem are a legal piece and a private note sent by a teacher to his student's parents. Since clay tablets are virtually indestructible by natural forces, the small number of such finds in Palestine is probably due to the difficulty of reaching, and clearing large areas of, the Late Bronze Age strata where they may be assumed to abound. Archaeological method is tending more and more toward the meticulous study of small plots of ground; the chances are against hitting upon Canaanite patrician houses or official residences. What finds of this kind are made will be made pretty much by chance; so far, that has meant hardly more than twenty tablets from Palestine proper, twelve of which came from one large Canaanite residence at Taanach.

[1] W. F. Albright, "A Teacher to a Man of Shechem about 1400 B.C.," *BASOR* 86, April 1942, pp. 28–31.

The two Shechem tablets were found in August, 1926, and were published by F. M. Th. Böhl during the subsequent autumn.[2] The first, Shechem No. 1350, was found in the immediate vicinity of the house of Sheikh Salim, only twenty inches below the ground surface in debris disturbed when the house was built in 1909. The fragment was 3.5 cm. by 2.5 cm., and was the lower part of a tablet; Böhl reports that the break was ancient.

All that remains are seven lines of names; four are on the obverse face, of which the middle two run around to end on the reverse, while the three on the reverse are written so as to interleave with the extensions of the lines coming around from the other side.

(1) Witness: Kanabi*lak* (or Kanabi*ru*)
(2) Witness: Hab-addu, son of Naṣibtu
(3) Witness: Suar*da*ta, son of Palsîyu
(4) Witness: Ya*da*[*h*-ad]du
(5) [Witness: *a*]*h*-abi
(6) Witness: Yantin-addu
(7) Witness: Baʾlu-badi

(The material in brackets is reconstructed, while the material in italics represents uncertain readings of at least partially preserved syllables.)

Each line begins with the Akkadian word for "witness," written out in syllables.[3] This word is the regular designation for witness in the Hammurapi law-code; sections 122–123 from that code suggest the importance of witnesses; when a man wants to leave valuables in the care of another man, he must show the valuables to witnesses and put the matter in writing, or risk being unable to claim his possessions should his "friend"

[2] "Anhang: Die bei den Ausgrabungen von Sichem gefundenen Keilschrifttafeln," *ZDPV* XLIX, 1926, pp. 321–327 and Pls. 44–46.

[3] Our tablet is unique in this feature among published texts; other witnessed legal documents list the names with the Akkadian ideogram which stands for this word in front of each name, or with the preposition "before" in front of each name, or with the designation "witness" written syllabically at the head of the list and not in front of each name. Professor Oppenheim of the Chicago Assyrian Dictionary project has very kindly shown me, however, two unpublished texts from Ur, one clearly dated to the middle of the 13th cent., which employ the syllabic writing for "witness" in front of some names in a list and the ideogram in front of some others. Hence the manner of writing in our text is no longer unique.

prove dishonest. Without witnesses and contract he has no legal case.[4]

Similarly, the word for witness regularly designates the gods who are guarantors of the suzerainty treaties known from the Hittite realm in the fourteenth and thirteenth centuries B.C. And then there exist innumerable records of legal action of various sorts, notably an ever-increasing number from Ugarit in Syria dated to the fourteenth and thirteenth centuries, which close with a list of witnesses.[5]

The names on the Shechem tablet come from at least two linguistic groups.[6] Three are made up of a west-Semitic verbal form and the god-name Hadad (Addu); thus, Yadah-addu means "May Hadad know," Yantin-addu means "May Hadad grant," and Hab-addu perhaps means "Protect, O Hadad." Palsîyu is paralleled by *Plsy* in Ugaritic and by Phoenician names which use the verbal root *pls*.[7] Judging from Hebrew and Phoenician, the root *pls* calls up the notion of fair judgment when it is yoked to a god-name, as it is in the Phoenician names. Naṣibtu is probably a Semitic feminine name (Albright assumes she was a harlot). Ba'lu-badi links the Canaanite Baal to an uncertain element (Böhl suggests *padû* "to redeem" while Albright suggests *ba'di* "on my behalf" as more probable). The fifth witness' name is mostly lost, although it has a Semitic final

---

[4] *See* the trans. of T. J. Meek in *ANET*, p. 171.

[5] *See*, e.g., J. Nougayrol, *Le palais royal d'Ugarit IV, Mission de Ras Shamra IX*, Paris, 1956, Texts 17.137; 17.28; 17.319; 17.316; 18.02 and several others.

[6] Here I am heavily dependent upon Dr. Albright's article and upon R. T. O'Callaghan, *Aram Naharaim*, Rome, 1948, pp. 51–70 and 149–155 (the latter being the Appendix on Indo-Aryan names prepared by P.-E. Dumont). Cf. H. L. Ginsberg and B. Maisler (Mazar), "Semitised Ḫurrians in Syria and Palestine," *Journal of the Palestine Oriental Society* XIV, 1934, pp. 251–252 for a different view on Palsîyu.

[7] The root probably also appears in the name Palz/sum in a 17th-cent. text from Khafajah near Baghdad and in the name Pala/ṣiya in another Old Babylonian text. Both names can be Amorite. For the former, *see* R. Harris, "The Archive of the Sin Temple in Khafajah (Tutub)," *Journal of Cuneiform Studies* IX, 1955, p. 94 (Text Kh. 1935, 60, 1. 18); and for the latter, *see* J. B. Alexander, *Early Babylonian Letters and Economic Texts, Babylonian Inscriptions in the Collection of J. B. Nies VII*, New Haven, 1943, Text 89:6. I am indebted to Prof. I. J. Gelb for pointing out the former and to Miss Harris' doctoral dissertation for its reference to the latter.

element meaning "father." There is almost certainly not enough room before the final element for the word "witness" and the *Yadah* proposed by Albright, but it is difficult to say what would fit the available space.

The first name, Kanabilak, remains a puzzle, although it is clearly not Semitic. Suardata in line 3 bears an Indo-Aryan name meaning "given by heaven,"[8] while his father bears a Semitic name. This recalls the situation depicted by the Amarna Letters of people with Indo-Aryan names in prominent positions interspersed with Semites, presumably a reflection of a former situation when Indo-Aryans were the ruling-class minority throughout the Hurrian sphere. As a matter of fact, a man named Shuwardata (the same name rendered by a scribe with different linguistic background) figures prominently in the region around Hebron in the Amarna Letters.

The combined evidence from the names, the format and the over-all pattern of cuneiform finds in Syro-Palestine, tends to support Albright's fourteenth-century date for our tablet against Böhl's date in the thirteenth century, although both are possible.

The second Shechem tablet, No. 1378, was found in the northern of the two rooms of a Canaanite house located just south of the spot where 1350 was found and at a much greater depth.[9] The tablet was 5 cm. by 3 cm. in size, and was nearly whole, but half of each of the seven lines on the reverse side was lost because the upper right-hand corner was chipped away. On the obverse were thirteen lines; some chipping, and the fact that two cuneiform signs used by this writer are almost identical in form, make the reading tentative in spots. The three principal renderings of the text differ widely at these points.[10] What follows depends most closely upon Albright's treatment.

[8] So Dumont, in O'Callaghan, *Aram Naharaim*, p. 152, No. 70.

[9] Sellin's description, in "Die Ausgrabung von Sichem," *ZDPV* XLIX, 1926, p. 319, is tantalizingly brief and incomplete, while Böhl's information is confusing (*ibid.*, pp. 321–322). Böhl says that both tablets were found on August 19, but his wording implies that the second date should be August 29, and the object registry from that summer implies the same.

[10] Böhl, *ibid.*, pp. 325–327; Albright, pp. 30–31; and B. Landsberger, "Assyrische Königsliste und 'dunkles Zeitalter'," *Journal of Cuneiform Studies* VIII, 1954, p. 59, n. 121. *See* also Albright's translation in *ANET*, p. 490.

To Birashshena say: Thus Banîtî-[   ] *thy* [   ].
For three years up to now you have had me paid. Is
there no grain or oil or [   ] that you might send?
What is my offense that you do not pay me (or: reply to
me)? The youngsters who are with me continue to learn[11]
—their father and their mother alike am I, all the time
[   ] I am angry [   ]. Now [behold] whatever
[there is] under the two feet (that is: at the disposal) of
[my lord, let him send] to me, and let him apprise me.

The recipient in Shechem was a man with an Indo-Aryan
name which probably means "possessing an army of heroes" or
"whose men are heroes."[12] The writer's name is half broken away
and is uncertain, since its first element begins with the ambiguous
sign which may be either *ba* or *ma*. If Banîtî is correct, Albright
then proposes a feminine form of the verb meaning "to create"
followed by the name of a goddess: Goddess X is my creatress.
The writer may, then, be a woman, who teaches her pupils
music and dancing. It would seem more likely, however, that
he is a man, an instructor of budding scribes. The children have
been at their schooling for some time and have gone a distance
to get there, so that a letter must be sent in lieu of a visit. In
the scribal schools of Mesopotamia the master is regularly the
"father" of his pupils. And finally if Landsberger's understanding
of line 15 is correct ("I am angry"), the letter sounds a bit more
like the sort of thing a man of stature and authority would write
(see also the tone of the last line). In short, some Shechemite

---

[11] The interpretation here depends upon whether we read *ma* or *ba*
as the fourth syllable of the Akkadian verb form which makes up line 11
of the text. The former yields the meaning here given, while the latter
leads to Böhl's understanding that the young people will criminally assault
their parents or Landsberger's claim that sexual abuse may be at issue.
See on this disagreement and on other matters pertaining to the scribal
schools the brilliant discussion by Landsberger and his colleagues (including Albright) in C. H. Kraeling and R. M. Adams, eds., *City Invincible*,
Chicago, 1960, pp. 94–123, esp. p. 106.

[12] Landsberger reads the name Birazina from the photograph, but I
cannot agree with him. Böhl and Albright were able to study the original
tablet at length and their reading is to be accepted now that the tablet is
lost. The name may be a peculiar spelling of Birazina anyway; see O'Callaghan, pp. 58 and 60, Nos. 26 and 49, and Dumont, pp. 150–151, Nos.
26 and 49.

sons of a leading Shechemite family have gone off to the scribal school at a town some distance away, and their father has failed to pay their tuition on time. Again the fourteenth century B.C. seems to be the most likely date for this valuable vignette.

Appendix 4

Water Sources in the Vicinity

The source of Shechem's water supply and the means whereby water was made readily available to the inhabitants of the city is not known with any degree of certainty. That Shechem had a water system wholly within the protection of its defense walls or had a means of conducting water into the city which was hidden from enemy detection and protected from destruction seems likely. Such a precaution was a military consideration which no ancient Palestinian city could ignore.

Whatever the earlier defense requirements of the city, the primary defense perimeter of Shechem, built during the Hyksos period, can still be traced as Chapter 5 has indicated. Wall A describes a gradual curve from the tripartite Northwest Gate south and east until it ends just north of the limits of the present village of Balâṭah. Dr. Sellin dug for some distance in 1913 beyond this point in the direction indicated by the curve of Wall A, but was unable to find a continuing wall. In all probability, the wall stones had been robbed out and used in other buildings when that part of the defense wall was no longer in use. The arc described by Wall A indicates that the Middle

Bronze Age defense walls of Shechem were roughly circular in shape, enclosing an area of approximately a dozen acres, and that the southern part of this defense system curved through the northern half of the present-day village of Balâṭah. The Middle Bronze Age defense system, in part at least, served as the city walls of later ages or served as the foundations for later defense measures down to Hellenistic times.

Since there is no natural spring within this circular defense system, water would have to have been made available to the city by one of three methods: cisterns, wells or conduits.

Cisterns. The results of the seven or eight campaigns undertaken by the German Archaeological Institute between 1913 and 1934 failed to indicate any substantial evidence of cisterns or associated water systems. The Drew-McCormick Archeological Expeditions at Shechem in 1956–1957–1960 and 1962 also failed to uncover cisterns or associated waterworks. This statement assumes that the stone-lined, flask-shaped structure (5099A, 2.50 m. deep by 1.75 m. in diameter) found in Field V, Area 3, in 1960 (Drew-McCormick Archaeological Expedition Reports, Field V, 1960) was not a cistern but a grain storage bin. The remains of a similarly shaped structure of about the same size, which may have been a small cistern, was found by the German excavators near the surface of the tell, west of Field VII and northeast of Field VI. It was plaster-lined and was at the approximate level of the Iron II houses found in Field VII. In any case, there is no evidence to indicate extensive use of cisterns as a means of supplying water for the city of Shechem.

Wells. No well has been discovered in Shechem. The nearest known ancient well is the Well of Jacob which lies approximately 300 m. south-southeast of the Shechem city limits. While the location of the Well of Jacob is historically one of the best-attested sites in Palestine, at least since New Testament times, the recorded depth of that well has been a matter of some uncertainty. It is only in relatively recent history that any accurate soundings have been made. One of the first attempts to measure the depth of the well was that of an unnamed French ecclesiastic in 1704 (*Relation historique d'un voyage nouvellement fait au Mont de Sinai et à Jerusalem,* Toul, 1704). The good monk records that on his visit to the Well of Jacob he let a pebble fall down its shaft, and as the pebble left his fingers he began to recite "not very slowly, yet not very fast" the following formula, *"Gloria Patri et Filio et Spiritu Sancto: sicut erat in principio, et nunc, et semper, et in saecula."* He asserts the pebble was heard to strike the bottom (*sic!*) just as the last syllable was pronounced. Unless the French monk could recite the office at an unbelievably rapid rate, the formula cannot be said in less than five seconds, and to repeat it "not very slowly, yet not very fast" requires seven seconds' time. Since a free-falling body accelerates at a given rate, the supposed depth of Jacob's Well can be calculated. If the recitation of the formula took five seconds, the well is approximately 402 feet deep, but if the time was seven seconds, the calculated depth would be almost doubled. One must conclude that reverence for the Patriarch Jacob's digging ability markedly influenced the monk's remembrance of the length of the time required by his falling stone.

The *Survey of Western Palestine, Memoirs,* (Vol. II, 1882, pp. 172–176) records the depth of Jacob's Well as 75 ft. and notes that the upper part of the well is lined with masonry and the lower part had been cut into layers of limestone. The same report, however, notes that Robinson had in 1838 found the depth of the well to be 105 ft. The writer had occasion to talk with Haj Raf'q of Balâṭah who was hired to clean out the well in 1935. He insisted that it had been measured at the time of cleaning and that its depth was 46 m. (approximately 138 ft.). The records of the Public Works Office in nearby Nablus seem to confirm this depth. In an average summer (summer being the time of the year when the water table is lowest) the level of water stands at a depth of between 23 and 25 m. below the surface of the ground, which surface at Jacob's Well is just below 500 m. above sea level.

In 1957 a well, Karim Dolih, was driven at a low point in the Shechem Pass (approximately 500 m. above sea level) at about 100 m. west-southwest of the site of Shechem. In the course of driving this well, water was first encountered in limited quantity in limestone layers at between 18 and 20 m. depth. Karim Dolih was driven to a depth of 34½ m. (*ca.* 104 ft. 9 in.) where "hard black stone" (basalt?) was struck and where water in quantity enough to supply continuous pumping through a

12-cm. pipe was encountered. Jacob's Well stands at the eastern extremity of the valley which forms the pass between Mt. Ebal and Mt. Gerizim, and Karim Dolih is to the west of Jacob's Well and within the pass between these two mountains. A depression in the valley floor causes the present level of the surface at Karim Dolih to be about the same as that of Jacob's Well. Thus Jacob's Well and Karim Dolih seem to tap the same water table. Further, both Jacob's Well and Karim Dolih indicate that in order to reach a good supply of water, a well of over 20 m. is necessary. Both of the wells mentioned are situated on the valley floor from which the mound, on which the Hyksos city of Shechem was built, rises. As a result of this mound, the city of Shechem is from 12 to 25 m. above the surrounding valley floor. Consequently, any well dug within the city down to the water table would have to be very deep indeed, i.e., between 32 and 55 m. in depth. Wells to this depth are not unknown in ancient Palestine, but they are exceedingly rare and obviously very difficult to dig.

Conduits. Perhaps the most obvious reason why cisterns and wells have not been found in the city of Shechem lies in the fact that nearby and continuous sources of water are to be found on the slopes of Mt. Ebal and, especially, Mt. Gerizim. A survey of the slopes east of the high point of the pass between these two mountains indicates that there are ten springs, two of which might have served as a water supply for the city of Shechem.

(1) Ain el-Fashura is a spring of moderate size with a continuously running supply of water located at an elevation of about 600 m., about 1,600 m. south of Shechem on the southeast slope of Mt. Gerizim. The remoteness of this spring from the site, particularly in the light of larger springs nearer by, rules it out as a possible water source for the site.

(2) Ain Sarin, a small spring at 575 m. elevation on the east slope of Mt. Gerizim, is approximately 1,400 m. south of the site. The smallness and remoteness of this spring preclude it as a possible water supply for the city.

(3) Ain es-Subyan, a small spring located at 550 m. elevation on the eastern slope of Mt. Gerizim, at about 1,100 m. south of the site, is likewise too small and to remote to be an adequate water supply for the site.

(4) Ain Abū Hammer is located on the eastern slope of Mt. Gerizim approximately 900 m. south of the site at about 510 m. elevation. It is too small and too remote from the site to be considered a possible water supply source.

(5) Ain Zanqa is located on the northeast slope of Mt. Gerizim at about the 540-m. elevation, 500 m. southwest of the site, but is a periodic spring and flows only in winter.

(6) Ain Askar on the southeastern slope of Mt. Ebal is a large, free-flowing spring which currently supplies the village of Askar and the surrounding neighborhood with water. It is at an elevation of approximately 550 m. and is about 700 m. northeast of the site of Shechem. While this spring is large enough to be an adequate supply of water for the site, its location and distance rule out the probability of its use as a water supply for Shechem.

(7) Ain Bassa is a small spring on the south-southeastern slope of Mt. Ebal at an elevation of 525 m. There are indications that it was used in Roman times as a source of water supply for a Roman villa. However, Ain Bassa is a small spring and would not afford an adequate supply of water for a city. It is located within 200 m. of the site of Shechem.

(8) Ras el-Ain is located about 2,000 m. to the west of the site of Shechem in the direction of the city of Nablus, and at the present time is used by that city as part of its water supply. The spring is located at the 615-m. level on the northwest slope of Mt. Gerizim and is a large, free-flowing spring. Its distance from the site of Shechem militates against its use as a water supply to that site. However, there is evidence that a Roman water conduit connected this spring with the next one listed.

(9) Ain Dafna—the exact site of the source of this spring is difficult to determine because its waters have become part of a rather complicated water supply originally used by the Romans and still used by the contemporary city of Nablus. In the course of trying to determine the location of this spring, a complex of cisterns and tunnels was found, including a Roman aqueduct 850 m. in length, 1 m. in width and 1½ m. in height. This long tunnel ran from the old mosque in the city of Nablus to a point underneath the federal penitentiary located between Nablus and Balâṭah. Prison authorities were somewhat reluctant to have this

water system explored and the fact made known that a series of tunnels ran under the second-largest jail in Jordan. Permission was granted, but the keeper of the prison and a guard stationed themselves at the entrance of the water system.

The jail is located about 800 m. due west of the site of Shechem in the pass between Mt. Gerizim and Mt. Ebal at an elevation of about 550 m. Access to the system was by means of a 13-m. vertical shaft of modern construction which led into a Roman cistern. The modern shaft penetrated the round vaulted roof of the cistern and a wrought-iron ladder permitted descent. The cistern was 3.30 m. in width and 5.95 m. in length. The high point of the barrel-vaulted roof was 3.50 m. above the present earthen floor, which was under approximately 30 cm. of water. The cistern, including the vaulting, was constructed of carefully hewn and fitted stones, 45 cm. long, 25 cm. wide and approximately 25 cm. thick, and the whole chamber oriented in a north-south direction on its long axis. A steady and generous stream of water bubbled up through the clay floor of the cistern in the northwest corner of the chamber and flowed out through a crude hole, not large enough to admit a man, in the eastern wall. This hole was approximately 3 m. from the northern end of the chamber and at floor level. A second stream of water flowed into the cistern through a crude opening of similar size and location in the western wall of the cistern. It is believed, because of its direction of flow and of reports from the local municipal water authorities, that the second stream of water comes by means of a tunnel from Ras el-Ain, mentioned above. Above the hole which admitted the stream of water in the western wall was the opening of a conduit approximately 50 cm. wide and 1.20 m. high. The sides of this conduit were made up of hewn and fitted stones, and it was covered by large semidressed stone slabs laid across the top. Its bottom entered the cistern at about 1.75 m. above the cistern floor. At a distance of approximately 1.50 m. back in the conduit from the opening into the cistern, it was completely blocked by a wall of stone and cement.

A second opening, having the same dimensions and appearance as the first, was found in the northern end of the cistern but only 1.20 m. above the floor of the cistern. It likewise had been blocked in a manner similar to the first. A third opening, of the same dimensions and construction as the first two, was discovered in the eastern wall of the cistern directly above the crude hole which served as the outlet for the stream of water. The third conduit was of the same height as the first above the cistern floor (1.75 m.) and the two were directly opposite one another in the cistern. When the third was entered, it was discovered that it was in depth only the width of the cistern wall (approximately 25 cm.); beyond that point its bottom was the same level as the floor of the cistern. Thus the conduit was 50 cm. wide and 3 m. high, and was discovered to be 4 m. long with about 40 cm. of water flowing in it.

At a distance of 4 m. due east from the opening in the eastern wall of the first cistern, a second and smaller cistern was discovered. It was 1.65 m. wide, 3.75 m. high and approximately 3.50 m. in length. The second cistern was likewise oriented north-south on its long axis and was located completely south of the midpoint of the larger cistern. It was evident that at one time the 4-m.-long conduit which joined the two cisterns entered each of the two cisterns at approximately 1.75 m. above the floor of each and was approximately 1.20 m. high and 50 cm. wide, but at a later time the floor had been lowered approximately 1.75 m., causing the floor of both cisterns and the conduit to be at the same level. On the northern end of the eastern wall of the second cistern and 1.75 m. above the floor of the smaller cistern, was a conduit-opening 50 cm. wide and 1.20 m. high, of construction similar to all of the other conduits. It was closed by a wall of stone and cement at a distance of approximately 2 m. from the opening.

The stream of water flowing from the 4-m.-long connecting conduit was by means of an S-shaped cement channel directed south and then east into a cement-lined water tunnel 1 m. wide and 1.50 m. high. The general direction of this tunnel was east and it ran for approximately 25 m., at which point it opened into a well-shaped chamber (approximately 3 m. in diameter) which served as the bottom of a second 13-m. shaft of modern construction which rose perpendicularly to the surface. Water flow was eastward, constant but not rapid, and varied from 30 to 40 cm. in depth. A water tunnel 1 m. in width and 1.50 m. in height, cement-lined, led in a northerly direction from the well-shaped chamber for 180 m., at which point it emptied into a large cistern filled with water to a depth of more than 4 m. The cistern was approximately 8 m. by 13 m., but owing to the depth of water it could not be examined carefully.

The water of this cistern is part of the water supply of the modern city of Nablus. It has been assumed that the cement-lined water tunnel mentioned above is, because of its dimensions and the appearance of hewn stone through cracks in the cement, a Roman water conduit which has been cemented over in recent times. The 850-m.-long tunnel, mentioned earlier, appears to be of Roman construction and runs from a point near the old mosque in Nablus to a point near the prison and is part of that city's water system. The eastern opening of this tunnel could not be found, but it probably opens into the last-mentioned cistern, which is probably the source of the water taken from the well near the old mosque.

One hundred meters west of the prison on the outside eastern wall of a building used by the Jordan Highway Department is a painted-over notice which reads, "The Roman Channel is 2.30 m. down from this stone." The nature of this "channel" is not known. It is not deep enough to be part of the 850-m.-long tunnel conducting water to Nablus, but it may be part of one of the blocked conduits which at one time emptied water into the first-mentioned cistern.

That there was a highly complex waterworks associated with Ain Dafna is evident. *The Palestine Exploration Fund, Map XI*, 1879, indicates the presence of what must have been a large cistern at the foot of Mt. Ebal. This was north of Ain Dafna and connected to it by a water channel, but there is no known evidence of the existence of either today.

Ain Dafna remains a definite possibility as a source of water supply for the city of Shechem, although no conduits thought to be older than the Roman period were found leading from that source in the direction of the site. In addition, Ain Dafna is 400 m. away from the walls which surround Shechem, and this militates against its having been used as a water source for that city.

(10) Ain Balâṭah is the closest continuously running large supply of water to the city of Shechem. Until 1960 it remained

the only source of water supply for the village of Balâṭah. With the coming of piped water from Nablus to the village in 1961–1962, the old spring at Balâṭah was no longer relied on as completely as once it had been. The exploration of the source of the water thus became a possibility. The author had been informed by members of the village that their water supply came through a long tunnel, and permission to explore the tunnel was sought from the authorities.

On July 17, 1960, permission having been granted by the Mukhtar of Balâṭah, Selman Suleiman, the author, accompanied by the Mukhtar's son and Mr. Mustafa Tawfiq, the Drew-McCormick Expedition's foreman, prepared to enter and examine the water tunnel. Its entrance is to be found in one of four barrel-vaulted chambers (probably of Roman construction) now almost completely buried, located behind (i.e., south of) the new mosque at Balâṭah. Specifically, the entrance to the tunnel is at a point 7.70 m. west and 12.70 m. south of the center of the minaret of the new mosque, and approximately 4 m. below the present surface of the ground. At this point water issues from the tunnel into a receiving basin, 91 cm. square, located in the center of the southern half of the barrel-vaulted chamber. The latter is 1.90 m. wide, approximately 4 m. long and 3.50 m. in height at the center of the vaulting (cf. the plan, Fig. 109). It is evident that a recently constructed wall had been built along the center of the length of the vaulted chamber from floor to ceiling so that only half of the vault is immediately apparent. The author was informed by the natives that this had been done to divide the approach to the water, thus permitting the women to approach from one side of the wall and the men from the other.

Our plan had been to have the Mukhtar's son carry a gas-pressure lantern for light. He was to be followed by the writer carrying compass, small tape for measuring widths and heights, a long tape for measuring lengths, and an air-flight bag full of equipment including flash cameras. Mr. Tawfiq was to follow in order that he could help with the measurement of the length of the tunnels. When we had passed through the opening of the wall of the vaulted chamber, we entered a small enclosure and the entrance of the tunnel was immediately apparent. The tunnel entrance was approximately 40 cm. wide and 70 cm. high. Mr. Mustafa Tawfiq became aware at this point that he had claustrophobia and felt that he could not enter the tunnel. The Mukhtar's son and the writer proceeded to crawl through the tunnel to its end and discovered that it was approximately 85 m. in length and varied considerably in width and height. At one point, the tunnel became so narrow that the writer and a flight bag containing the camera equipment could not both get through at the same time, and at this point, a decision was made that another exploratory effort would have to be made if photographs were to be taken.

On July 31, 1962, a team of four men, each having one specific job to do, attempted the second exploration of the tunnel. Dr. James Ross of Drew University was to proceed first with flash camera equipment. Dr. Siegfried Horn of Andrews University was to follow and measure widths and heighths of the tunnel. Dr. Horn was followed by the writer, who was responsible for the measurement of horizontal and vertical angles by means of a theodolite. Dr. Bull was followed by Mr. Aziz Mohammed Jodila, the Field V foreman, who was to aid in the measurement of the length of the tunnel.

The entrance (Point A on Plan, Fig. 109) consisted of three courses of semi-hewn stones on each side and a roof made up of a series of rough-hewn slabs lying across the top of the tunnel. On the floor a channel had been cut, approximately 20 cm. wide and 12 cm. deep. This served to conduct the major part of the rapidly running water, which in some places became as deep as 24 cm. Almost at once, the tunnel diminished in width so that it was 27 cm. wide by 70 cm. high. For some of the more corpulent members of the expedition, such as the writer, this became a very difficult place through which to squeeze. Beyond that narrow point, however, the tunnel gradually became wider and higher, until at a distance of 10.20 m. from the entrance (cf. Point A) it was 40 cm. wide and 1.10 m. high. The tunnel at Point A was made of four courses of rough-hewn stone on either side of the channel and covered with rough-hewn slabs, and continued to have this construction and dimensions for the next 18.80 m. to Point B. The direction of the tunnel from the entrance (Point A) to Point B was 270 degrees true. At Point B the tunnel

was approximately 20 cm. higher in elevation than it was at the
entrance.

At Point B the tunnel turned in a southwesterly direction
(198 degrees true) and broadened into a tunnel, 57 cm. wide
by 79 cm. high. This was made of three courses of rough-hewn
stone on either side and covered by rough-hewn slabs. This
section ran for 4.70 m., and in the course of that distance, gained
about 10 cm. elevation (cf. Plan, B–C). The conduit then turned
in a westerly direction (266 degrees true) and measured 60 cm.
wide by 81 cm. in height, had the same general construction as
the section immediately before it, and was 5.10 m. in length
(Plan, C–D). The tunnel then led into an irregularly shaped
chamber made up of small unhewn stones. This was approximately 3.65 m. in length by 65 cm. in width and 3.50 m. in height.
The top of this irregularly shaped chamber was closed over by
unhewn stones. The structure appeared at one time to have been
a well, the entrance to which had been subsequently covered
over. In the course of traversing this chamber the water channel
ran for 2 m. in a northwesterly direction (292 degrees true) (cf.
Plan, D–E) and then 1.65 m. in an easterly direction (244
degrees true) (Plan, E–F), during which time the elevation of
the channel was raised 5 cm. in height. This crudely-fashioned
chamber was contiguous to a well-fashioned long chamber with
a pointed-vault ceiling. The pointed vault was made up of carefully fitted rough-hewn limestone blocks approximately 15 cm.
by 15 cm., and 30 cm. in length. The cross-section on the plan
shows the dimensions in centimeters. This chamber ran for some
distance in a southwesterly direction (205 degrees true; cf. Plan,
F–G). As one proceeded in that direction, an entrance opened
into a small passage on the left at about 2 m. distance. It was
apparently an old entrance into the chamber now blocked by
rubble. Here a lintel (90 cm. long, 45 cm. wide, 15 cm. thick),
which may not be *in situ*, was seen about 1.50 m. above the
bottom of the old entrance. On the under face of the lintel and
incised in it, is what might be described as a sunburst or central
disk from which emanated divergent lines (*see* sketch on Plan).

Farther along, the tunnel opens into a somewhat larger
round or barrel-vaulted chamber of the same general construction and orientation (cf. Plan, F–G, and sections). The two
vaulted chambers form a single chamber 12.75 m. long, oriented

205 degrees true, in the course of which the elevation of the water tunnel rises 25 cm. The water channel in the barrel-vaulted section was along the western side of the chamber, while the eastern side was made up of a platform of earth and stone to a height of 38 cm. and a width at the southwestern end of the chamber (i.e., at Point F) of about 1.65 m. The extreme eastern side of this chamber was piled high with rubble, dirt and large stones, to the height of the vault, making measurement of the width of the chamber, except at the southwestern end, difficult.

At this end (Point G) an obstructed opening led to the southeast (to the left as one goes up the tunnel) and turned abruptly in a northeasterly direction (to the left as one goes through the opening) into a blocked tunnel which was so filled with debris as to make exploration impossible.

The southwestern end of the barrel-vaulted chamber (Point G) ends at a solid stone face. In the lower right (as one faces the southwestern end of the chamber) the solid stone face had been cut through and a water tunnel of carefully hewn and fitted stone had been built so that it extended 20.90 m. in a southwesterly direction (239 degrees true) from the opening in the rock face of the chamber (cf. Plan, G–H). The water tunnel was 50 cm. wide with 78-cm.-high sides made up of three (occasionally two) layers of well-hewn sandstone blocks. The top of the tunnel comes to a point or ridge (44 cm. above the height of the sides) formed by a series of two stone blocks (approximately 50 cm. in length and 30 cm. in width) fitted in such a way as to form a 60-degree angle at the peak or ridge of the tunnel. At a distance of 14.35 m. along this water tunnel, an opening 60 cm. in diameter had been cut through the top and through two limestone slabs whose combined width was 85 cm. Above this opening arose a cylindrical well-like shaft, 60 cm. in diameter, to a height 1.47 m. above the stone slabs (cf. Plan, G–H, and section). The shaft was formed of small unhewn stones; it had been closed by large rough-hewn slabs of stone laid across the top. The height of the shaft from the bottom of the tunnel to the stone slabs covering the shaft was 3.07 m. The elevation of the water channel rose approximately 20 cm. in the course of this 20.90-m.-long tunnel (from Point G to Point H on Plan).

At Point H the character of the tunnel changed, although the

direction remained the same (239 degrees true) for a distance of
1.50 m. (H–I on Plan). The top of the tunnel at this point was
covered with rough-hewn stone slabs (approximately 1.20 m.
above the floor) and the sides of the tunnel (approximately
50 cm. apart) were composed of semi-hewn stones of various
sizes. At Point I the water course turned abruptly south (177
degrees true) into a water tunnel, 3.80 m. long (cf. Plan, I–J),
the bottom part of which was rough-hewn out of solid rock and
varied from 25 to 40 cm. in width. The upper part of the sides
was made up of unhewn stones set directly on the hewn rock
sides of the water course. The top of the tunnel was covered with
rough-hewn stone slabs at a height which varied from approximately 1 to 2 m. above the floor of the tunnel. At its southern
extremity the conduit opened into a natural cave 80 cm. deep,
2 m. wide and approximately 2 m. high from the floor of the
cave, on which the water was 30 to 50 cm. deep. A large source of
cold water could be felt gushing up from under a large stone in
the southeastern section of the cave. A number of large unhewn
stones were present. The elevation of the water channel in the
southern end at Point J was approximately 5 cm. above the
elevation in the northern extremity at Point I.

Water flowing from the spring cave through the channel
cut from bedrock flows in a northerly direction (i.e., 357 degrees
true) until it reaches Point I, where the stream is diverted
abruptly into a northeasterly direction (i.e., 059 degrees true)
and into the carefully constructed water tunnel H–G. That the
stream of water is diverted from its original northerly course
seems evident from the fact that the stones which cause the
course of the water to be redirected in a northeasterly direction
are semi-finished stones unlike those found in the tunnel leading
from the spring cave. Further, they lie across (from floor to
ceiling) the rock-cut channel leading from the spring cave.
However, it should be noted that the eastern side of the rock-cut
channel could not be traced at Point I. Additional evidence that
the channel at one time continued in a northerly (i.e., 357
degrees true) direction from the spring cave beyond Point I
was seen in the fact that the rough-hewn slabs which cover it
were seen continuing in a northerly direction over the top of the
semi-finished stone wall which blocked and diverted the water

into Section G–H. Emphasis has been placed on the change of direction at Point I because the rock-hewn channel tunnel (I–J), if extended for approximately 100 m., would meet the probable course of Wall A of Shechem as it curves through the northern half of the village of Balâṭah.

The dating of the various sections of the Balâṭah water tunnel is difficult. All of the pottery taken from it was Byzantine or later. Other pieces of pottery taken from the spring cave and/or the rock-cut channel (Plan, I–J) were too water-eroded to be useful in dating.

The different types of construction used in various sections of the water tunnel, however, do suggest general dates for parts of it. The rock-hewn channel I–J, with built-up sides of unhewn stone and covering of rough-hewn oblong slabs of stone, has been called pre-Roman because of the crudeness of its construction and the fact that its original water course has been redirected by a later hand into what is obviously an example of Roman engineering and construction at its best, the carefully constructed 20.90-m.-long water conduit labeled G–H. This well-engineered conduit empties into a well-constructed, low, barrel-vaulted chamber which is also probably Roman. The barrel-vaulted chamber is connected directly with a well-constructed pointed-vault chamber which suggests to the author that it is late Roman or Byzantine. The presence of a lintel incised with a design which is similar to many Byzantine decorative forms tends to confirm a Byzantine dating for this section. The crudity of construction of the rest of the tunnel (Plan, F–A), with its semi-hewn or unhewn stone sides covered with crudely hewn oblong slabs, suggests only that it was post-Byzantine or even modern. The fact that much of the tunnel from the pointed-vault chamber to the receiving basin at the entrance (Plan, F–A) has been covered in cement, particularly in the lower courses of stone, prevents careful examination of the construction.

In the absence of, or unlikely use of, other water sources noted above, Ain Balâṭah, with its spring cave and the rock-cut channel leading in the general direction of Shechem, plus its proximity to the walls of that city, argues strongly that it was once used as the source of ancient Shechem's water supply. Since the cave, its spring and the water tunnel are under approximately

4 m. of earth and stone, confirmation of the rock-hewn channel's extension in a northerly direction beyond the point of its present diversion (Point I on Plan) will have to await future archaeological excavation. That Shechem got its supply of water from the nearby copious water source, Ain Balâṭah, via a conduit which led that water underground and under its defense system into the city, seems probable.

Appendix 5

The Stratification of the Temple Forecourt

This book has made abundantly clear the importance of "sections" for the understanding and interpretation of the data gathered by an archaeological expedition. The reader may be wondering just how a section is read and the information gleaned from it integrated into the reconstruction of the history of the city as a whole. The best way to answer this question is to look over the archaeologist's shoulder as he reads one of the crucial sections from the expedition's files. The trench, opened in 1962 in the vicinity of the Late Bronze Age altar and *maṣṣēbāh* (Field V, Area 13) was a relatively small operation, but it produced results of the greatest significance for the long history of the sacred area of ancient Shechem. These results are recorded in Section B–B (Fig. 110), and supplemented by Section A–A (Fig. 110), and the section made in 1960 by cutting back the northern face of the courtyard fill.[1] We begin the reading of Section B–B from the bottom upward.

[1] Fig. 49. The reader will be helped in following the argument of this appendix by the plans for the various phases of the courtyard temple (Figs. 63, 64, 69, 71). Section A–A represents the southern and B–B the northern face of the excavation.

Temenos 2. The most conspicuous feature of Section B–B is Wall 983–983A–938. This is the eastern wall of the Central Court, which, as noted on page 107, retained the same line throughout the history of *Temenoi* 2–5. Its three phases appear clearly in the section. The earliest surface associated with this wall is the "plasterlike floor" running up to the preserved top of Wall 983. The subfloor make-up of "dark-brown earth" is the same type of soil as that underlying *Temenos* 2 (939) floors elsewhere in Field VI, and the pottery above and below the floor is early MB II B in type. Since the courtyard temple was erected on an area deliberately leveled to receive it, the absolute level of this floor is of some significance. It corresponds almost exactly with 939 phase floors to the east and with Street 9.[2] This floor, therefore, is the surfacing of the Central Court during *Temenos* 2, extending from Wall 983 to an unknown western limit, possibly Wall D itself, or, less probably, an early phase of Wall 914.[3]

Temenos 3. The case is less clear with the next higher floor level on Section B–B, the thin "plasterlike floor" laid over "red-brown earth." Neither of its limits is secure, its eastern end being cut by a foundation trench and its western extremity not appearing in the section. There can be little doubt that this floor ran up to Wall 938A when that wall stood at a higher level than at present. Its absolute level associates it with *Temenos* 3 (902)

[2] Comparative Table of Absolute Levels.

	Street Elevations	Nearest Field VI Floor	Phases in Forecourt
1.	14.70		
2.	14.60	No 909–910 floors preserved	
3.	14.35		
4.	14.19	901 phase, 14.63	901 phase, 14.60
5.	13.93		
6.	13.65	902 phase, 13.73	902 phase, 13.75
7.	13.32	939 phase, 13.23	939 phase, 13.20
8.	13.20		
9.	12.90		

The streets begin in the 939 phase a little lower than the corresponding temple floors and build up during that phase to a slightly higher level. This condition was corrected at the foundation of the 902 phase, and thereafter the temple floors remained 0.30–0.50 m. higher than the street.

[3] The Welter section (Fig. 22) shows Wall 914 founded considerably higher than would be expected for a wall belonging to *Temenos* 2. If it is eliminated from consideration, we have no other candidate for the western wall of the Central Court except Wall D itself.

floors and with Street 6,[4] and the "red-brown" make-up is a common feature of known 902 floors. The associated pottery is developed MB II B. On this evidence the floor may with confidence be identified as the surfacing of the *Temenos* 3 Central Court.[5]

Temenos 4. As Section B–B shows, the *Temenos* 4 builders dug a deep foundation trench to the stump of old Wall 983, and erected their new wall on the foundation courses of Wall 938A. As elsewhere in Field VI, they employed a heavy fill of "gray-brown earth" mixed with charcoal and plaster flecks. Over this they laid a make-up of ash and destruction debris as a foundation for their plaster floor. This surface clearly predates Wall 925A, since it is cut by the foundation trench for that wall. Originally it probably extended west of the line of Wall 925A, and, although we cannot now be absolutely sure of its western limit, it may well have been terminated by the lower courses of Wall 914.[6] The pottery associated with this surface is MB II B and its absolute level agrees with that of the nearest 901 floor.[7] The surface may, accordingly, be identified as that of the Central Court during the *Temenos* 4 period, bounded on the east by Wall 938, and on the west (hypothetically) by an early phase of Wall 914.

The deep foundation trench sunk by the builders of *Temenos* 4 in search of the line of Wall 983 is significant, showing as it does that this line was of sufficient importance that its location had to be established even if this meant a deep excavation through the fill. The explanation offered in the text of this book, namely that the definition of the limits of the Central Court was

---

[4] See n. 2, above.

[5] The western limit is again not secure. On the evidence cited in n. 3 above we conjecture a reuse of Wall D for this purpose.

[6] Wall 914 is clearly a wall of at least two phases. The lower courses are not battered and suggest a freestanding wall. Its level of foundation would associate it with *Temenos* 4. This conclusion is supported by the fact that the *Temenos* 4 (901) phase succeeded a major destruction and reconstruction of the site, when a new western wall might be expected. If Wall 914 was founded for that purpose in this phase of construction, the care taken to recover and re-establish the line of old Wall 983 is all the more remarkable.

[7] See no. 2 above.

crucial for the position of the altar, seems to be the readiest and most convincing way of accounting for the manifest interest in the line of Wall 983.

Section B–B goes a long way toward clearing up the difficulties associated with later phases of *Temenos* 4. It shows clearly that the various walls involved (925A, 985A, 938, and 989) were not founded at the same time. Wall 985A is founded above the level of the 901 floor, leaving it intact, whereas the foundation trench for Wall 925A cuts through it. The most obvious, and therefore probably the correct, explanation of these facts is that in the second phase of *Temenos* 4 the Central Court consisted of a paved area between Walls 925A and 938, when the latter stood at a level higher than its present preserved top. It was thus exactly analogous to the earlier courtyards except that its surface was paved rather than plastered. During a third stage this pavement was dug out at its western end, and Wall 985A was set in to make the small room with clay floors, oven and store-jar. The pavement to the east was retained as a courtyard for this new establishment.

Temenos 5. All remains of the Central Court of the 909–910 temple were destroyed and a great pit dug down into the debris, to a level just above Wall 985 in Section B–B. This was then filled in again for *Temenos* 6. The high level of the 909–910 walls can be seen in Fig. 72, while the tip lines of the new courtyard fill, thrown in from the top of Wall 914, can be seen in Fig. 49.

Temenos 6. The mass of fill was laid in to form the forecourt of Fortress-temple 1a. In Section B–B this fill includes all layers from the pavement level upward to the "packed white *huwwar*." Careful study of the intermediate layers indicates that they had no structural function, but represent various stages in the filling process.[8] On top of this fill the *Temenos* 6 builders placed a double layer of surfacing (packed lime topped by bricky red earth) as foundation for a pavement of irregular-shaped stones, which in turn was surfaced by a layer of white plaster.[9] This

[8] A selection of pottery from this fill is published in *BASOR* 169, Feb. 1963, pp. 58 f.

[9] Promptly dubbed by the site supervisor "the Via Sacra." The whole area was irreverently known as "the phone booth."

elaborate construction covered the whole of the excavated area, and appears in Section A–A sloping sharply up toward the top of Wall 914, although its connection with Wall 914 has been destroyed by a German trench. The most likely hypothesis to account for these stratigraphic facts is that, in the process of laying the fill for Temple 1a, Wall 914 was raised to provide a consolidating wall in the fill and to serve as a base for the stairs leading up to the Temple entrance.[10] The cobbled and plastered surface has an architectural function only as an approach road leading up to the entrance of the fortress-temple. Although the pottery remains are scanty, its date is stratigraphically secure. It belongs to the earliest phase of the fortress-temple.

Temenos 7. The Fortress-temple 1b phase presents two peculiar stratigraphic features. (1) The whole excavated area is covered with a layer of gray brick and brick dust in which occasional whole bricks are found, all laid horizontally. In Section A–A this layer slopes sharply upward toward the temple entrance immediately above the Temple 1a surfacing. The northern face of the excavation (Section B–B) shows the gray bricks intact and topped by a layer of white bricks, which however does not extend over the whole area, but forms a kind of curbing only on the western end of the section.[11] (2) The layer overlying the gray brick is unique among the fills found in the temple courtyard, a thick deposit of *huwwar* chips with very little earth among them. It seems highly unlikely that chips of limestone rock would be deliberately and laboriously produced for use merely as a make-up layer. It is much more probable that they once formed the interior of some kind of structure. This is borne out by the nature and state of preservation of the bricks on which the *huwwar* chips lay. No roadway in the entire history of the temple possessed a brick pavement, and the intact bricks recov-

---

[10] The upper phase of Wall 914 is battered to the west, and consequently was intended to hold back a mound of earth on the western side of the wall. This was probably the remains of the old MB II B bank which must have been in bad repair and in danger of slippage. When the fill was completed for Fortress-temple 1a, the top of Wall 914 was broadened to form a support for the stairs to the temple entrance. The existing remains of Wall 914, therefore, represent a weirdly composite picture of its history. This gave the supervisors chronic headaches until its history was worked out.

[11] For photograph *see* Fig. 50.

ered in the excavation show no evidence of having been walked over. The chips probably functioned as the interior composition of a large structure of which the brick layers were the foundation. The location in front of the temple would indicate that the brick structure was the basement of an altar composed of a compact mass of *huwwar* chips consolidated and held in place by a layer of plaster, some fragments of which are still preserved and appear in Section B–B.

Temenoi 8–9. In the construction of *Temenos* 8 the altar just described was in part demolished, and its core used in the *Temenos* 8 fill. Immediately above this early altar the builders erected an altar of their own. Only the foundation stones of this structure now survive *in situ*. Section A–A shows them packed in a fill of "gray-white *huwwar*." Only a few badly disturbed stones survive at the very top of Section B–B. Stratigraphically this structure belongs to *Temenos* 8 or 9, the Late Bronze Age fortress-temples, but, as the sections eloquently show, the precise connection has been destroyed by German excavation. The evidence may with a fair degree of confidence be taken to show that this spot was the location of the great altar during the entire history of the fortress-temples from their foundation to their final destruction.[12]

The dating of the altar foundation by ceramic evidence is rendered difficult by the fact that very little pottery is found in the courtyard fills and the few sherds recovered are suspect because of their location so near to the surface, exposed since the German excavations. The only pottery which can be used in evidence is that securely located in the gray-white *huwwar* layer. The majority of these sherds are too fragmentary to allow meaningful drawing. Field identification of the pottery indicates that it is to be dated to the Late Bronze Age and two bowl fragments correspond precisely to Nos. 1 and 3 in *BASOR*, 169, Feb. 1963, Fig. 23. However, the paucity of pottery evidence makes the section which we have studied a textbook case of the fundamental importance of stratigraphic evidence in the interpretation of archaeological results.

[12] *See* p. 99, where it is noted that Sellin may have found part of the *Temenos* 8 altar, in which case the final one of stone would be *Temenos* 9.

Appendix 6

Two Pottery Groups of Middle Bronze Shechem

While there is general agreement as to the varieties of pottery types representing the Middle Bronze Age in Palestine, work at establishing chronologically significant type distinctions for phases within the MB period has been to date largely inconclusive. Except for the work of Albright in his Tell Beit Mirsim volumes,[1] attempts at such definition have proceeded on the basis of purely typological considerations, i.e., observing taxonomic principles for the arrangement of materials into presumed developmental sequences. This work has principally involved analysis of tomb pottery, in that this source renders a more copious supply of whole forms with which to work.[2]

Typologies of this sort, however, remain, as they must, merely tentative constructions. Definitive work demands that typological analysis be checked by reference to stratigraphic

[1] W. F. Albright, *The Excavation of Tell Beit Mirsim*, Vols. I, Ia (*AASOR* XII, XIII; New Haven, ASOR, 1931, 1932).

[2] Cf. Kathleeen M. Kenyon, *Excavations at Jericho, I. The Tombs Excavated in 1952–1954*, London, British School of Archaeology, 1960, for a recent attempt in this regard.

data. Whereas Albright's pioneering work at Tell Beit Mirsim, with an eye to the stratigraphic factor, established the broad lines of the MB sequence, a more detailed stratigraphy and fresh excavation methods have been needed to pinpoint more subtle chronological factors. It is only with the advent of newer methods, including techniques of debris and section analysis, that a more refined consideration has become possible. The application of these new techniques at Shechem has provided a basis for more detailed study of the Middle Bronze pottery type-chronology.

The plates included here (Figs. 111 and 112) represent some preliminary results of these studies. While we should in no case have expected to find any radical disjunction between the pottery horizons of these phases, it is significant that some distinct tendencies do mark their differences. Figures 111 and 112 illustrate the horizons of *Temenos* phases 4 and 6 (Wall A) respectively. It should be noted that the tendencies observable here correlate well with distinctions separating the MB II B and II C periods as illustrated by Strata E–D at Tell Beit Mirsim and by Megiddo Strata XI–X.

Among the tendencies that call for particular notice, the most obvious is seen in the development of cooking pots. The wheel-made, round-bottomed variety, which, in a hole-mouth form, had already largely displaced the cruder, handmade, flat-bottomed type by the *Temenos* 4 period, begins in *Temenos* 6 to show a distinct tendency favoring an everted rim (cf. Fig. 112: *v, w, y*). This development continues in the next (*Temenos* 7–Wall B) phase and eventuates in the typical LB rim type.

Other features include the development during the Wall A–Fortress-temple 1a (*Temenos* 6) phase in both platter bowls and water jars of a characteristic beveling or angling of the outer transition of the rim (see Fig. 112:*h, j, m, n*), this as opposed to the generally rounded transitions of earlier phases. While traditions in store-jar rims are fairly constant, there is a tendency to accentuate features in the later period (cf. Fig. 111:*l* and Fig. 112:*r*). Less certain is the distinction to be seen in the apparent replacement of the curvilinear flaring neck of Fig. 111:*a* by the straight neck of Fig. 112:*a*, and we might also mention that a rather bright red, slow-fired ware, with small to medium lime grits (cf. Fig. 112:*c, m, o*), as well as a slow-fired gray ware with similar grits (cf. Fig. 112:*r*), likewise tend to become numerically significant during the Wall A phase.

Finally we should also notice the appearance in the *Temenos* 6 phase of the small cup-like bowls (Fig. 112:*s, t*). Very similar forms make their appearance first in Megiddo X (cf. G. Loud, *Megiddo* II, Pl. 44:7). The unusual profiled ring base (Fig. 112:*f*) also draws our attention, as does the painted jar or jug fragment (Fig. 112:*u*). An almost exact parallel to the latter is found at Megiddo in Stratum X (*ibid.*, Pl. 42:6).

Based, as it is, on the study of stratigraphically located sherd groups, further work on the pottery from Shechem can be expected to contribute substantially to our understanding of the type-chronology of Palestinian pottery, not only in the Middle Bronze Age,[3] but throughout the first two millennia B.C. While our remarks here are necessarily abbreviated, it is hoped that these plates, as a supplement to those already published in *BASOR* 169, will offer a preliminary review of Shechem's pottery profile.

[3] It may be noted that we have four stratified phases (*Temenoi* 2–5) belonging to MB II B (*ca.* 1750–1650 B.C.). These will be published in detail by Dan C. Cole. For MB II C (*ca.* 1650–1550/40 B.C.) we also have several groups of pottery which can be separated stratigraphically into four main phases: (1) The erection and first use of Wall A and Fortress-temple 1a (*Temenos* 6): this phase is represented by the selection in Fig. 112, which comes from Building 110 in the East Gate, described in Chap. 5, and from the courtyard fill of Fortress-temple 1a, a selection of which is published in *BASOR* 169, Feb. 1963, pp. 58–60, Fig. 25; (2) the foundation phase of the Wall B fortification system; (3) the second or Orthostat phase of the East Gate: the painted sherds published in *ibid.*, p. 60, Fig. 26 are from the leveling fill for the roadway through the gate for this phase; and (4) the final destructions of the city and its fortifications shortly after the middle of the 16th cent. Whether the rebuilding of the temple as Fortress-temple 1b (*Temenos* 7) belongs to phases 2 or 3 above probably cannot be proved ceramically because the phases are so close together that the ceramic changes are subtle, and it is dangerous at this stage of our knowledge to make them overly precise. The pottery of these phases will be published by the writer of this Appendix.

Appendix 7

Some Black- and Red-figured Attic Ware

NANCY R. LAPP

Fragments 1–5 in Fig. 113 are probably part of one Attic black-figured *krater* from a little after 500 B.C. A chariot scene is portrayed, a very common subject on large black-figured vases. No. 1 shows the driver's arm holding the reins; No. 2, a fragment from the rounded upper body of the vase, depicts part of two horses' heads, one behind the other; Nos. 3 and 4 are too worn to interpret but the incised lines may indicate parts of garments; No. 5 (cf. *BASOR* 161, p. 53, Fig. 20) depicts a male figure in front of the forelegs of a horse. Nos. 1–5 are examples of late black-figured technique. The incisions are particularly poor; the schematic branch-and-vine design used as a filling device in the background is a late feature. Some pieces are very worn, although Nos. 2 and 5 are fairly well preserved. The clay is typically Attic red; figures and designs are done in black paint with some use of purple.

Similar Attic black-figured column *kraters* dated between 550 and 490 B.C. are shown in *Corpus Vasorum Antiquorum* (*CVA*), Louvre 12 (France 19), III H e, Pls. 164–189. Chariot scenes occur frequently (note Pls. 169:1–2; 170:5–6; 171:2–3;

etc.), and the schematic branch-and-vine filling ornaments are common particularly in the later vases (cf. especially Pls. 182:8; 183:3; 185:2; 187:1 and 188:1, all dated about 500 to 490 B.C.).

No. 6 is an early red-figured piece, a little earlier in date than the *krater* above—that is, probably from the latter part of the sixth century B.C. It depicts part of a chariot wheel behind the tails of horses. There are good relief lines. The tails, as well as the chariot wheel, are partly reserved, as in red-figured style, but purple paint and incised lines are added, which are characteristic of black-figured technique. The piece is therefore transitional between the black-figured and red-figured styles.

No. 7 shows the two hands of a chariot driver in red-figured style. Similar paint and ware, as well as incised lines and the purple paint, of a chariot scene again, indicate the same vessel as fragment No. 6. One other small fragment (not shown) was found which has black relief lines and purple paint, probably part of the same scene.

No. 8 is an outline drawing with relief lines, most likely portraying a soldier's cuirass. Since it is drawn in outline on red ground and with the lower part of the body in black, it is to be classed with black-figured pottery. In the red-figured period this type of cuirass is replaced by the leather cuirass. For another case of the cuirass being left light, like gleaming metal, see Graef and Langlotz, *Die Antiken Vasen von der Akropolis zu Athen* I, Pl. 36, No. 611a.

The red-figured fragment, No. 9, is our latest example of the red-figured technique. It portrays an arm of a dancing figure with castanets. The edges of the figures are not as exact as our other pieces. It dates about 480 B.C., or even into the second quarter of the fifth century.

The remaining fragments are part of black- or red-figured *kraters*, most likely the same vessels as described above.

No. 10 is a small piece of the lower rim of a black-figured *krater* with the common ivy pattern. No. 11, probably from the same vessel, is from the horizontal part of the rim. On a side of the fragment not visible in the photograph is a part of the ivy-leaf pattern of the exterior lower rim as No. 10. For a similar combination of patterns, see *CVA, op. cit.*, Pl. 173:1.

No. 12 is another fragment of a rim. The carelessly made

circles (deteriorated ivy leaves) are on the lower exterior side, while on the upper side, not shown in the photograph, are poorly made lotus buds. For an exact parallel see the *petit cratère à colonnettes* pictured in *CVA, op. cit.*, Pl. 187:2. It is an Attic black-figured vessel, dated 490–480 B.C.

Another rim fragment, No. 13, has good relief lines and a band of purple paint. Perhaps it is part of the same red-figured vessel as fragments 6 and 7.

No. 16 is a part of the heavy foot of a large Attic *krater*. No. 17 is another fragment of the same vessel shown in profile. Note the band of purple paint about a centimeter wide at the very bottom. Nos. 14 and 15 are parts of the lower body just above the foot of the same vessel. Remains of a narrow purple band at the top of the foot separating it from the lower body can be seen on all four sherds. Compare the black-figured *kraters, CVA, op. cit.*, noted above, with similar heavy feet and lower bodies with rays in reserve. See especially Pls. 166:5; 169:1; 171:3; and 178:1–2, although the reserved rays in our vessel are narrower and less carefully made.

Thanks are due especially to Miss Dorothy Hill of Walters Art Gallery, Baltimore, Maryland, for her consultation and suggestions, though any inadequacies in the above should not be charged to her account.

Summary of Contexts

Almost all these fragments of black- and red-figured vessels are from the southeastern corner of Field VII. No. 9, the latest example of figured ware, is the only example from Field IX; it is from a Stratum V context. Most of the Field VII sherds are well sealed below Early Hellenistic floors or surfaces. The Hellenistic peoples built their structures on debris from earlier occupations—mainly Iron II and Early Persian (Stratum V). Non-imported wares also indicate this. The earliest context for any of these fragments (Nos. 1 and 7) is below what the excavators believe to be an early phase Stratum IV (IV B) metaled surface, Locus 1229–1232–1234. The pottery below this surface was almost exclusively Stratum V or earlier. Five fragments (Nos. 3, 5, 10, 15, and 16) are from the leveling fill of more than a half-meter beneath Stratum III B structures toward Stratum IV plastered Surface 1216.

Implications for the Date of Stratum V

The date of these fragments and their contexts indicates that these sherds are a part of Early Persian (Stratum V) debris. Since these imported wares can be dated closely, they are important for determining the absolute dates of Stratum V. As noted above, the latest example of figured ware, No. 9, dates *ca.* 480 B.C. Allowing time for its importation into Palestine and consideration for its value, a conservative terminus for the end of Stratum V at Balâṭah would be the end of the first quarter of the fifth century B.C. or *ca.* 475 B.C. Other pieces, notably Nos. 1–5, 10–11, 14–17, and particularly No. 12, date probably a little after 500 B.C., while the remainder discussed above may be put in the late sixth century. Some fragments of imported pottery not discussed here may be a little earlier, but the intrinsic value of these vessels and thus the possibility that they may have been preserved over a period of time should be considered, as well as the length of time it may have taken them to reach Palestine. The half-century between *ca.* 525 B.C. and 475 B.C. would perhaps be adequate for all of the imported wares of Stratum V. Comparative and typological study of the local wares of Stratum V, as well as consideration of any other evidence, will have to test this hypothesis.

Notes

Footnotes to Chapter 1

¹ Quoted by Johannes Hempel in ZAW 51, 1933, p. 157. The translation is the author's, revised at two places, from its publication in *BA XX*, 1957, p. 20.

² That is, not far from the size of the state of Rhode Island or the slightly smaller grand duchy of Luxemburg.

³ There are two such references, both of which refer to the city as *skmm*, the second *m* being understood today as a dual ending or else the enclitic *ma*. One of these references is among certain figurines on which were written the names of enemies of Egypt in Palestine and southern Syria. The figurines were broken as a magical way of crushing the enemies: *see* G. Posener, *Princes et Pays d'Asie et de Nubie*, Brussels, 1940, p. 68; J. A. Wilson, *ANET*, p. 329; W. F. Albright, *BASOR* 81, pp. 16–21. The second reference is in the Khu-Sebek inscription on a stele from Abydos, dated to the reign of Sesostris III: *see* Wilson, *op. cit.*, p. 230.

⁴ *Antiquities of the Jews* IV. viii. 44.

⁵ *See* M. Avi-Yonah, *The Madeba Mosaic Map*, Jerusalem, 1954; R. T. O'Callaghan, S.J., "Madaba (Carte de)," *Dictionnaire de la Bible, Supplément*, V, cols. 627–704; Victor Gold, "The Mosaic Map of Madeba," *BA* XXI, 1958, pp. 50–71.

⁶ " 'Askar" means "military camp" in Arabic, and Dr. Albright has suggested that it may go back to a Roman military installation once placed there. In any event, it is very doubtful that the ancient tradition is correct in identifying 'Askar with Sychar in John 4:5. It is much more probable that Sychar is a very ancient textual corruption of Sychem (Shechem), and that the Samaritan woman who met Jesus at Jacob's Well came from

243

the neighboring Shechem and not from Sychar which, if at 'Askar, is so much farther away. Of course, as our archaeological work has shown, Shechem as a city on the old tell was no longer in existence, but it is highly probable that a village has always existed where the village of Balâṭah now is. Roman-Byzantine remains in this village, including provision for water in water tunnels from Gerizim springs, are still to be found.

[7] Jerome, *Pilgrimage of the Holy Paula*, xvi; *Quaest. in Gen.*, c. XLVIII, No. 22.

[8] E. Robinson and E. Smith, *Biblical Researches in Palestine: A Journal of Travels in the Year 1838*, II, p. 292, n. 2.

[9] See C. R. Conder and H. H. Kitchener, *Survey of Western Palestine. Memoirs*, II, London, 1881, pp. 204–205.

[10] It would have been more accurate to say that the site of the old city was forgotten after the 6th cent. A.D. The words are those of A. Eckstein, *Geschichte und Bedeutung der Stadt Sichem* (Dissertation presented to the Faculty of Philosophy at the University of Leipzig), Berlin, 1886 (49 pp.). This work is not available to me, and the quotation is taken from an article of F. M. Th. Böhl, "De Geschiedenis der Stadt Sichem en de Opgravingen aldaar," *Mededeelingen der Koninklijke Akademie van Wetenschappen*, Amsterdam, Afd. Letterkunde, Deel 62, Serie B, 1926, pp. 1–24. The translation is that of S. H. Horn.

[11] So Johannes Hempel in ZAW 51, 1933, pp. 156–169, n. 3.

[12] For the first detailed publication of this hoard known to me, *see* the Appendix by von Bissing to the article of Böhl cited in n. 10 above. Members of our staff in 1962 were able to find Scheurleer collections in an art museum in The Hague (musical instruments) and in the Allard Pierson Museum in Amsterdam (Greek and Roman antiquities), but no trace of the bronzes. According to von Bissing they had been given numbers in the Scheurleer inventory ranging from V.A. (*Vorderasien*) 109 to 120. The Allard Pierson Museum had purchased Greco-Roman items numbered from 1 to about 8,000, no part of them bearing the letters V.A. It appears that von Bissing had recalled the objects when the Scheurleer Museum was closed. Inquiries produced the information that the von Bissing collection was broken up and sold in Berlin before World War II.

[13] *Anzeiger der kaiserlichen Akademie der Wissenschaften in Wien*. Phil.-Hist. Klasse, 51. Jahrgang 1914, VII, pp. 35–40; and XVIII, pp. 204–207.

[14] Sellin was dating his findings on the basis of his Jericho work, where things dated "Israelite" are actually Middle Bronze Age, seven hundred years earlier. His "Canaanite" discoveries in 1913–1914 are said to have been few in number, perhaps because "Canaanite" in the Sellin and Watzinger work at Jericho meant Early Bronze Age and earlier.

[15] The 1913–1914 discoveries were never properly published, including detailed plans and sections of the great Northwest Gate. What happened to the 850 arrowheads is also unknown.

[16] Sellin, *ibid.*, VII. Trans. by S. H. Horn.

Footnotes to Chapter 2

[1] *See* A. Alt, "Jerusalems Aufstieg," *Zeitschrift der Deutschen Morgenländischen Gesellschaft* 79, 1925, pp. 1–19 (reprinted in his *Kleine Schriften*, München, 1959, III, pp. 243–257); and also F. M. Th. Böhl in his article

on the history and excavations of Shechem in *Mededeelingen der Koninklijke Akademie van Wetenschappen,* Amsterdam, Afd. Letterkunde, Deel 62, Serie B, 1926, pp. 1–24.

2 My colleague, Krister Stendahl, brought this passage to my attention.

3 The one major exception is at the southeastern end of Ebal where a spring makes it possible for the village of 'Askar to exist there (*see* Appendix 4).

4 Cf. the 100-ft.-deep well cleared in the excavation of Lachish, its mouth opening on top of the city wall. *See* Olga Tufnell, *Lachish III: The Iron Age,* London, 1953, pp. 92 f.

5 Khirbet Mahneh et-Tahta ("the Lower") to distinguish it from Khirbet Mahneh el-Foqa ("the Upper") where the spring issued from the mountainside.

6 The summary of modern literary form-critical and tradition-history investigation of the biblical traditions about Shechem is that of Eduard Nielsen, *Shechem, A Traditio-Historical Investigation,* Copenhagen, 1955. While this book is a discursive and wide-ranging discussion covering 384 pp., it shows how and why a detailed discussion of Shechem throws one into the midst of nearly all the major problems connected with the early history of Israel.

7 There are two groups of the Egyptian magical texts in which the Asiatic enemies of Egypt are listed. The second or Brussels group is the later of the two, probably dating from the second half of the 19th or the early part of the 18th cent. *See* W. F. Albright in *The Bible and the Ancient Near East* (G. E. Wright, ed.; Garden City, N. Y., 1961), p. 333 (where he dates both groups between *ca.* 1925–1825 B.C., following his earlier treatment in *BASOR* 81, Feb. 1941, pp. 16–21; 83, Oct. 1941, pp. 30–36); J. A. Wilson, *ibid.,* p. 304; Posener, *loc. cit.*

8 *See* the writer in *The Bible and the Ancient Near East,* p. 88, and n. 68 for pertinent references. When one considers the re-establishment of the city-state system implied as taking place between the time of the first and second group of execration texts, and at the period when important officials leave their names in major cities, we are led to suggest that the MB II A period must begin during the 19th cent., and scarcely later than the time of Sesostris III. In recent articles my revered teacher, W. F. Albright, has proposed lowering the date to *ca.* 1800 B.C., but for the above-cited reasons I have had difficulty in compressing the chronology of the Middle Bronze Age to that extent: *see* his "Abram the Hebrew: A New Archaeological Interpretation," *BASOR* 163, Oct. 1961, pp. 36–54; and "The Chronology of Middle Bronze I (Early Bronze–Middle Bronze)," 168, Dec. 1962, pp. 36–42.

9 The "letters fit the period from approximately the 30th year of Amenophis III to approximately the end of Akhenaten's reign, i.e., *ca.* 1376–1350 B.C.": so the most recent survey of the question by Edward F. Campbell, Jr. in *BA* XXIII, 1960, pp. 2–22; *see further* his *The Chronology of the Amarna Letters,* Baltimore, 1964.

10 *BA* XXIII, 1960, pp. 19–20.

11 A. Alt has argued that the story of Jacob's migration from Shechem to Bethel, preceded by a purification ceremony (Gen. 35), suggests that in later Israel an annual pilgrimage was held as a journey from Shechem to Bethel: "Die Wahlfart von Sichem nach Bethel," *Kleine Schriften* I, pp. 79–88.

¹² Jacob's words to his two sons in v. 30, "You have made me odious," literally "stink," "among the inhabitants of the land," suggest that covenant violation is meant. A solemn oath has been violated.

¹³ The only tradition regarding a conquest of north central Palestine, besides that of Shechem in Gen. 34, can possibly be seen in Josh. 12:17, 24 within a list of kings Joshua conquered. Among them is listed "the king of Tappuah," a dependencey of Shechem, only some six miles to the south at Tell Sheikh Abū Zarad—a site which must have had a history closely paralleling that of Shechem, judging from the surface exploration there by the writer and members of the Shechem excavation staff in 1960 and again in 1962. The other is "the king of Tirzah," five miles northeast of Shechem at Tell el-Fâr‘ah, another probable dependency. It is difficult, however, to know how to assess the historical meaning of this chapter. It appears to be a secondary compilation, which lists kings of cities which elsewhere are said not to have been conquered by Israel (e.g., Gezer, Dor, Megiddo, Taanach, etc. Cf. Judg. 1:27–29).

¹⁴ *See further* the writer's *Biblical Archaeology* (rev. ed., London, 1962; Philadelphia, 1963), Chap. V; and John Bright, *A History of Israel*, Philadelphia, 1959, pp. 122–27. Both of these have references to other sources.

¹⁵ For summaries of the fresh treatment of the Deuteronomic tradition now possible, *see* G. von Rad, *Studies in Deuteronomy*, London and Naperville, Ill., 1953; G. Ernest Wright, *Deuteronomy* (*Interpreter's Bible*, II, New York and Nashville, 1953).

¹⁶ *See* Stanley Gevirtz, "Jericho and Shechem: A Religio-Literary Aspect of City Destruction," *Vetus Testamentum* XIII, 1963, pp. 52–62, wherein there is a rejection of the views of A. M. Honeyman, "The Salting of Shechem," *ibid*. III, 1953, pp. 192–195. *See also* F. Charles Fensham, "Salt as Curse in the Old Testament and the Ancient Near East," *BA* XXV, 1962, pp. 48–50.

¹⁷ The Samaritans are called "Shechemites" by one of the sources used by Josephus, *Antiquities,* XI, 340 ff. *Note also* Sirach 50:25-26.

Footnotes to Chapter 3

¹ About 1955 surveyors of the Jordan government appropriated for the government 13½ *dunams* (Blocks 39 and 40 of the Nablus land survey) in the tell's western sector because the great ruins prevented any further agricultural use. Hence our rental requirement is only for 41 *dunams.*

² This object is reported to be 60 cm. high, 36 cm. wide, and a depression exists on the top, 30 cm. in diameter, surrounded by the four "horns." It is probably the same as one from the Shechem excavations now preserved in the Leiden Museum. The second incense altar, mentioned below, is a later type and probably Hellenistic in date.

³ The report of the spring campaign was published in *ZDPV*, 49, 1926, pp. 229–236, together with some photographs, including those of the two incense altars (Pl. 31 b and c).

⁴ For Sellin's report of the summer campaign, 1926, *see ibid.*, pp. 304–320. The preliminary report on the cuneiform tablets was published by F. M. Th. Böhl in *ibid.*, pp. 321–327, with photographs and drawings of the tablets on Pls. 44–46. For Albright's treatment *see* his article, "A

Teacher to a Man of Shechem about 1400 B.C.," *BASOR* 86, Apr. 1942, pp. 28–31. For a more detailed story of the 1926 campaigns *see* Böhl, *De Opgraving van Sichem; Bericht over de Voorjaars-campagne en de Zomer-campagne in 1926,* Zeist, Netherlands, 1927; 40 pp.

⁵ *ZDPV* 50, 1927, p. 266.

⁶ *Ibid.*, pp. 265–274.

⁷ *ZDPV* 51, 1926, pp. 119–123.

⁸ A brief article on his work during the summer of 1928 was published in *Forschungen und Fortschritte,* Vol. 4, No. 31 (Nov. 1, 1928), pp. 316–317; and also a note about his excavation of a Byzantine octagonal church on the top of Mt. Gerizim appeared in *ibid.*, No. 32 (Nov. 10, 1928), p. 329. A somewhat longer edition of the first was unpublished but was submitted to the Department of Antiquities (on file in the Palestine Archaeological Museum). A briefer statement of his work, "Balata-Shechem (1928, 1929, 1931)" is also on file. His only substantial review of his work, however, was published in 1932 together with some excellent plans in *Archäologischer Anzeiger, Beiblatt zum Jahrbuch des Archäologischen Instituts,* 1932, III/IV, Cols. 289–314.

⁹ In this he was followed by no less a scholar than Kurt Galling, *Biblisches Reallexikon,* Tübingen, 1937, Col. 511, though Galling, of course, did not identify it with the temple of Judg. 9.

¹⁰ For the "final" report on the 1934 excavations with prognosis, *see* Sellin and Steckeweh, *ZDPV* 64, 1941, pp. 1–20.

¹¹ H. Thiersch, "Ein altmediterraner Tempeltyp," *Zeitschrift für die Alttestamentliche Wissenschaft,* Vol. 50, 1932, pp. 76–78 (n. 4). Trans. by S. H. Horn.

¹² *Ibid.*, pp. 303–308. Quotations are from a translation by S. H. Horn. For a lengthy review of the whole situation, an attempt to summarize the status of the excavations and an appeal for the creation of a special German school where Palestinian archaeology could be furthered and men trained in the discipline, *see* Johannes Hempel, *ibid.*, Vol. 51, 1933, pp. 156–169.

Footnotes to Chapter 4

¹ The following preliminary reports of our excavations may be listed: G. Ernest Wright, "The First Campaign at Tell Balâṭah (Shechem)," *BASOR* 144, Dec. 1956, pp. 9–20; G. Ernest Wright, "The Second Campaign . . .," *BASOR* 148, Dec. 1957, pp. 11–28; Lawrence E. Toombs and G. Ernest Wright, "The Third Campaign . . .," *BASOR* 161, Feb. 1961, pp. 11–54; Lawrence E. Toombs and G. Ernest Wright, "The Fourth Campaign . . .," *BASOR* 169, Feb. 1963, pp. 1–60. Summaries of these by the same authors are to be found in *Revue Biblique* LXIV, 1957, pp. 230–233; LXV, 1958, pp. 253–260; LXIX, 1962, pp. 257–266.

See also: Walter Harrelson, Bernhard W. Anderson and G. Ernest Wright, "Shechem, 'Navel of the Land,'" *BA* XX, 1957, pp. 2–32; Howard C. Kee and Lawrence E. Toombs, "The Second Season of Excavation at Biblical Shechem," *ibid.*, pp. 82–105; Edward F. Campbell, Jr., "Excavation at Shechem, 1960," *BA* XXIII, 1960, pp. 102–110; Robert J. Bull, "A Re-examination of the Shechem Temple," *ibid.*, pp. 110–119; G. R. H. Wright, "The Architectural Recording of the Shechem Excavation," *ibid.*, pp. 120–126; G. Ernest Wright, "Archaeological Fills and Strata," *BA* XXV, 1962, pp. 34–40; Ovid R. Sellers, "Coins of the 1960 Excavation at

Shechem," *ibid.*, pp. 87–96; Edward F. Campbell, Jr. and James F. Ross, "The Excavation of Shechem and the Biblical Tradition," *BA* XXVI, 1963, pp. 2–27.

James F. Ross and Lawrence E. Toombs, "The Excavation of Biblical Shechem," *Archaeology* 14, 1961, pp. 171–179; Bernhard W. Anderson, Robert J. Bull, James F. Ross, Lawrence E. Toombs and G. Ernest Wright, "Shechem," *The Drew Gateway* XXXII, 1962, pp. 127–172; Siegfried H. Horn, "The Excavation of Shechem," *Review and Herald* for Nov. 2, 9, 16 and 23, 1961; Siegfried H. Horn, "The Scarabs from Shechem," *Journal of Near Eastern Studies* XXI, 1962, pp. 1–14; G. Ernest Wright, "Selected Seals from Balâṭah (Shechem)," *BASOR* 167, Oct. 1962, pp. 5–13; Frank M. Cross, Jr., "An Inscribed Seal from Balâṭah (Shechem)," *ibid.*, pp. 14–15; G. Ernest Wright, "1600 Years of Shechem and its Pillars of the Covenant," *Illustrated London News*, No. 6471, Vol. 243 (Aug. 10, 1963), pp. 204–208.

2 Other members of the 1957 staff, in addition to Dean Anderson, Dr. Steckeweh, Mr. G. R. H. Wright and me were the following: David M. Graybeal of Drew was camp and expedition manager; Ovid R. Sellers was recorder and our expert on scarabs and coins; field supervisors were Robert J. Bull, Robert W. Funk, William R. Farmer, H. Neil Richardson and Lawrence E. Toombs; Howard C. Kee was in charge of the pottery sorting; James T. Stewart served as photographer; student assistants were George W. Buchanan and Paul Hollenbach of Drew, Edward F. Campbell, Jr., Robert G. and Jean Boling, Paul W. and Nancy Lapp, Lawrence W. Sinclair of Johns Hopkins University, Lee C. Ellenberger of McCormick and Arthur E. Talbert of the University of Chicago. Spiridion Jahshan was foreman, assisted by Mustafa Tawfiq, Mohammed Mustafa, and Yusuf Jadullah from Balâṭah. The representative from the Department of Antiquities was Mr. Farah Ma'ayeh.

3 We did not know all this at the time of digging. The interpretation of the stratigraphical situation was worked out subsequently by Paul W. Lapp, who at my suggestion took the problem of the chronology of Hellenistic pottery as a subject for his dissertation. *See* his *Palestinian Ceramic Chronology, 200 B.C.–A.D., 70,* New Haven, 1961, now obtainable only from my office, Rm. 102, 6 Divinity Ave., Cambridge 38, Mass. His wife, Nancy R. Lapp, will publish a companion dissertation on the pottery of the 4th and 3rd cents. B.C.

4 For the meaning and importance of an archaeological section, *see* Appendix 1 by Prof. Toombs. Other members of the staff in the Third Campaign: assisting Robert Bull in Field V were H. Neil Richardson, Henry O. Thompson and Herbert B. Huffmon; assisting James F. Ross in Field VI were Joseph A. Callaway, James Mays and Maury Luker; assisting Edward F. Campbell in Field VII were Siegfried H. Horn, E. Jerry Vardaman, Clinton D. Morrison (before his transfer to the chief architect's crew), Jack R. Irwin and Sami Rashid, who was the representative of the Jordanian Department of Antiquities; assisting the chief architect, J. Stanley Chesnut; assisting Paul Lapp in ceramic recording, Tracy Luke, and in Hellenistic pottery analysis, his wife, Nancy R. Lapp; John S. Holladay, Jr. was part-time assistant to the photographer for color pictures and otherwise assistant supervisor in Field VII; Daniel P. Cole was in charge of pottery washing and sorting; Mrs. Herbert Huffmon was assistant in both the managerial and recording departments. Spiridion Jahshan was

again chief foreman, assisted by Mustafa Tawfiq and Yusuf Jadullah of Balâṭah.

⁵ I was again Archaeological Director, assisted by Lawrence E. Toombs as Associate Director in charge of field operations and by Paul W. Lapp, by then Director of the American School in Jerusalem, in pottery analysis; he also was in charge of recording where he was assisted by Ovid R. Sellers and George M. Landes. Edward F. Campbell, Jr. was again assistant director and treasurer, and Vivian (Mrs. Robert J.) Bull was again camp manager and assistant treasurer. G. R. H. Wright was chief architect, assisted by J. Stanley Chesnut and David Voelter. Lee C. Ellenberger was photographer, assisted by William G. Dever for color pictures. Mr. Rafiq Dajani was the representative of the Department of Antiquities. Assisting Robert Bull in Field V were J. Alberto Soggin and William G. Dever. Assisting James Ross in Field VI were Robert Schnell, Joe D. Seger and Roger S. Boraas. A special section in Field VI was Area 2, supervised by Daniel P. Cole, assisted by Byron C. Shafer. Assisting Edward F. Campbell, Jr. and Siegfried H. Horn in Field VII were Albert E. Glock, John S. Holladay, Jr., Hanna E. Kassis, H. Darrell Lance, and Prescott H. Williams, Jr. Assisting Joseph A. Callaway, supervisor of the new Field IX, were Delbert R. Hillers and Murray B. Nicol (Roger S. Boraas joined them during the final two weeks). Mrs. Joseph A. Callaway, Mrs. George M. Landes and Mrs. J. Alberto Soggin assisted Henry O. Thompson, who was in charge of pottery washing and sorting, and they also took charge of pottery mending, public relations and medical matters. Mustafa Tawfiq was chief foreman, assisted by Yusuf Jadullah and Aziz Mohammed Jadullah—all of Balâṭah. Fuad Zogbi of Bethlehem was draftsman.

⁶ A similar feature in Samaria Period VIII is interpreted in this manner by Kathleen M. Kenyon: see *Samaria I. The Buildings,* London, 1942, pp. 112–115.

⁷ *See* for detailed description of her methods Kathleen M. Kenyon, *Beginning in Archaeology,* London and New York, 1952; and also the book by one of her teachers, Mortimer Wheeler, *Archaeology from the Earth,* Oxford, 1954. On drawing a balk or section, *see* Appendix 1 below.

⁸ It is to be hoped that this is a more judicious way of stating the matter than is to be found in the book of the Dutch and British archaeologists, trained by Miss Kenyon, H. J. Franken and C. A. Franken-Battershill, *A Primer of Old Testament Archaeology,* Leiden, 1963. It would appear to this writer that this work is lacking in perspective and proportion, and seems largely lacking also in any sense of gratitude, indebtedness or respect for the great men of the previous generation on whose shoulders we all stand. Professor Franken seems to imply that the only good archaeological work is that done by Miss Kenyon and her pupils. In any case, it is European and never American! The basic nature of Albright's work, which has towered over the field, is scarcely acknowledged or understood. This type of loyalty to one's teacher is commendable, but it scarcely exhibits any breadth in spirit or in grasp of the total field.

⁹ In 1956 I dated the pottery from this locus too early, preferring a date around 800 B.C. or "between *ca.* 850 and 750 B.C." (*BASOR* 144, p. 19). This is because in 1956 the pottery of the 9th and 8th cents. was still not well known and ceramic development in Iron II (the archaeological period between *ca.* 900 and 550 B.C.) could not be clearly delineated. The publication of *Samaria* III (London, 1957), and the excavation of Hazor,

Tirzah and Shechem, together with a number of other sites in Israel, is doing much to clarify the situation. Preliminary reports are always hazardous, because initial conclusions not infrequently must be revised on fuller evidence.

10 *See further* my remarks in my stratigraphical and chronological survey of "The Archaeology of Palestine," in *The Bible and the Ancient Near East* (The W. F. Albright *Festschrift*), Garden City, N. Y., 1961, pp. 73 ff.

Footnotes to Chapter 5

1 The date of this excavation is given by Sellin, *ZAW* 50, 1932, pp. 303–308.

2 The precise height is given as 8.50 m. (*ca.* 28 ft.) by Sellin from a 2-m.-wide pit he dug alongside it (*ZDPV* 49, 1926, p. 320). Welter, on the other hand, in *Archäologischer Anzeiger*, 1932, III/IV, cols. 289–314, gives the height as 10 m. for part of its length (*ca.* 32 ft.). The Jordanian Department of Antiquities is scheduled to clear away the debris piled against it by John Hyrcanus to cover it. When that is done, to quote Dr. F. M. Th. Böhl, "the city of Shechem would become one of the most impressive monuments in all Palestine" (trans. by S. H. Horn from *De Opgraving Van Sichem.*)

3 *See* Yigael Yadin, "Hyksos Fortifications and the Battering-Ram," *BASOR* 137, Feb. 1955, pp. 23–32; and W. F. Albright, *The Excavation of Tell Beit Mirsim, Vol. II. The Bronze Age, AASOR,* XVII; New Haven, ASOR, 1938, pp. 27 ff.

4 Another exceedingly important discovery of Prof. D. A. Kuschke of Mainz, for which we are deeply in his debt.

5 The dimensions here given are only rough approximations given from measurements taken from this plan. A special study is to be made of the Northwest Gate and its measurements by our expedition's architect, G. R. H. Wright.

6 After the preliminary report of the 2nd campaign the interpretation given here for the Northwest Gate was suggested to me for the East Gate by Yigael Yadin. There was no question but that Yadin was correct with regard to the symmetry of the dimensions, but at the time I could not bring myself to accept the idea of sliding doors because of the lack of parallels. I recall suggesting to the staff in 1960 that the gate may have been closed by beams.

7 For description and review of the evidence for the typical door and gate, and the sockets in which they turned, *see* Rudolf Naumann, *Architektur Kleinasiens,* Tübingen, 1955, pp. 155–165.

8 *See* Naumann, *ibid.,* pp. 290 ff. and Fig. 366.

9 Kathleen M. Kenyon, *Digging Up Jericho,* London and New York, 1957, Chap. 9 and Pl. 44 A; *Archaeology in the Holy Land,* London and New York, 1960, pp. 178 ff.; and E. Sellin and C. Watzinger, *Jericho,* Leipzig, 1913—the Red Wall.

10 According to figures submitted to me by Prof. R. B. Y. Scott, a 6-cubit, or 1-reed, wall should average about 2.667 m. (8 ft., 9 in.) in width. *See further* the summary of his recent studies of weights and measures in *BA* XVII, 1959, pp. 22–40. The common cubit was about 17½ in.

11 Gordon Loud, *Megiddo* II, Chicago, 1948, pp. 6–8, 78–87 (for

dating *see* my remarks and chart in *The Bible and the Ancient Near East*, pp. 88–89 and p. 108, n. 71).

[12] Kathleen M. Kenyon, *Archaeology in the Holy Land*, p. 174.

[13] *See* W. F. Albright, *Tell Beit Mirsim* II, pp. 17 ff.

[14] Trans. by S. H. Horn from Welter's report on his summer campaign in 1928 to the Department of Antiquities (unpublished). These same conclusions were published by Welter in *Forschungen und Fortschritte*, Vol. 4, No. 31 (Nov. 1, 1928), pp. 316–317.

[15] *Archäologischer Anzeiger*, 1932, Cols. 289–314.

[16] *See* Yadin, *loc. cit.* (n. 3) for a recent summary with references, to which should be added Yadin, *et al.*, Hazor I, Jerusalem, 1958, esp. Chap. 1.

[17] *See* my report of the 1st campaign, *BASOR* 144, p. 15.

[18] Welter, who found the outer one in his section to the East Gate, appears to have thought that it was simply a revetment to hold the earth in place for the heavy Wall B and gate above it (*see* his article, *loc. cit.*, n. 15).

[19] *See* the final published discussion of the question by Sellin, in which he summarizes his differences of opinion with Welter, *ZDPV* 64, 1941, pp. 1–20, esp. section III of the article.

[20] This means that the well-preserved building here is of a later era, but precisely which is unknown. It may be Late Bronze, Iron Age or Hellenistic. From the existing ruins I would judge that it is earlier than the 9th cent. Wall E (see below), but there is now no possibility of finding out.

[21] *See further* my survey in *The Bible and the Ancient Near East*, pp. 88–91, and Chart 6.

[22] For samples of this pottery, see *BASOR* 169, Feb. 1963, pp. 51, 60 and Fig. 26. The stratification is certain and little uncontaminated with later intrusions within MB II C. For my dating of Megiddo IX as *ca.* 1500–1468 B.C. and the strong indication that none of the bichrome ware belongs to Stratum X (MB II C), though Gordon Loud assigns it to both strata, *see* my remarks in *The Bible and the Ancient Near East*, pp. 91 and 109, n. 85.

I am deeply indebted to Mrs. H. J. Franken-Battershill for her assistance in 1957 with regard to our Shechem red-painted white-slipped ware. She carefully went through the pottery collections of the Palestine Archaeological Museum, looking for parallels to our sherds. She wrote at the time that her search drew a virtual blank, except for one special piece, our B57 Pottery Reg. 865, which is a double-handled painted jug, not yet published.

Footnotes to Chapter 6

[1] *See* ZDPV 49, 1926, pp. 304–320. Trans. by S. H. Horn.

[2] *Archäologisher Anzeiger*, 1932, cols. 289–314. Trans. by S. H. Horn.

[3] *ZDPV* 49, 1926, Taf. 16–17, following p. 264. Tafel 16 is a view "from the north" in the terminology of both Sellin and Welter. We prefer to call Tafel 16 a view "from the west." Actually, the view looks in a direction which is about 30 deg. south of east. On top of a wall to the right in Tafel 16 is a cylindrical stone which may be what Welter was talking about but not what Sellin was referring to.

[4] *ZDPV* 64, 1941, pp. 1–20. Trans. by S. H. Horn.

[5] H. Thiersch, "Ein altmediterraner Tempeltyp," *ZAW* 50, 1932, pp. 76–78.

[6] *ZAW* 51, 1933, pp. 156–169.

[7] *See* articles on "Sichem" and "Altar" in *Biblisches Reallexikon,* Tübingen, 1937, cols. 477–478 and 14 respectively. In the second, Galling speaks of the building as "at one time certainly a temple."

[8] W. F. Albright, *The Archaeoolgy of Palestine* (Penguin Books, 1st ed. 1949), pp. 90 (Fig. 15) and 104. Albright uses the inaccurate dimensions of Welter; unable to measure the remains oneself, one would naturally suppose that Welter's article in *Archäologischer Anzeiger* (see n. 2) was the one to follow.

[9] Galling, *op. cit.* (article "Altar," col. 14), suggests that this platform should be regarded as the altar itself, because it is very similar to the hearth-form. A good Bronze Age example of the latter was found by Petrie at Tell el-'Ajjûl (*Ancient Gaza,* I, London, 1931, Pl. VI). *See* Appendix 5, however, for the interpretation of Lawrence E. Toombs.

[10] In 1960 this spot was treated as Field V, Area 2, from which two small groups of pottery were recovered. In our Pottery Reg. V.2.1 (Aug. 3, 1960) are sherds 7427–7432; in V.2.2 (Aug. 5, 1960) are sherds 6113–6115. A few more pieces were recovered in 1962. They were saved but not registered because they were undistinguished body sherds.

[11] In the report of the summer campaign of 1926 (*ZDPV* 49, pp. 304–320), Sellin wrote: "Certain evidence for the dating of the outermost supporting wall [the *temenos* wall, our Wall 900—Figs. 22 and 59] and therefore also of the temple is provided by Late Mycenaean sherds found in the earth fill of the latest part of the terrace. Accordingly, it [*sic!* the wall?] and the temple should be put into the thirteenth century." Unfortunately, this is too sweeping a conclusion for so generalized and imprecise an observation. That Wall 900 was used as a support for the fill of the temple's court and that Mycenaean sherds (imported from Greece into Palestine between *ca.* 1375 and 1225 B.C.) appear in the latest fill of the court is important. Both temple and court were probably in use therefore at least as late as the 13th cent. But this evidence says nothing about the time when either Wall 900 or the temple was erected. We shall see that while used together, they did not originate in the same period.

[12] *See ZDPV* 51, 1928, pp. 119–123.

[13] Quoted from an unpublished report filed with the Department of Antiquities (*see above* pp. 33–34). One might suppose that the stones had slid down the slopes by natural forces of time and erosion, were it not for two facts: (a) W. F. Albright who was present in the country at the time was an independent witness confirming Schmidt's report. He writes: "I was then in Palestine and saw the stone [the large *Maṣṣēbāh* 1] after it had been set up by Sellin where it had been found, and also after Welter had dumped it into a neighboring trench; it was broken further in the process" (*BASOR* 169, p. 15, n. 14). (b) Albright's memory to the effect that it was broken further is sustained by one difference in its height as Sellin reports it (1.52 m.) and as we found it (1.45 m.), and by the fact that the end of the base is broken off (see below). Anyone qualified to dig in Palestine and who saw that stone for the first time should know that nothing like it had ever been reported before.

[14] Dr. F. M. Th. Böhl of Leiden in his independent account of the

1926 campaign tells us something about this foreman. He was Franz Datodi, the son of an Italian father and a German mother who spoke, in addition to Arabic, at least four European languages. With his brothers he had worked previously for Sellin and Watzinger at Jericho in 1908, with Reisner at Samaria in 1910, and again with Sellin at Shechem in 1913 and 1914. Under him were five Arab assistants who had worked for Sellin in Taanach as early as 1902 (Böhl, *De Opgraving van Sichem,* 1927. A copy of this work is not available to me; I am working from an English translation made for our expedition by S. H. Horn).

¹⁵ Böhl, *ibid.* See *also* the photograph, taken in the summer of 1926 by Kurt Galling, in Fig. 72.

¹⁶ In analyzing a large number of ancient buildings, Scott's figures for the common cubit average at about 445 mm., with a slight variation either way which cannot be precisely controlled because of the imprecision of the ancient architects. The long cubit is one handbreadth, or one-sixth longer than a common cubit. An approximation for it of 525 mm. would mean: a 50 by 40 long-cubit building should be 26.25 m. by 21.00 m. This is certainly very close to the actual size.

¹⁷ *See* Gordon Loud, *Megiddo II. Seasons of 1935–1939,* Chicago, 1948, pp. 102 ff. The Megiddo temple is 16.50 by 21.50 m., with walls 3.50 m. thick. The cella is 9.50 by 11.50 m.

¹⁸ Cf. also Kathleen M. Kenyon, *Archaeology in the Holy Land,* London and New York, 1960, p. 203, n. 1.

¹⁹ *See* W. F. Albright, *From the Stone Age to Christianity* (Anchor ed., 1957), pp. 204–206; A. Scharff and A. Moortgat, *Ägypten und Vorderasien im Altertum,* München, 1950, pp. 321 ff.; and H. Schmökel, *Geschichte des alten Vorderasien,* Leiden, 1957, pp. 1954 ff., 213 ff.

²⁰ In our records this material was found in B60 pottery baskets V.4.15, 16, 25, 26 (and closely associated in the same earth layer but east of the wall, Basket V.4.27). From the baskets the following sherds were saved which were identified as of Late Bronze date: 6027, 6029, 6033–6035, 6435–6437 and 6882–6883.

²¹ *See* S. H. Horn, "Scarabs from Shechem," *Journal of Near Eastern Studies* XXI, 1962, pp. 8–9.

²² Sir Leonard Woolley, *Alalakh,* Oxford, 1955, pp. 59 ff., Fig. 35 and Pl. XIV. The pottery found in Level VII dates from the MB II B–C period in Palestine, and the dating given by the excavator and others, including C. F. A. Schaeffer, *Stratigraphie Comparée et Chronologie de l'Asie Occidentale,* London, 1948, pp. 98–107, is much too high. Stratum VI with its Late Bronze I painted ware cannot begin much before *ca.* 1550 B.C., nor can the pottery of VII extend so far back into the 18th cent. Cf. W. F. Albright, *BASOR* 144, Dec. 1956, pp. 26–30, esp. p. 27. It is my personal view that Alalakh VII cannot be dated by the late 18th-cent. cuneiform tablets found in the palace. The pottery requires the supposition that these tablets were a family archive held over from a previous generation.

²³ *ZDPV* 49, 1926, p. 313.

Footnotes to Chapter 7

¹ *ZDPV* 49, 1926, Taf. 29, following p. 272.

² Fig. 69 (901 palace), Room 2, Rooms 4–6 in its original phase, and a third above Wall 938. In Fig. 64 (902), Rooms 11 and 12.

[3] Alan Rowe, *The Topography and History of Beth-shan,* Philadelphia, 1930, pp. 10–17 with plan in Fig. 1 and photographs in Pls. 16–22. The author, dating largely by scarabs, assigned it to a period at least a century too early (the so-called "Thothmes III" Stratum).

[4] *BASOR* 169, pp. 1 ff.

[5] *See* Kathleen M. Kenyon, *Digging Up Jericho,* pp. 85–92; *Archaeology in the Holy Land,* pp. 63–67; and esp. R. de Vaux, *Revue Biblique* LIV, 1947, pp. 397–403; LV, 1948, pp. 545–548, 558–559; and LXII, 1955, pp. 550–553. In Israel this culture has been called "Yarmukian": *see* M. Stekelis, "A New Neolithic Industry: The Yarmukian of Palestine," *Israel Exploration Journal* 1, 1950–1951, pp. 1–19. For critical discussion with bibliography, *see* J. Kaplan, "The Neolithic Pottery of Palestine," *BASOR* 156, Dec. 1959, pp. 15–22. For a more general description and evaluation, *see also* Emmanual Anati, *Palestine before the Hebrews,* New York, 1963, pp. 263–269.

[6] *See* my article in *BASOR* 122, April 1951, pp. 52–55; and Robert J. and Linda S. Braidwood, *Excavations in the Plain of Antioch. I. The Earlier Assemblages, Phases A–J,* Chicago, 1960, pp. 509–511. In northern Mesopotamia copper seems first to appear in the Halafian painted pottery culture. In the Plain of Antioch pottery much like the Yarmukian or Neolithic B appears in a brief interlude (Phase D) between the Halafian and the painted pottery culture which followed, Obeidian. The Plain of Antioch in its Phases C and E shows dominant influence from the east. Only in Phase D does the connection down the Orontes River to Palestine appear before the third millennium.

[7] Gordon Loud, *Megiddo II,* Chicago, 1948, pp. 78 ff.

[8] R. A. S. Macalister, *The Excavation of Gezer,* I, London, 1912, pp. 236–238. This wall is difficult to understand. While the description is not very clear, and the nature of the construction said not to be uniform, it is described as an earthen bank lined with stone. At one point the inner face is said to be a wall 6½ ft. high, 2 ft. 2 in. thick. A sloping bank of earth capped with stones sloped up to this wall, so that the width of the whole at the base was 6½ ft.

[9] The widths of the 939 and 902 courtyard compounds were *ca.* 14 m. (46 ft.), while the second phase extension of 901 made it *ca.* 16.50 m. (54 ft.).

[10] *See* Rudolf Naumann, *Architektur Kleinasiens,* p. 390, Figs. 475 and 476.

[11] That is, in addition to the fortress-temples of Shechem and Megiddo, the typical Canaanite "broadhouse" temples of the third and second millennia mentioned in the last chapter, and a rather strange and atypical structure excavated by Immanuel Ben-Dor and M. Dothan at Nahariyah, and dating from Middle Bronze Age: *see* Ben-Dor, *Quarterly of the Department of Antiquities in Palestine* XIV, 1944, pp. 1–41; and Dothan, *Israel Exploration Journal 6,* 1956, pp. 14–25. A fine broad-roomed temple found at Hazor and dated in the Middle Bronze Age had towers and portico added in the Late Bronze Age; *see* Y. Yadin, *BA* XXI, 1958, pp. 34–39.

Footnotes to Chapter 8

[1] *See above,* p. 242, n. 16.

[2] Judg. 9:46. In 9:4 it is called "the House of Baal-berith," on which see below.

[3] The phrases used surely indicate this: "And Abimelech fought against the city . . .; he took the city, and killed the people . . .; and he razed the city and sowed it with salt."

[4] The Hebrew word here, the plural of baʻal, "lord," surely means either the officials, which is improbable, or else the leading male citizens who controlled the city's affairs—that is, in the terms of local government in modern New England, those legally qualified to vote in town meeting. Vv. 2, 3 and 6 indicate that the latter is meant.

[5] From the way the stories are put together, the antecedent of "heard" would appear to be the news of the city's destruction in the preceding verse. If this was another or independent fragment of oral tradition, the precise antecedent is not so certain.

[6] J. T. Milik, "Notes d'épigraphie et de topographie palestiniennes," Revue Biblique LXVI, 1959, pp. 556 f., 560–562. The word appears only one other time in the Old Testament, in 1 Sam. 13:6, where it seems to mean a cave in which people took refuge. Milik shows that in post-biblical Hebrew it is used for rock-cut tombs.

[7] The people who made him king are "all of the baʻălê of Shechem and all Bêt-Millô." Are the latter one special group of the former or a completely separate entity? The passage can be interpreted either way and still be within the bounds of good Hebrew style. Yet since Bêt-Millô is simply another name for the temple precincts (see below), then the first is the proper interpretation as v. 4 makes clear.

[8] This position is also adopted by E. Nielsen, Shechem, A Traditio-Historical Investigation, Copenhagen, 1955, pp. 164–167. This book is an excellent review and study of the history of the Shechem traditions with full discussion of each disputed point and full bibliography. It is also an eloquent demonstration of how history-of-tradition studies in themselves alone produce little history without the external referents which archaeology in its fullest sense alone can provide.

[9] See my remarks in Biblical Archaeology (rev. ed., London, 1962; Philadelphia, 1963), p. 131; The Bible and the Ancient Near East, Garden City, N. Y., 1961, p. 110, n. 96; my review of Lachish III in Vetus Testament V, 1955, pp. 97 ff.; and my description in Grant and Wright, Ain Shems Excavations V, Haverford, 1939, pp. 68–71.

[10] This indeed appears to be the dominant reading according to Brooke and McLean, The Old Testament in Greek, Vol. I, Part IV, Cambridge, 1917, p. 833. It has strong support particularly in the A group of manuscripts. In the words of Harry M. Orlinsky in a letter (Mar. 11, 1963): "In the case of A(lexandrian) and B (Vaticanus) groups in Judges, sound method leads one to recognize the priority of a reading in the A group, unless and until a different reading in the B group is proved superior."

[11] See BASOR 169, Feb., 1963, p. 30, n. 35.

[12] This term is translated by the RSV as "a strong tower." Yet, while this is possible, it is also possible that a town under the strong influence of Shechem may well have had a Migdāl-temple in it. If so, then Migdal-ʻŌz may have been its name, and the second term, a noun meaning "strength," could be an appelative of deity comparable to Migdal-Gad (Josh. 15:37). The latter means, "fortress-temple of Gad," a divine title referring to a deity as "(Good) Fortune." ʻŌz is frequently cited as an attribute of deity in the Old Testament. In addition, it is a theophorous element in a number of proper names in the Old Testament, as well as in Phoenician and on Hebrew seals (e.g., Z. Harris, Grammar of the Phoenician Language, New

Haven, 1936, p. 131). For example, Uzziah ("My Strength is Yahweh"), the great king of Judah *ca.* 783–742; or Uzziel ("My Strength is El"), an even more common name. In the case of the *Migdāl* at Thebez the epithet surely refers to El. It is to be noted also that its location is said to be *in the midst of* the town and that Abimelech broke through the town's defenses before he laid siege to it.

[13] See W. F. Albright, *From the Stone Age to Christianity* (Anchor ed., 1957), Chap. IV, esp. pp. 236 ff.; John Bright, *A History of Israel,* Philadelphia, 1959, Chap. 2; the same author's *Early Israel in Recent History Writing: A Study in Method,* London, 1956; and G. Ernest Wright, *Biblical Archaeology* (rev. ed.), Chap. III.

[14] Göttingen, 1922. This introduction was published separately in English translation as *The Legends of Genesis,* London, 1901.

[15] The predecessor of Hebron, the latter not appearing until later (Num. 13:24). The importance of Mamre as a pilgrimage center in the New Testament era is indicated by the fact that Herod the Great built an elaborate compound there. Hebron, where the Patriarchal burial Cave of Machpelah traditionally existed, was also provided with a building over the spot by Herod commensurate with the importance of the place to Jewish pilgrims. See A. E. Mader, *Mambre; die Ergebnisse der Ausgrabungen im heiligen Bezirk Râmet el-Ḫalîl in Südpalästina, 1926–1928,* Freiburg, 1957; and Joachim Jeremias, *Heiligengräber in Jesu Umwelt,* Göttingen, 1958.

[16] An unknown type of money.

[17] See W. F. Albright, *From the Stone Age to Christianity* (Anchor ed., 1957), p. 279; George M. Mendenhall, BASOR 133, Feb. 1954, pp. 26–30; Martin Noth, *Gesammelte Studien zum Alten Testament,* München, 1957, pp. 142–154; and Folker Willesen, *Vetus Testamentum IV,* 1954, pp. 216–217. The last-mentioned draws attention to a South Arabian inscription in which "ass" designates a covenant alliance.

[18] Contrast E. Nielsen, *Shechem,* pp. 216 ff., who takes the root *yrh* behind Moreh to mean "to throw lots and thereby obtain oracles." This to me is highly speculative, lacking solid support in the uses of the root and its derivatives in the Old Testament.

[19] The Greek or Septuagint translation places the ceremony, not at Shechem, but at Shiloh. Prof. Harry M. Orlinsky, after study of the text critical problem at my request, concluded: "I believe that the original LXX (Septuagint) read 'Shiloh' in its Hebrew *Vorlage* and that the Palestinian Recension substituted 'Shechem' for it. . . . Thus the Palestinian Recension simply adjusted original 'Shiloh' to 'Shechem' to accord with the reading in the current Hebrew text. In other words, I regard these as authentic variants in different Hebrew text-traditions. While I assume that Masoretic 'Shechem' is original, and that a supposed original 'Shiloh' leads us nowhere, the case must be solved by other data than text criticism." In this case, I would suggest that the decision for an original "Shechem" is based simply on the difficulty in understanding how an original "Shiloh" could have been changed to "Shechem," whereas the importance of Shiloh in the period of the Judges and its presence in Josh. 18:1 as the place where the assembly of Israel was held for final tribal allotments would provide sufficient reason for the harmonistic change of the text from "Shechem" to "Shiloh" preserved in the Septuagint's text tradition. See BASOR 169, p. 28, n. 31.

[20] See George E. Mendenhall, *Law and Covenant in Israel and the*

Ancient Near East, Pittsburgh, 1955; John Bright, *A History of Israel,* Chap. 4; G. Ernest Wright, *Biblical Archaeology,* (rev. ed.), pp. 99–101; and the same with Reginald H. Fuller, *The Book of the Acts of God* (Anchor ed., 1957), pp. 86–98.

21 This rendering of the Hebrew requires the reading *'ēlāh,* instead of *'allāh,* with the Hebrew text behind the Septuagint.

22 The Hebrew text has the consonants *mṣb* which have been given vowels by the Masoretic editors *muṣṣāb.* Commentators generally agree that this makes no sense and that the simplest change is to read the consonants instead as *maṣṣēbāh,* "sacred pillar." See, e.g., George Foote Moore, *Judges* (*International Critical Commentary;* New York, 1901), p. 244; W. Nowack, *Richter-Ruth* (*Handkommentar zum Alten Testament;* Göttingen, 1900), pp. 86–87; K. Budde, *Richter* (*Kurzer Hand-Commentar;* Freiburg, 1897), p. 72; and H. W. Hertzberg, *Die Bücher Josua, Richter, Ruth* (*Das Alte Testament Deutsch;* Göttingen, 1959), p. 205; and Nielsen, *op. cit.,* pp. 123 ff. and p. 142. Dr. Albright would prefer a different and much more elaborate solution (*see BASOR* 169, pp. 28–29, n. 32). It is clear from a letter of Harry M. Orlinsky about the Septuagint traditions regarding this verse that much more needs to be said and done with regard to the text critical question than the commentators cited above have done. Yet this matter cannot be dealt with at this point.

23 The subject of the "God of the Fathers" cannot be treated here. The most comprehensive recent study is that of my colleague, Frank M. Cross, Jr., "Yahweh and the God of the Patriarchs," *Harvard Theological Review* LV, 1962, pp. 225–259. *See also* the discussion of W. F. Albright, *From the Stone Age to Christianity* (Anchor ed., 1957), pp. 243 ff.

Footnotes to Chapter 9

1 Ernst Sellin, *Wie Wurde Sichem eine israelitische Stadt?,* Leipzig, n.d., but Preface on p. 4 was written in Berlin, May 26, 1922.

2 *Ibid.,* p. 47. Sellin's minute source analysis of Judg. 9 and his textual emendations at crucial points, which lack any real textual basis other than a theory of how the chapter ought to read, do not commend themselves, of course, today. *See* the review and evaluation of E. Nielsen, *Shechem,* pp. 19 ff.

3 F. M. Th. Böhl, *Mededeelingen der Koninklijke Akademie van Wetenschappen,* Amsterdam, Afd. Letterkunde, Deel 162, Serie B, 1926, pp. 1–24; and *De Opgraving van Sichem,* Zeist, 1927. Neither of these works is available to me except in translations made for the use of our staff by S. H. Horn.

4 Dr. Böhl is interpreting the Amarna Letters as testimony to an invasion of Hebrew tribes. This interpretation has today been given up by leading scholars: *see,* e.g., Edward F. Campbell, Jr. in Appendix 2.

5 *Das System der zwölf Stämme Israels,* Stuttgart, 1930. *See also* his *The History of Israel,* London, 1958, Chap. II.

6 *See* W. F. Albright, *Archaeology and the Religion of Israel,* Baltimore, 1st ed. 1942; 3d ed., 1953, pp. 103–105, and *see* Nielsen, *op. cit.,* p. 36, no. 1, who, though he does not mention Albright, supports the same view. *See also* John Bright, *A History of Israel,* Philadelphia, 1959, pp. 146–147.

7 For an interesting sociological analysis of the situation in Canaan,

see George E. Mendenhall, "The Hebrew Conquest of Palestine," *BA* XXV, 1962, pp. 66–87. This article has given many readers a false impression that Israel's strong traditions of holy war, the biblical tradition and the archaeological evidence for a concerted effort to capture a number of city-states during the second half of the 13th cent., can be disregarded. This is not Professor Mendenhall's true view, he informs me; to this article there should be added Professor Menhenhall's chapter, "Biblical History in Transition," *The Bible and the Ancient Near East* (G. E. Wright, ed.; Garden City, N. Y., 1961), pp. 32–53.

[8] "The List of Levitic Cities," *Louis Ginzberg Jubilee Volume*, English Section, New York, 1945, pp. 49–73.

[9] *See* Frank M. Cross, Jr. and G. Ernest Wright, "The Boundary and Province Lists of the Kingdom of Judah," *Journal of Biblical Literature* LXXV, 1956, pp. 202–226, esp. pp. 224–226.

[10] Further support of the hypothesis that during the 10th cent. "Mt. Ephraim" becomes an official governmental term for a province, is to be found in later writings, particularly in the prophets, where Ephraim is used as a synonym for the Kingdom of Israel. Manasseh rarely appears at all. *See,* e.g., Isa. 7:2, 9; Jer. 7:15; 31:9, 18, 20; Ezek. 37:15; Hos. 4:17, 5:3 ff., etc.

[11] *Géographie de la Palestine* II, Paris, 1938, pp. 81 and 460.

[12] 1 Kings 16:24 says only that Omri purchased the hill of Samaria. That there was a small village upon it is known from the excavations there, as pointed out in my article, "Israelite Samaria and Iron Age Chronology," *BASOR* 155, Oct. 1959, pp. 13–29.

[13] *See* Chap. 10.

[14] In the report of the first campaign (*BASOR* 144, p. 19; *BA* XX, p. 23, Fig. 8) a reuse of the gate, as indicated by I.3.Loc. 1, was dated to the 9th cent., with destruction dated between 850 and 750 B.C. Following the 1962 campaign it became clear that this view was mistaken and that locus and gate repair are to be assigned to Stratum VI (*see below*).

[15] On the basis of the narrative in Gen. 35, Albrecht Alt postulated that there was an annual pilgrimage from Shechem to Bethel ("Die Wahlfahrt von Sichem nach Bethel," *Kleine Schriften* I, München, 1953, pp. 79–88). Precisely what this would have involved with regard to rites of worship is difficult to say. Perhaps there would have been reflected here the transfer of the Shechem cult of El-berith to Bethel, but of this we have no certain knowledge.

[16] *See* 1 Kings 15:19–20; Yigael Yadin, *Israel Exploration Journal* 9, 1959, pp. 184–187; *Scripta Hierosolymitana* III, Jerusalem, 1960, pp. 1–17; Frank M. Cross, Jr., *BASOR* 163, Oct. 1961, pp. 12–14; and for summary *see* my remarks in *Biblical Archaeology* (rev. ed), pp. 163–164.

[17] *ZDPV* 49, pp. 309–310. Trans. by S. H. Horn.

[18] Thus Johannes' plan in *ibid.*, Tafel 12 (following p. 264), cannot be correct. Welter's stone-by-stone drawing in Fig. 10 is correct and shows the problem of the two strips of wall, labeled in our Fig. 73 5902 and 5702(?). The last mentioned may be the only hint remaining of the Temple 2 rear wall, but this is by no means certain since 5702(?) could belong to an earlier phase of the granary.

[19] In Fig. 73 there is an unexplained feature in Room B at Point *b*. Five large stones are in a row, resting squarely on the Temple 1 wall and carefully lined up with its inner edge. That is, whoever put them there

was very conscious of the Temple 1 and had laid bare its socket at this point. Yet the stones are the unhewn boulder type used in the granary but not in either Temple 1 or in Temple 2. Furthermore, the top of the Temple 1 wall is completely preserved as it was leveled for the brick superstructure, except for the surfacing of small stones and plaster. The stones may be seen in Welter's stone-by-stone drawing, Fig. 10. Hence they are granary masonry but on the axis of Temple 1. Since they make no architectural sense where they are, one can only conjecture that they represent something from a period within Strata VI–I. It would not be surprising that they date from the Hellenistic period, for example, where builders were always digging deep for foundations, reusing old stones which they had encountered, etc.

[20] See W. F. Albright, *Tell Beit Mirsim III. The Iron Age*, New Haven, 1943, pp. 22–24.

[21] These figures are only approximate, taken from plans.

[22] Yadin, *et al, Hazor II*, 1960, Pl. XVIII:5; *Israel Exploration Journal* 12, 1962, p. 92 and Pl. 12:A.

[23] For discussion see Benjamin Mazar, *BA* XXV, 1962, pp. 106–109.

[24] See "Israelite Samaria and Iron Age Chronology," *BASOR* 155, Oct. 1959, pp. 13–29, esp. pp. 23–24.

[25] Correcting the Hebrew "Tiphsakh" on the basis of Greek mss.

[26] Again correcting a corrupt Hebrew text by means of the Greek translation.

[27] The earliest from the 10th cent. were found in Niveau III at Tell el-Farʻah (Tirzah) by Père R. de Vaux; *Revue Biblique* XLII, 1955, Pl. VI, pp. 575, 580. For an 8th-cent. example at Hazor (Strata VI–V), see *BA* XXII, 1959, p. 15, Fig. 11 (upper left) and XXI, 1958, p. 29, Fig. 1; and Yigael Yadin, *et al, Hazor III–IV*, Jerusalem, 1961, Pls. II XXIV–XXV. For three fine examples which appear to be the same size as the Shechem house, see C. C. McCown, *Tell en-Nasbeh I*, Berkeley and New Haven, 1947, pp. 206 ff. When first found, one of them was considered to be a temple, and a church service was held "in the Israelite sanctuary" on May 8, 1927; W. F. Badé, *Excavations at Tell en-Nasbeh, 1926 and 1927*, Berkeley, 1928, pp. 39–40.

[28] The statement just made about country forts is based upon information concerning the Buqeiʻah forts provided by Frank M. Cross, Jr. (unpublished); note also the ʻAin el-Qudeirât fort in the Negev (Woolley and Lawrence, *Palestine Exploration Fund Annual*, III, London, 1914, p. 65); and the fortifications on the summit of Tell el-Fûl (Gibeah of Saul; see *BASOR* 52, Dec. 1933, p. 7, Fig. 1).

[29] This has been suggested to me by Prof. Abraham Malamat of Hebrew University.

[30] For detail see my analysis in *BASOR* 167, Oct. 1962, pp. 6–8.

[30a] S. H. Horn during the winter of 1963–1964 noted a comparable specimen in the antiquities' catalogue of a California dealer.

[31] For photograph see *BA* XX, 1957, p. 23, Fig. 8, where it was dated much too early.

[32] See Frank M. Cross, Jr., "An Inscribed Seal from Balâtah (Shechem)," *BASOR* 167, Oct. 1962, pp. 14–15. In our records it is B60, Reg. 26.

[33] The ware of the handles is generally reddish-brown, typically with a marked reddish cast and a dark center. Certain, though not all, of the

inscribed wine-jug handles found by Prof. J .B. Pritchard at Gibeon are quite similar to these of Shechem V. Elsewhere I have suggested the possibility that the Gibeon handles may be dated to the Shechem V period, in any case not before the second half of the 6th cent. My colleague, Frank M. Cross, Jr., had independently arrived at the same date by study of the paleography: see Pritchard, *Hebrew Inscriptions and Stamps from Gibeon*, Philadelphia, 1959; this writer's review of Pritchard's *The Water System of Gibeon* in *Journal of Near Eastern Studies* XXII, 1963, p. 211, n. 1; and Frank M. Cross' treatment in *BASOR* 168, Dec. 1962, pp. 18–23.

[34] For other examples of the same motif on stamps of the period, see Y. Aharoni, *Excavations at Ramat Rahel. Seasons of 1959 and 1960*, Rome, 1962, Fig. 9:9–12.

[35] See W. Wroth, "Ridgeway's Origin of Currency and Weight Standards," *The Classical Review* VI, 1892, pp. 470–473; *Guide to the Catherine Page Perkins Collection of Greek and Roman Coins*, Museum of Fine Arts, Boston, 1902, pp. 29–30; Ridgeway, "On Mr. Wroth's Review of Ridgeway's Metallic Currency," *The Classical Review* VII, 1893, p. 80; G. F. Hill, *A Handbook of Greek and Roman Coins*, London, 1899, p. 206, n. 1; P. Gardner, *The Types of Greek Coins*, Cambridge, 1883, Pl. III:28; B. V. Head, *Coins of the Ancients*, London, 1881, Pl. IV:1–5; *Historia Numorum*, Oxford, 1887, p. 264. The identification of the Shechem coin as possibly belonging to the Thasos series was first suggested by the late Leo Kadman, *BASOR* 144, Dec. 1956, p. 20, n. 17.

[36] G. F. Hill, *op. cit.*, p. 158.

[37] See J. Meshorer, "An Attic Archaic Coin from Jerusalem," *'Atiqot* III, 1961, p. 185. The author dates the coin to the earliest possible time, between 555 and 546 B.C., and believes it to be earlier than the Shechem example. Miriam S. Balmuth of Harvard University, who is working on the origin of coinage in her dissertation, has called my attention, however, to an article by Colin M. Kraay, "The Archaic Owls of Athens: Classification and Chronology," *Numismatic Chronicle*, Ser. 6, Vol. 16, 1956, pp. 43–68, who pushes the date of the series down to 500 B.C. or later.

Footnotes to Chapter 10

[1] In 1956, by this means, I discerned at the East Gate three phases which I dated to the late 4th–3d cents. B.C., 3d-early 2d cents. B.C., and the second half of the 2d cent. B.C.–a range which has proved approximately correct; we now know of four strata instead of three, and the second campaign in 1957 and the fresh balk cutting by Dr. Lapp in 1962 revised the preliminary stratigraphical observations of the first campaign: see *BASOR* 144, p. 13.

[2] *Loc. cit.* I was mistaken in 1956 in assuming that these coins dated the Hellenistic tower on the slope at the East Gate. This tower we now consider as belonging to Stratum II of *ca.* the first half of the 2d cent.

[3] See the survey of our 1960 coins by Ovid R. Sellers, *BA* XXV, 1962, pp. 87–96.

[4] *BASOR* 148, p. 27.

[5] *Palestinian Ceramic Chronology, 200 B.C.–A.D. 70*, New Haven, 1961.

[6] What follows is a slightly revised version of my article on "The Samaritans at Shechem," *Harvard Theological Review* LV, 1962, pp. 357–366.

7 A great body of literature has arisen around this problem, and it is not the purpose of this brief discussion to present a complete review of the scholarly debate. Suffice it to say, the main problem with which the literature has been concerned is whether or not there were two Jadduas and two Sanballats, and the consequences of affirmation or denial of this central question. In addition to the literature cited in the review article of H. H. Rowley (*see* n. 20), *see* among others V. Tcherikover, *Hellenistic Civilization and the Jews*, Philadelphia, 1959, pp. 42 ff. The necessity of explaining the archaeological data from the Shechem tell seems to us to lead to the necessity of a new review of the problem, a solution to which otherwise appears to have reached an impasse.

8 Josephus, Loeb ed., VI, p. 532.

9 Marcus, *ibid.*, Appendix C.

10 *Antiquities* IX, p. 291.

11 IV.v.9. This title evidently refers to a province which included not only the Damascus area but northern Palestine as well.

12 The date would have to have been during the winter or spring of 331.

13 *Op. cit.*, VIII.10; trans. by J. C. Rolfe, Loeb ed.

14 *Chronicon*, Armenian text, II, p. 223, ed. Aucher (= II, 114, ed. Schoene). The references are those of Marcus, as are those in n. 15 and 16.

15 P. 496, ed. Bonn.

16 *Op. cit.*, II, p. 229, ed. Aucher (= II, p. 118, ed. Schoene).

17 *Op. cit.*, pp. 524–525.

18 J. W. Crowfoot in *Samaria I. The Buildings,* London, 1942, pp. 24 and 27.

19 *Note also* the reference in Sirach 50:25–26 to two nations with which the author is vexed and to a third which "is no nation . . . the foolish people that dwell in Shechem" (RSV).

20 In 1955 H. H. Rowley published a survey of the account of Josephus regarding the building of the Samaritan temple, with full bibliography, and concludes that it is entirely untrustworthy: "Sanballat and the Samaritan Temple," *Bulletin of the Johns Rylands Library* 38, pp. 166–198. Heretofore, most treatments of the question have centered in Josephus' confusion of late 5th- and late 4th-century events. Rowley surveys three main solutions which have emerged: (1) that of Torrey who combined both events and dated Nehemiah in the 4th cent.; (2) that of a large number of scholars who see a kernel of truth in the tradition about the building of the temple, but deny the trustworthiness of its accompanying elements, including the relation of a Sanballat to it; and (3) those who transfer the temple's erection back to the 5th cent. Rowley believes that each of the three views is very problematical. Yet as for Rowley's objection that there was no time to erect the temple in the approximately nine months between Alexander's permission to build it and Sanballat's death, in the Josephus account, one could note that such an observation can scarcely be used for or against the tradition's historicity. The temple, for example, might have been virtually complete before Alexander's appearance at Tyre; and Sanballat's visit to Alexander, and the present to him of 8,000 troops, was a drastic measure designed to secure official approval for a program already well under way with the blessing of the Persian court. Be that as it may, the treatment of Ralph Marcus and the historical-archaeological observations added above put the whole issue in a new light, so that it must be reconsidered, even though it must be granted that Josephus has confused

events in two centuries. For our purposes here, however, the chief issue is to explain the sudden rebuilding of Shechem about the time when Josephus claims the Samaritan temple was erected. The tradition of Eusebius and Syncellus would provide the simplest explanation for Shechem's reoccupation as Samaria's replacement.

21 The fall, 1962, issue of the *Harvard Theological Review* (*see* n. 6).

22 Dr. Lapp's vivid story of the first excavations of the cave appeared in his "Archaeological Newsletter" from the Jerusalem School, dated Feb. 1, 1963. *See* Frank M. Cross, Jr., "The Discovery of the Samaria Papyri," *The Biblical Archaeologist*, XXVI, No. 4, Dec. 1963, pp. 110–121.

23 Josephus, *Antiquities*, Loeb ed., vol. XII, p. 154.

24 *Ibid.*, XII, pp. 257 ff. In his comments on this story, Ralph Marcus notes that in 2 Macc. 6:2 the temple is named instead Zeus Xenios, rendered by the RSV as "Zeus the Friend of Strangers." He believes that this was more probably the correct name.

25 *Ibid.*, XIII, pp. 9, 281; *War*, I, p. 66. It is possible that the battle of Alexander Jannaeus (107–76 B.C.) with Demetrius III (95–78 B.C.) which took place at or near Shechem in 88 B.C. may have marked the city's end, but at this time it would appear that our evidence fits best with the earlier rather than the later date: *Antiquities*, XIII, pp. 372–383; *War* I, pp. 90–98. For a survey of the reign of John Hyrcanus into which the Shechem evidence is to be fitted, *see* E. Schurer, *A History of the Jewish People in the Time of Jesus Christ* (2d ed., trans. by John MacPherson, Edinburgh, 1890), Vol. I, i, pp. 279 ff.

26 It was probably these events which led to the final and definite split between the Samaritans and Jerusalem Jews. Further confirmation of this suggestion is Frank M. Cross, Jr.'s demonstration that the Samaritan script began its independent history at this time: *see* his "The Development of the Jewish Scripts," *The Bible and the Ancient Near East* (G. E. Wright, ed., Garden City, N. Y., 1961), pp. 133 ff. *See also* the forthcoming monograph by James D. Purvis, *The Origin of the Samaritan Sect*.

Index